The Political Economy of Pension Policy Reversal in Post-Communist Countries

Why do governments backtrack on major policy reforms? Reversals of pension privatization provide insight into why governments abandon potentially path-departing policy changes. Academics and policy-makers will find this work relevant in understanding market-oriented reform, authoritarian and post-communist politics, and the politics of aging populations. The clear presentation and multi-method approach make the findings broadly accessible in understanding social security reform, an issue of increasing importance around the world. Survival analysis using global data is complemented by detailed case studies of reversal in Russia, Hungary, and Poland including original survey data. The findings support an innovative argument countering the conventional wisdom that more extensive reforms are more likely to survive. Indeed, governments pursuing moderate reform – neither the least nor most extensive reformers – were the most likely to retract. This lends insight into the stickiness of many social and economic reforms, calling for more attention to which reforms are reversible and which, as a result, may ultimately be detrimental.

Sarah Wilson Sokhey is an Assistant Professor in the Department of Political Science at the University of Colorado, Boulder, a Faculty Associate at the Institute of Behavioral Science, and an Associate Fellow at the International Center for the Study of Institutions and Development at the Higher School of Economics in Moscow. Her work on comparative political economy and post-communist politics has appeared in Party Politics, Europe–Asia Studies, Business & Politics, and Economics & Politics. Her research has been funded by the International Research & Exchanges Board (IREX) and the Social Science Research Council (SSRC).

The Political Economy of Pension Policy Reversal in Post-Communist Countries

SARAH WILSON SOKHEY

University of Colorado, Boulder

CAMBRIDGE
UNIVERSITY PRESS

University Printing House, Cambridge CB2 8BS, United Kingdom

One Liberty Plaza, 20th Floor, New York, NY 10006, USA

477 Williamstown Road, Port Melbourne, VIC 3207, Australia

314–321, 3rd Floor, Plot 3, Splendor Forum, Jasola District Centre, New Delhi – 110025, India

79 Anson Road, #06-04/06, Singapore 079906

Cambridge University Press is part of the University of Cambridge.

It furthers the University's mission by disseminating knowledge in the pursuit of
education, learning and research at the highest international levels of excellence.

www.cambridge.org
Information on this title: www.cambridge.org/9781107189850
DOI: 10.1017/9781316995822

First published 2017

Printed in the United States of America by Sheridan Books, Inc.

A catalogue record for this publication is available from the British Library.

Library of Congress Cataloging-in-Publication data
Names: Wilson Sokhey, Sarah, author.
Title: The political economy of pension policy reversal in post-communist
countries / Sarah Wilson Sokhey, University of Colorado.
Description: Cambridge, United Kingdom ; New York, NY : Cambridge
University Press, 2017. | Includes bibliographical references and index.
Identifiers: LCCN 2017026527 | ISBN 9781107189850 (alk. paper)
Subjects: LCSH: Pensions – Government policy – Former communist countries. |
Post-communism – Economic aspects – Europe, Eastern. | Former communist
countries – Economic policy.
Classification: LCC HD7196.S598155 2017 | DDC 331.25/2091717 – dc23
LC record available at https://lccn.loc.gov/2017026527

ISBN 978-1-107-18985-0 Hardback

For my parents, Eugene C. Wilson, Jr. & Julia A. Wilson who always care, a whole awful lot

But Mousie, thou art no thy lane,
In proving foresight may be vain:
The best-laid schemes o mice an men,
   Gang aft agley,
An lea'e us nought but grief an pain,
   For promis'd joy!
           To a Mouse, Robert Burns

Contents

Figures and Tables

Figures

Tables

Preface

Scholars have debated whether politicians and citizens can possibly back the right policy options given their own relatively short timeframes and perhaps limited ability to think ahead. Pension politics put the dilemma of long-term planning in stark relief: politicians must adopt policies to solve problems that are several generations away.

I began researching the politics of a particular pension reform – often referred to as pension privatization – in 2005. Pension privatization caught my interest as a unique type of social reform, but also as one that had similarities with other market-oriented reforms. This reform directs mandatory retirement contributions to individual accounts which are privately invested. A citizen's future benefits depend on returns to this account, be they negative or positive. The introduction of pension privatization – to date in 30 countries around the world – represented a fundamental shift in thinking about social security. No longer were national retirements systems based on the principle that workers were entitled to benefits earned over their career; instead they were based on the idea that workers themselves were responsible to invest and plan for their own old age.

Since the first introduction of pension privatization in Chile in 1981, much has changed. In the summer of 2008, a Russian expert on pension reform noted that it was a shame that I was nearing the end of my dissertation research: big changes in the pension system were on the horizon. Although his references to big changes was ambiguous at the time, he was ultimately proved right. Despite the potential costs and the presence of several alternative reform options, Russia adopted a radical market-oriented pension privatization reform in 2001. The next ten years saw the implementation of the reform and then its subsequent reversal. In December 2012, the Duma voted to begin backtracking on the system. Today the system adopted in 2001 is virtually gone. And the

Russian reversal was ultimately part of a larger global trend in backtracking on what had been intended to be a fundamental restructuring of pension systems.

My research on pensions began – albeit in a very different form – as a dissertation written at The Ohio State University. As I was concluding my dissertation research on the influence of corporate lobbying on pension privatization, a global financial crisis was in full swing and governments were beginning to cut and eliminate contributions to individual accounts set up as the second tier of national social security systems. At the University of Colorado, I shifted my research to explain the surprising turnaround in social policy reforms. Although pension privatization did fundamentally redefine social security in some countries, in others it clearly did not.

I received a tremendous amount of help and encouragement along the way. At Ohio State, I am grateful for a supportive and encouraging committee that helped me approach a challenging topic. I owe Sarah Brooks a great deal of gratitude not only for introducing me to the world of pension politics, but also for her guidance along the way. Her uncanny ability to both simplify or complicate issues at the right time of a project structure the way I think about research in general. Timothy Frye introduced me to the world of post-communist politics, generously lending his time even after leaving Ohio State. His invaluable help with field research, his understanding of the nature of Russian and post-communist politics, and the community of scholars he has fostered have strengthened all parts of my research. Marcus Kurtz always offered insightful comments and questions urging me to consider all possible alternative explanations and the larger implications of the project. His ability to see the big picture helped me to better understand why my own research was interesting. Last in alphabetical order, but very certainly not least, Irfan Nooruddin has gone very far above and beyond in mentoring me as an early graduate student and throughout my time as a faculty member. His own work has played a central role in how I think about politics, and his willingness and ability to offer professional advice has repeatedly proven essential in helping me navigate academic waters. I doubt I can fully live up to the model of mentorship or research embodied in any of my advisors, but at least I know the standard to which to aspire. If I succeed even partially in emulating them, I will be very glad.

I also benefited from a network of then graduate students at Ohio State who have gone on to great things. I am grateful to Quintin Beazer and Dinissa Duvanova, my fellow Buckeyes who also work in the world of political economy and Russian politics. They have seen parts of the book presented at various times and in various stages and have also offered helpful comments and insights. Their own work has been inspiring and has helped focus my own thinking on the nature of post-communist politics. Quintin's work on bureaucratic politics across the regions on Russia has made me think more seriously about the role of political institutions and bureaucratic discretion in influencing economic outcomes. Dinissa's research, including her book *Building Business in Post-Communist Russia, Eastern Europe, and Eurasia* (Cambridge University Press,

2013), pushed me to consider more seriously the role played by businesses and business associations in Russian policymaking.

As I was completing the final draft of this manuscript, a good friend from graduate school – Danielle Langfield – passed away very suddenly and unexpectedly. Danielle was a smart, funny, and caring friend; it is a great tragedy that her own time was cut so short.

Finally, Delia Dumitrescu is the best friend I could have found in graduate school; among her many great qualities no one has ever been quite so good at convincing me that I just might be right about something!

I am especially appreciative of scholars who have taken an active interest in the project and generously shared their own research in addition to providing detailed comments about the work. Thomas Remington has been incredibly supportive of this work. His own current research comparing welfare state politics in Russia and China has been very beneficial in influencing my thinking about my own work. I also benefited from a conference at Emory University, organized by Thomas Remington, in the fall of 2015 at which I was able to present research related to the book. Linda Cook has also been supportive of this project throughout its development and offered useful comments and suggestions at different stages. Her extensive body of work on the communist and post-communist social contract contain ideas which are central to the development of my arguments here. Israel Marques provided helpful comments on a portion of this work presented in Moscow in the summer of 2015. His own research about which individuals and business support social policy is insightful and innovative and is inspiring exciting new research into these questions.

In Russia, I have benefited from the support of a wide array of wonderful and helpful people. I am grateful to Sergei Guriev and the Center for Economic and Financial Research (CEFIR), which hosted me while I was conducting the dissertation research which inspired this project. At CEFIR, I received feedback and encouragement from Markus Eller, Scott Gehlbach, Irina Denisova, Natalia Volchkova, and Ekaterina Zhuravskaya. I am also grateful to Timothy Frye and Andrei Yakovlev for establishing and directing the International Center for the Study of Institutions and Development (ICSID) at the Higher School of Economics in Moscow which has hosted me during recent research trips to Russia and which holds regular conferences that have allowed me to collaborate and receive feedback in a very intellectually stimulating network of scholars.

I owe an enormous debt of gratitude to the Russian experts who met with me – sometimes on multiple occasions over several years – and provided invaluable insight into the workings of the Russia pension system and its reform. To maintain their anonymity and confidentiality, I do not identify them by name here. This does not, however, in any way diminish my enormous appreciation for their help without which this project would certainly not have been possible.

I have benefited from a stellar group of colleagues at the University of Colorado. A number of my colleagues read parts of this book at its various stages of development and offered helpful comments and advice, including Scott

Adler, Andy Baker, Carew Boulding, David Brown, Jennifer Fitzgerald, Joseph Jupille, and Amy Liu. Amy Liu read and commented on drafts, and endured more conversations about pensions than might be reasonable. I also owe a special thanks to Andy Baker who went far beyond the typical collegial obligations and read the entire manuscript and provided detailed comments. Gathering these perspectives and comments on the project has made this final product much better than it would otherwise have been. I am also grateful to the Institute of Behavioral Science (IBS) at the University of Colorado, Boulder for providing support and resources for my research during my time in Colorado.

Others have made the process of completing the book a much easier one. Joseph B. Schaffer provided early research assistance on the project, for which I am grateful. Eve Baker and Timothy Passmore provided incredibly helpful editorial assistance in thoroughly proofreading the manuscript and doing so on a short timeline. At Cambridge University Press, I am grateful to Robert Dreesen who made the review and publication process a pleasant experience. I would also like to thank two anonymous reviewers for Cambridge University Press who provided thoughtful and constructive comments which have greatly improved the manuscript. All errors – substantive, methodological, typographical, and otherwise – are, of course, my own.

I thank *Europe–Asia Studies* for permission to reprint portions of the following article: Sarah Wilson Sokhey, 2015, "Market-Oriented Reforms as a Tool of State-Building: Russian Pension Reform in 2001," *Europe–Asia Studies*, Vol. 67(5), pp. 695–717, copyright by the University of Glasgow and reprinted by permission of the publisher Taylor & Francis Ltd (www.tandfonline.com) on behalf of the University of Glasgow. Parts of this article, specifically the sections discussing the politics behind the adoption of Russia's pension reforms, appear in Chapter 5, "Russia's Staggered Reversal of Pension Reform."

The Skvortsov family has been part of my Russian life since I first visited the country with an undergraduate study abroad program in the fall of 2002, and is responsible for introducing me to Russian life and a country very dear to me. Larissa Skvortsova, Anna Skvortsova, Alexei Skvortsov, and Andrei Skvortsov are now a very welcome and regular part of my trips to Russia. And they have continued to graciously let a strange American student come stay with them over the years and throughout the research done for this book. Спасибо большое за все!

This book is dedicated to my parents – Eugene C. Wilson, Jr. and Julia A. Wilson – who have stood behind me in all of my endeavors. They have had more influence on this project, and all of my work, than they likely realize. From a very young age, they taught me through their words and deeds that "unless someone cares a whole awful lot, nothing's going to get better, it's not." This sentiment has inspired me to pay attention to issues like pensions for which the consequences may seem far down the road but for which we must plan today. A book on pension reform is perhaps a strange way to thank them for all of their years of love and support; nonetheless – thank you!

Finally, I could not ask for a better partner than Anand whose love, humor, generosity, and artistic abilities including and extending far beyond book covers – not to mention his intellectual support of this project – make everything possible and for which I am grateful, always forever. Although the research began long before, this version of the manuscript was written almost entirely after the arrival of our son, Ronan. How lucky I am to have had such a delightful and welcome companion while finishing this project!

Note on Transliteration

I transliterate Russian-language sources using the Modified Library of Congress system recommended by the Department of Modern Languages at Cambridge University. This transliteration system is used by all major libraries in the United Kingdom and the United States of America. I make a few exceptions to this system. I use common spellings of names (as in Yeltsin instead of Yelt'sin) or the spelling used by the author. I also make exceptions for Russian words that are commonly used in English-language texts to follow existing conventions (such as *Kommersant* instead of *Kommersant'*).

PART I

INTRODUCTION AND THEORY

1

Introduction

Explaining the Puzzling Reversal of Pension Privatization

> I am not entirely sure whether our pension reform will really deliver on all its promises.
>
> Former Polish Minister of Finance, Leszek Balcerowicz[1]

> But one simple recommendation is clear: all countries should begin planning now.
>
> *Averting the Old-Age Crisis*, World Bank, 1994[2]

> You have to understand that pension reform has nothing to do with pensioners ... it has to do with *future* pensioners.
>
> President of a private pension fund, Moscow, Russia, Fall 2007[3]

On the day that the Russian government overhauled the national pension system by introducing partial pension privatization in December 2001, just one hundred protesters gathered outside of the Duma to oppose the measures.[4] On the days that the Russian government voted to backtrack on that same pension privatization reform in December 2012 and 2013, there are no reports of any protests whatsoever. Indeed, survey evidence from the time shows that as much as 50 percent of the public was unaware that the government was reversing course.[5] In Russia, as in many other countries which reversed, pension privatization came in and out, not with a bang but a whimper.

Pension privatization – a radical, potentially path-departing reform – was reversed in about a third of the countries in which it was introduced. This

---

[1] Quoted in Barr and Rutkowski (2005, p. 158).

[2] *Averting the Old Age Crisis: Policies to Protect the Old **and** Promote Growth* (emphasis in the original), World Bank, Oxford University Press, 1994, p. 23.

[3] Interview with head of private pension fund, October 25, 2007.

[4] "Duma OKs Bill Aimed at Pumping up Pensions," *The Moscow Times*, July 16, 2001.

[5] Levada survey organization, nationally representative sample of Russian citizens, October 2014.

backtracking cannot be explained by a public backlash to market-oriented reform nor solely by the partisanship of the government nor by a shift in policy advice from international organizations. Instead, backtracking on pension privatization resulted from politicians' short-term fiscal incentives and the failure of the reform to be strongly supported by public or private interests in some countries. The case of pension privatization challenges some of our conventional wisdom about when market-oriented reform will survive by revealing the connected relationship between fiscal pressures, potential domestic stakeholders, and the nature of the reform initially adopted.

Pension privatization directs mandatory social security contributions to individual accounts which are privately managed and invested. I choose to focus on pension privatization because it highlights several key dimensions of market-oriented reforms. The three opening quotes reveal, in order, that pension reform entails uncertainty (whether the reform will deliver on all of its promises), long-term planning (for a social issue that will emerge decades later), and a time inconsistency problem (today's changes affect tomorrow's pensioners). Uncertainty is common to all reforms to varying degrees. The need for long-term planning and a time inconsistency problem are also common challenges, but are especially pronounced for pension reform. These characteristics make pension privatization an excellent case of a market-oriented reform adopted for long-term benefits which are gained by incurring short-term costs. Why would such reforms ever be adopted? And if politicians and citizens overcome the barrier of the significant political, fiscal, and social costs of adopting such reforms, why would these same actors subsequently reverse them? Furthermore, how and to what extent do governments abandon what were intended to be radical market-oriented reforms?

The recent trend in pension privatization emerged as a radical market-oriented reform adopted in Chile in 1980 which subsequently spread to countries in Europe and to Australia. The Chilean reform was not the first time such a system had been considered. During the post-World War II era, Central Provident Funds were introduced in many British colonies and subsequently influenced other social policies. The Central Provident Fund of Singapore was initially established in 1955 and entailed mandatory contributions to individual retirement accounts; it was subsequently expanded to cover expenses for healthcare and housing (Vasoo and Lee 2001). In a handful of cases, cities like Hong Kong and Singapore and federal governments like India and Nigeria have experimented with pension privatization at the subnational level or for government employees (Dave 2006, Casey and Dostal 2008). Hong Kong introduced a Mandatory Provident Fund in 2000 which, like the system in Singapore, is based on mandatory contributions which finance future benefits.

Pension privatization has spread to countries around the world. Modern pension privatization has been referred to as a, "revolution in the postwar social contract" (Orenstein 2008). Research has found that pension privatization did indeed change citizens' voting behavior (Kerner). Kay (2009) further finds that the creation of individual privatized pension accounts made politicians more politically vulnerable to economic fluctuations – which influenced returns to retirement savings – despite the argument that pension privatization would help insulate elected officials from these pressures. Pension privatization was promoted as a way to reduce long-term pension costs, spur the development of domestic capital and financial markets, and increase citizens' savings (World Bank 1994). In short, pension privatization was supposed to be a complete overhaul in how countries and citizens thought about social security.

Despite the potential benefits of pension privatization, critics were skeptical of its merits even when it was initially introduced (Kay 2000). Governments have subsequently backtracked in about a third of the countries that incurred the significant political and fiscal costs of pension privatization. Reversals of pension privatization suggest several important questions: Why are new policies sometimes highly resilient to challenges while in other cases they are abandoned or significantly revised?

In many ways, pension privatization is a reform that – once adopted – we would have expected to survive. Pension privatization created new interests groups including citizens, private pension funds, and bureaucrats who were invested in its survival. Because pension privatization attempted to rewrite the roles of the retirement game, there is every reason to suspect that its implementation could be self-reinforcing. Path dependency arguments, for instance, point out a myriad of reasons that policy change is highly unlikely.

Table 1.1 summarizes my central argument. My explanation links the reasons for the adoption of pension privatization – and the reasons for adopting a moderate degree of pension privatization – with its reversal. Contrary to conventional wisdom, I argue that countries that pursued more moderate degrees of pension privatization – not the most or least extensive reformers – were the most likely to backtrack when financial crisis heightened fiscal pressures on governments. In this case, politicians faced significant fiscal benefits from reversing but were not blocked by domestic stakeholders. When reforms were moderate, citizens were less invested in the reform's survival and private pension funds profited less extensively from it. In short, moderate reforms constitute a distinct type of pension privatization which was more likely to be overturned. In countries with limited or extensive pension privatization, financial crisis was not likely to provoke a turnabout in pension privatization.

The reversal of pension privatization is not the only interesting question. Countries also varied in how they abandoned pension privatization (whether in a one-time move or in several staggered measures) and whether they abandoned the reform wholesale or partially. The nature of domestic politics and a country's unique fiscal pressures determined the way in which reversals were pursued. When pension privatization was being heavily promoted by the World Bank and spread to countries around the world, it was often discussed as if pension privatization constituted one uniform type of policy. The reversals of

TABLE 1.1 *Summary of Main Argument*

	Keep pension privatization	Reverse pension privatization when financial crisis hits
Limited pension privatization	The limited degree of pension privatization makes the fiscal benefits of reversal small.	
Moderate pension privatization		Pension privatization diverts a valuable short-term source of revenue and is not strongly backed by domestic stakeholders. Domestic politics and the country's fiscal situation determines the nature and degree of reversal.
Extensive pension privatization	Although extensive pension privatization generates significant fiscal incentives to reverse, citizens and private pension funds support for the reform make reversal politically infeasible.	

pension privatization, however, highlight just how different pension privatization was in different countries.

Countries varied in the type and degree of reversal: Russia pursued a staggered, complete reversal of pension privatization over two years; Hungary instituted a one-time, complete reversal; and Poland adopted a staggered, partial reversal. Domestic political battles and the country's fiscal situation explain why reversals looked different across countries.

In Russia and Poland, the government was concerned about a potential public backlash (for different reasons) and the possibility of a backlash from private investors. In Russia, Putin and United Russia backed the introduction and reversal of pension privatization; citizens might have viewed this dramatic turnaround in policy negatively. In Poland, competitive domestic politics led politicians to more carefully consider how to reverse course on pensions. Introducing reversals slowly over time allowed these governments to learn about the response from the public and private investors. In Hungary, the government faced a much tighter fiscal situation than either Russia or Poland prompting Fidesz to completely redirect second-tier (privatized) contributions back to general government revenue despite the possibility of objections from citizens or private pension funds (neither of which manifested in Hungary).

The reasons for reversal are linked to why reforms were adopted in the first place and whether the initial reasons for adoption influenced subsequent reversals. Pension privatization was adopted due to pressures from international and domestic policymakers and fiscal pressures associated with the current and projected costs of social security. Notably absent from these explanations is any public demand for pension privatization. Instead, politicians had to convince citizens to accept this significant change in the rules of the social security game. The fiscal pressures of social security in the short and long-term play a central role in the adoption and reversal of pension privatization. Brooks (2009) shows that countries with very high levels of implicit pension debt – the cost of current obligations to retirees under the PAYG system – were unable to afford the financing gap created by pension privatization in which current contributions would be diverted away from covering current benefits. Governments in countries with very low levels of implicit pension debt did not face significant fiscal pressure to pursue pension privatization; their current social security systems were not very costly. Governments in countries with mid-range implicit pension debt were most likely to introduce pension privatization. Furthermore, of those that privatized, those with the highest levels of implicit pension debt privatized the least extensively and those with the lowest levels could afford to privatize pensions the most extensively. Again, those in the middle privatized to moderate degrees. Ultimately, that moderate degree of pension privatization would undermine the reforms in those countries.

The larger and more generalizable lesson is that reform may be hardest in countries where there is neither the least nor the greatest pressure to reform. Countries with the least need to reform will pursue limited reforms which are likely to be less costly and less controversial domestically and therefore more likely to stay in place. Countries with the greatest need to reform may implement more extensive measures which are more likely to become entrenched in society and therefore survive. As a result, countries that pursue moderate reforms have been at the greatest risk of reversal.

Existing works have provided invaluable insights into the political economy of market-oriented reforms and their consequences, but we still have many questions to answer. Scholars have often focused on when governments make progress on packages of reform rather than why particular measures will be pursued. Analysis has also focused much less on whether these reforms will stay in place.

This book seeks to address our limited understanding of why market-oriented reforms survive by examining the specific case of pension privatization. One explanation is that pension privatization simply went too far. Because pension privatization was such a radical step to redesign social security, citizens might have objected, the fiscal costs may have been too high, or the bureaucracy may have been too entrenched in the former pay-as-you-go (PAYG) system. Such an explanation would be in keeping with some current research that market-oriented reforms that are too radical may not survive for political reasons. Indeed, Przeworski (1991) explains the logic of the J-curve in which short-term reforms may be too politically unpopular to survive democratic contestation even if such reforms would yield long-term benefits.

Instead, I find that pension privatization was not reversed because it was too radical for society, but instead because the financing gap associated with pension privatization was not sustainable under certain circumstances. Furthermore, there is a tension between the fiscal cost of transitioning to pension privatization and the extent to which the policy is supported by groups in the public and private sector. More extensive pension privatization meant that the financing gap created by switching to a privatized system is higher. As pension privatization was pursued more extensively, pension privatization was backed more strongly by domestic stakeholders. More extensive pension privatization meant that private pension funds were making more money from the system and that citizens more closely linked their own retirement benefits with their private individual accounts.

Reversals of pension privatization were also not a backlash to globalization. One might think that pension privatization was simply the last straw in a series of market-oriented reforms which opened up countries' economies to risk associated with the international economy. Market-oriented reforms have indeed provoked a backlash in some cases. Again, we see that reversals in pension privatization do not fit within this common narrative about when and why reforms will survive.

Finally, the case of reversals in pension privatization reveals that backtracking was not an attempt to compensate citizens for the aftermath of the financial crisis. Citizens did not demand reversals. The financial crisis that began in 2008 prompted politicians to think about where they could get short-term sources of revenue. Financial crisis, then, created fiscal demands to reverse, but did not lead to public calls to eliminate the privatized pension systems. And in countries that had extensively pursued pension privatization, the financial crisis did not prompt calls for a reversal of pension privatization.

Broad Implications

Although the empirical question is specific to pension privatization, this book speaks to several important audiences and suggests wide-ranging implications in several areas: the welfare state, the political economy of market-oriented reforms, public policy, and post-communist politics.

The Welfare State & Rewriting the Social Contract

Pensions are important to study in their own right. Pensions are often one of the largest single areas of expenditures for states. Between 1990 and 2007, spending on old-age benefits in the OECD countries grew 15 percent faster than national income increasing from 6.1 to 7 percent of GDP with average OECD spending on pensions at about 17 percent of total spending.[6] In 2015,

---

[6] OECD. 2011. *Pensions at a Glance 2011: Retirement-Income Systems in OECD and G20 Countries.* Paris: OECD Publishing.

average OECD pension expenditures were up to 9 percent and projected to continue increasing. Spending is projected to increase – in some cases quite dramatically – in 20 OECD countries and decline in 13 others.[7] Pensions are also a central pillar of the welfare state. In the post-World War II expansion of the welfare state, the spread of national systems of social security was a central component of political new deals.

Pension privatization in particular was an attempt to rewrite the social contract on retirement, and it was an effort that succeeded in some cases but not others. Path dependency work provides conflicting expectations about whether we should have expected pension privatization to have generally survived or failed in most countries. On the one hand, path dependency arguments suggests that the rules of the game established by PAYG pension systems should have been very difficult to alter. On the other hand, once adopted, pension privatization set up a very different set of rules which path dependency arguments suggest should be self-reinforcing. Existing theories do a poor job of explaining *variation* in the survival of pension privatization and the corresponding attempt to rewrite the social contract. My argument and evidence offer insight into how the initial conditions under which pension privatization was adopted and the extent to which it was pursued explain why the social contract could be overhauled in some cases but not others.

The case of pension privatization also gives us insight into welfare state retrenchment and reinforcement. Pierson and others have written extensively about the shift in the 1980s in which governments like those of Reagan and Thatcher began attempting to find ways to cut back on the welfare state (e.g., Hacker 2008; Pierson 1994). Pension privatization is not clearly – or at least not entirely – retrenchment in that it does not cut benefits (necessarily although it may by effect) but rather changes where the benefit comes from and who bears the risk of its provision. The specific case of pension privatization, then, tells us more than just about this specific policy. It tells us about how governments are moving beyond simple retrenchment efforts that cut government benefits and opt instead to promote policies that reformulate the welfare state in a way that can privatize risk. The case of pension privatization also tells us about how short-term preferences of citizens and interest groups could either lock-in politicians to a certain course of action as it did in cases where pension privatization stuck, or enable politicians to pursue short-term fiscal goals as it did in cases where pension privatization was reversed.

Political Economy of Market-Oriented Reforms

Debates about welfare policy broadly and social security policies in particular are here to stay even if particular policies are not. A large body of work about the path dependency created by new policies – and pension policy in particular – suggests that change is difficult and relatively rare (e.g., Pierson 1994, 1998,

---

[7] OECD. 2015. *Pensions at a Glance 2015: OECD and G20 Indicators*. Paris: OECD Publishing.

2000, Hacker 2008, Rose 1990). Work on the political economy of market transitions, however, examines how political institutions make the adoption and survival of packages of reforms more likely (Frye 2010, Przeworski 1991, Hellman 1998).

This book contributes to our understanding of when market-oriented reforms will be adopted and abandoned by focusing on one particular reform instead of packages of reforms. This allows for a more detailed consideration of the relevant groups and interests, and a thorough examination of how fiscal and social pressures are filtered by the political system. Geddes (2003) warns against research designs which compare the influence of the same groups across different policies; she writes that, "[T]he researcher would be better off looking at similar policies in several countries than looking at several different policies within the same country" (p. 138). Different policies – like healthcare, pensions, the privatization of state-owned enterprises – entail different policy landscapes. In understanding why reforms fail, then, there are advantages to focusing on just one policy.

Pension privatization is particularly useful because it is a policy with long-term implications and short-term costs and is therefore the epitome of a market-oriented reform. Przeworski defined market-oriented reforms as an attempt to, "organize an economy that rationally allocates resources and in which the state is financially solvent" (p. 136). Pension privatization sought to accomplish precisely these goals in rationally allocating resources for retirement in a manner that was financially sustainable for governments. It is therefore a reform that is perfectly poised to evaluate arguments about how the short-term costs of implementing a reform that is argued to be necessary in the long run but costly at present. The central challenge, then, was overcoming the short-term obstacles to adopting a policy that was – as least in principle – going to have important long-term payoffs. In Przeworski's explanation of the J-curve, however, it was the politicians' short-term electoral goals which could be problematic: citizens would object to the short-term costs and politicians would cave.

By contrast, in my account citizens could be sold on pension privatization and other domestic interest groups like private pension funds might back its survival if the reform had been extensively implemented. Where pension privatization had only been moderately pursued, it was the politicians' own short-term fiscal incentives which provides a crucial part of the impetus to reverse pension privatization and redirect mandatory social security contributions back to the state. Particularly in the light of domestic post-communist political struggles, this offers an important twist on when and how market-oriented reforms may not survive.

Public Policy

Scholars have called for a renewed focus on policy-focused political science in which politics is, "centrally about the exercise of government authority for particular substantive purposes" (Hacker and Pierson 2014). By focusing on political battles over policy, we can gain a more accurate understanding of how institutions operate and how groups exert influence. This book does precisely this by examining how a policy adopted with a particular set of objectives – including altering the social contract on retirement – failed to take hold in some countries because of a combination of fiscal pressures, a wide variety of potential or actual domestic stakeholders, and domestic political conditions. The main argument is that the degree to which pension privatization was initially implemented played the central role in shaping how fiscal incentives, domestic stakeholders, and domestic politics resulted in reversals. Countries in which moderate pension privatization had been adopted were ultimately the most likely to backtrack.

From a public policy perspective, the book provides important insight into who the key domestic stakeholders were and the role that they played in domestic political battles about the adoption, implementation, and reversal of a radical and potentially path-departing kind of social security reform. No complete policy analysis can avoid a discussion of politics. There are differences in values and goals and tradeoffs inherent in any policy choice (Stone 2012). Social security is a prime example of how politics informs the policy process. Policymakers crafting retirement policies have sometimes focused on actuarial and fiscal analyses without considering whether these policies could be adopted or effectively implemented in particular political circumstances. Despite the importance of understanding political battles, Acemoglu and Robinson (2013) note that much policymaking in economics fails to consider politics and political economy. This book seeks to do just that by considering the political battles over values and ideas that have shaped social security policy.

I take no stance in this book on whether pension privatization is the best kind of social security reform or whether governments should have adopted it. I use the term "reform" in the general and more colloquial sense, not because there is a consensus that its introduction always improves outcomes we care about including providing for citizens in old-age or improving macroeconomic growth. Indeed, the results on pension privatization are mixed (Orenstein 2008). In some countries, it does appear to have boosted investment and in some countries the first waves of retirees are beginning to draw benefits from second tier accounts established by pension privatization.

Rather, I emphasize that regardless of which social security policies are ideal, changing the basic rules of the pension game every decade or so is not good policy. Retirement policy must be more forward looking. Even the Hungarian economist, András Simonovits, who opposed the introduction of pension privatization has called its reversal short-sighted and reactionary (Simonovits 2011). Debates over pension reform starkly illustrate that policymaking cannot be devoid of politics, but rather is inherently a tradeoff between competing preferences and goals. There is not perfect ideal solution to be adopted if only politics were not a concern. Rather, we must consider both which policies accomplish desirable goals and whether these policies are feasible.

Adopting national retirement policies which will only be abandoned in the near to medium term is not a good policy solution. The argument and evidence in this book contribute to our understanding of how domestic stakeholders influence the adoption, implementation, and reversal of policies thereby providing lessons for policymakers and scholars of public policy.

This book focuses on the critical question of why reversals occur and emphasizes the importance of the initial conditions under which reforms were adopted. The explanation is not as simple as just partisan alternations in power or a clear failure of the policy to accomplish any of its goals. Indeed, in some cases pension privatization was only just beginning to have the potential to provide the fiscal, social, and macroeconomic benefits for which it was ostensibly adopted at the time it was abandoned.

The explanation I offer gives insight into policymaking by illuminating the role of domestic stakeholders in either bolstering or undermining the survival of pension privatization. Kingdon (2003[1984]) writes that, "If one can specify what the initial conditions in a process are, and if one has good information about those conditions, then one can predict outcomes more reliably than if one does not know of the initial conditions" (p. 224). I go back to the initial conditions under which pension privatization was adopted which determined the extent to which it was pursued and which, ultimately, can help us explain why pension privatization failed in some countries. Doing so should help us better predict when other economic and social policies might also be abandoned.

Post-Communist Politics

To date, reversals in pension privatization have been a largely post-communist phenomena with the exception of Argentina and the United Kingdom. This suggests that there is something distinct about post-communist politics which explain why governments adopted a moderate degree of pension privatization which proved unable to survive in the long-run.

A number of studies have looked at different aspects of the Communist legacy and how it influences a wide variety of political and policy outcomes including social policy (Cook 2007, Marques 2016), tax politics (Appel 2011, Gehlbach 2008), patterns of protest (Robertson 2011, Robertson and Teitelbaum 2011), military and police reforms (Light 2012, Taylor 2011), and revolutionary politics including the Color Revolutions (Levitsky and Way 2011, Way 2008). As Frye (2010) notes, "if the watchword of the communist era was conformity, the watchword of the post-communist world is diversity" (p. 1). Post-communist diversity is especially evident in how the legacy of communism created similar challenges to which governments and politicians have widely varied responses across countries.

In this case, I argue that there is a particular aspect of post-Communist politics which resulted in the adoption of moderate pension privatization. The relatively high levels of implicit pension debt – the cost of current obligations to retirees under the PAYG system – created the pressure to reform but made more extensive pension privatization too costly. The result was ultimately that moderate pension privatization itself was too costly in the face of the financial crisis. In combination with domestic political battles, the fiscal pressures and lack of domestic support for keeping pension privatization resulted in reversals.

The surprising uniformity in the spread of the flat tax and pension privatization has been explained in part as a way for the post-communist countries to attract investment and due to the spread of a particular ideology (Appel and Orenstein 2013). Even within this seeming uniformity, however, there is often important variation. In this case, the nature and degrees of reversal of pension privatization across the region depended on the nature of partisan political battles within the country. In Hungary, the Fidesz victory allowed the party to swiftly and entirely abandon reform while in Poland, a more competitive party system resulted in a slower and more partial reversal. The very nature of reversal varied too. In Hungary, the holdings of individual accounts in the second tier were reacquired by the government, but in Poland the individual accounts continued to exist although smaller contributions were made to them. In Russia, the government began by suspending contributions to the second tier before moving to more permanent measures to marginalize the role of the second privatized tier of pensions.

The findings of this book bolster existing findings about how a Communist legacy can influence modern politics and policies, but emphasizes that there is a great deal of variation in how, when, and why the Communist legacy manifests. This is not a mere "history matters" argument, but rather a detailed examination of how similar fiscal and social pressures associated with a shared challenge – supporting aging populations – are refracted differently through distinct political prisms. In this way, the book's argument and evidence contribute to our understanding of post-Communist politics. More than two decades after the fall of communism we now have sufficient observations to draw stronger conclusions about post-communist politics in the region than we could before.

While many post-communist countries are competitive democracies today, democratic institutions have failed to take hold in others. The Russian case in particular lends insight into policymaking in an authoritarian regime. In Russia, pension privatization was both introduced, implemented, and reversed under the leadership of Vladimir Putin. Putin's political motivations for pension privatization were part of his larger political and economic strategy for consolidating power. In particular, market-oriented reforms were a way for Putin to undercut the power of influential oligarchs and consistent with a move to consolidate power over certain state bureaucracies. The policymaking process was dictated more by inter-ministry rivalries than pluralist interest group politics seen in more competitive democratic settings. The Russian case in particular emphasizes how elite politics and policymaking operate even for social policies that are typically thought to capture the public's attention and the attention of interest groups.

A Note about Terminology

Throughout the book, I use the terms *pension privatization* and *second pillar* reforms interchangeably. Pension privatization or second pillar reforms entail the creation of a system in which mandatory social security contributions are credited to individual accounts whose holdings are privately managed and invested. The risk, ownership, and management of retirement savings are thereby shifted from the state to private businesses and individual citizens. The state is still responsible for the central management and oversight of individual accounts. But given that systems of private property ownership typically entail state regulation and oversight, the central role of the state does not make this reform any less a kind of privatization. Privatization is a broad term that varies across sectors (factories, housing, utilities, education, healthcare, etc.) and often has unique characteristics depending on what is being privatized and how. The common element of privatization is that it shifts resources from state-owned to private hands.

Pension reform, however, has sparked debates about the correct terminology and in particular the correct terminology for this specific kind of reform. Some consider the term pension privatization misleading because of the state's central regulatory and management role. Others consider the term too ideological arguing that the privatization label makes it sound unduly market-oriented. As noted above, the state's central regulatory role does not alter the fact that resources were shifted from state to private ownership. In fact, the motivation was to put citizens' retirement savings in their own hands in part so that they would take greater responsibility and interest in providing for themselves in old age. Furthermore, there are few scholars – if any – who would contest that pension privatization is indeed market-oriented.

I also wish to avoid confusion by either introducing a new term for this reform or using alternate terms which can be ambiguous. Alternate terms for pension privatization or second pillar reforms include *individual account reforms, structural pension reform, funded reforms,* and *mandatory funded reforms. Individual account reforms* can include measures that are both mandatory and voluntary. The terms *structural* and *funded* (or even *mandatory funded*) reforms include measures like notional defined contributions which alters the nature of the pension system but do not establish individual accounts and do not entail private management. Instead, a system of notional defined contributions links contributions to benefits using a formula to link returns to savings.

Within pension privatization there is, however, significant variation. For instance, pension privatization can be included as part of a national retirement system in which there is more or less social pooling, meaning that there is more or less redistribution of retirement benefits. The extent of social pooling depends primarily on the design of the other tier in the system, i.e. the PAYG component and any voluntary savings. Within these varying degrees of social pooling or redistribution, however, the central characteristic of pension privatization is that some portion of mandatory social security contributions are directed to individual accounts which are privately invested and managed and whose benefits accrue to an individual. The variation in the type and degree of pension privatization has been extensively documented in previous work (e.g., Barr and Diamond 2008, Brooks 2009, James and Brooks 2001). And indeed, the argument made in this book draws on the variation in the degree and types of pension privatization to explain why it was reversed in some cases but not others.

The term *second pillar reforms* is used interchangeably with pension privatization in the text. *Second pillar reforms* comes from standard terminology of the World Bank in characterizing pension systems in which there is a first pillar consisting of the PAYG system, a second privatized pillar, and a third pillar based on voluntary savings. Some debate whether we should more accurately refer to *tiers* or *pillars* in pension systems. I prefer the term pillars because tiers imply that the different parts build on each other and tends to suggest that the PAYG portion is the largest tier which is not necessarily the case.

Throughout the book, a reversal of pension privatization refers to decreasing or eliminating contributions to the mandatory individual accounts established by pension privatization. Depending on how governments announced these moves, the reversal may be more or less obvious. In Kazakhstan, for instance, the holdings of ten private pension funds were consolidated into a Single Funded Pension Fund (UAPF) which is a joint-stock company owned by the Kazakh government. Important aspects of the pension privatization reform have been maintained including individual records of pension accumulations and payments which will determine future benefits. Although Kazakhstan is keeping elements of its previously privatized pension system, changes announced in 2013 and 2014 establish notional defined contributions rather than relying on actual individual accounts.[8] The main difference between the Kazakh reversal and other cases was how the governments framed their reversals in official announcements. The Hungarian government, for instance, simply announced that the holdings in the individual accounts were being transferred back into the state system and individual accounts would not continue to exist. In Kazakhstan, the leadership was careful to maintain that the three levels of pensions would continue to exist possibly making it sound like less of a reversal to the public.[9] Despite differences in how governments announced the moves, all reversals entailed the reduction or elimination of contributions to individual accounts which were privately managed and invested.

---

[8] For a complete description of the unique case of Kazakh pension reform in 2014, see an appendix to IMF Country Report No. 14/258, "The Republic of Kazakhstan: Financial System Stability Assessment," Washington, DC: IMF, July 8, 2014.

[9] *Kapital*, "V pensionnuiu sistemu Kazakhstana vnesut izmeneniia: Bazovuiu pensiiu budut naznachat' v zavisimosti ot stazha raboty," May 13, 2014.

Outline of Book

In the first part of the book, I present the variation in reversals of pension privatization, the inadequacy of existing explanations, and build on extant arguments to develop a new theoretical understanding about how the degree of reform affects its survival. In Chapter 2, I explain why our ex ante expectations about reversing pension privatization are conflicting, describe the trend in reversals, and explain why existing explanations are insufficient to account for backtracking on pension privatization. Reversals in pension privatization have been explained by focusing on the role of economic crisis and the cost of reform without taking into consideration how domestic politics filters economic crisis and fiscal pressure into policy outcomes. Furthermore, explanations of market-oriented reforms have generally advanced the idea that more extensive reforms were more likely to overcome opposition and create domestic stakeholders who would back their survival.

In Chapter 3, I present a theoretical basis on which to understand reversals in pension privatization. I highlight the fiscal pressure generated by pension privatization, the role of financial crisis in sparking debates about sources of additional short-term revenue, and the role of domestic stakeholders who would make backtracking politically undesirable. Pension privatization generates a financing gap – typically covered by deficit spending – by diverting current contributions away from paying current benefits and instead into individual accounts. When the financial crisis hit in 2008, governments were pressed to find a source of short-term revenue and one option was to eliminate or reduce contributions to the second privatized tier of pensions and use those funds instead for current spending. In countries with extensive pension privatization, domestic stakeholders in the form of citizens and private pension funds made the option of reversing pension privatization untenable. In countries with limited pension privatization, the costs of reversing compared to the fiscal gain from doing so made reversal politically undesirable. In countries with moderate pension privatization, however, pension privatization was most likely because of the short-term fiscal gain for politicians and the lack of opposition from domestic stakeholders. The causal story here reveals the complicated and connected influence of fiscal pressures and domestic stakeholders on the formation and sustainability of policy. In some countries, the pressure and ability to reform resulted in moderate reforms which did not fundamentally alter the social contract but were nonetheless fiscally costly for politicians to maintain in light of a financial crisis.

The next section of the book provides a variety of empirical evidence about why reversals in pension privatization occurred and why these reversal vary. In Chapter 4, I discuss global trends in the reversal of pension privatization and evaluate my expectations regarding when reversals will be most likely. I use an original dataset including all 28 countries that have adopted pension privatization. I find evidence that countries that adopted a moderate degree of pension privatization were indeed the most likely to abandon the reform. These cross-national trends confirm my theoretical expectations that one part of the conventional wisdom about adopting market-oriented reforms is wrong: more extensive reforms are not necessarily more likely to survive.

The cross-national evidence highlights the importance of the question about how and why countries rethought pension privatization. A wide variety of differences in domestic political conditions suggests that reversals would not all be handled in the same way. Exploring how countries reversed pension privatization – including the timing of reversals around elections, whether reversals were temporary, multi-step, or partial, and which groups were the most vocal in debates – reveals in greater depth the nature and logic of political battles surrounding backtracking.

The next three chapters present country case studies of reversals in pension privatization in Russia, Hungary, and Poland. The case studies test the causal mechanisms of my theory in greater depth and evaluate my expectations about how and to what degree reversals would occur in different countries. These instances of reversal reveal why backtracking was more likely in countries that had adopted moderate reforms. The other main purpose of the case studies is to explore the variation in reversals. As such, I have chosen countries where reversals occurred instead of including a case of non-reversal. The case studies hone in on how countries varied in their methods of pulling back on pension privatization and why some countries chose gradual and partial reversals (like Russia and Poland) and others entirely scrapped pension privatization in virtually a single legislative move (like Hungary).

In Chapters 5 and 6, I examine the Russian reversal of pension privatization. The Russian case is based on field research conducted over the course of seven years from 2006 to 2013 including interviews with bureaucrats, policy experts, politicians, and representatives of private pension funds.[10] Original survey questions from the fall of 2014 and the fall of 2015 provide additional insight into public opinion about Russia's reversal of pension privatization as it was happening. In Russia, a moderate degree of pension privatization was adopted and reversed under the same center-right party of power, United Russia, and under the same leadership of Vladimir Putin. When the financial crisis hit, the Russian government spent its fiscal reserves and was eager to find a new source of revenue. Furthermore, the Russian pension system had been running deficits since before the fall of communism. Because Russia had adopted a moderate degree of pension privatization, neither the public nor private pension funds were strongly invested in the continuation of the privatized pension

---

[10] Forty-two individuals were interviewed between 2006 and 2013. A summary of the interviews can be found in the appendix at the end of the book. Anonymized transcripts and/or recordings are available for many of the interviews. An anonymized version of the author's notes are available for all of the interviews.

system. Indeed, many Russian citizens were largely unaware of the changes in the pension system that were occurring.

The government tested the waters with legislation that initially reduced contributions to the privatized tier and gave citizens the option to keep their full contributions going to the second privatized tier. After little reaction from investors or domestic groups, a year later in December 2013, the government passed legislation nearly eliminating pension privatization for those currently in the system and phasing out the privatized system altogether for new labor market entrants. The Russian government has subsequently announced that it will maintain a portion of the privatized tier of pensions. The volatility in Russian pension policy is consistent with the story of reversals: Russian politicians reacted to the potential fiscal and economic benefits of pension privatization with minimal if any opposition from domestic stakeholders.

Chapter 7 addresses the Hungarian and Polish cases which give further insight into how and why the type of reversals varied. I explain how the Hungarian reversal was part of a right-wing government's attempt to avoid raising taxes or cutting spending amidst a financial crisis. The Hungarian reversal was more dramatic and complete than the Russian one, being passed in a single legislative measure that was never debated in the Hungarian parliament. Because Hungary had privatized pensions more extensively than Russia, the revenue to be gained by reversing was greater. The Hungarian government also faced a worse fiscal situation than Russia making it useful to end the financing gap caused by pension privatization. Although Hungary has privatized more extensively than Russia, like Russia pension privatization was not strongly supported by domestic stakeholders in the public or private sector. And the dramatic elimination of the privatized pension system in 2010 – which entailed transferring private pension fund holdings back to the national social security system – provoked very little reaction.

I leverage the Polish case in comparison to the Russian and Hungarian experiences to explore in greater depth the variation in the nature and degree of reversals in pension privatization. The Polish reversal has been the most gradual of the three and, to date, has been less extensive than in either Russia or Hungary. In Poland, pension privatization had received more overt public support than in neighboring countries with the government engaging in an extensive public relations campaign to promote the new system before its adoption in 1999. Nonetheless, in the aftermath of the financial crisis, the public and private pension funds were not sufficiently supportive of pension privatization – which was only partially pursued in their countries – to either have the will or ability to fight strongly for its survival.

Finally, in Chapter 8, I conclude the book with a discussion of the larger implications of the findings. The advantage of the empirical questions addressed here – why are there reversals in pension privatization and why there is variation in the nature and degree of these reversals? – is that their specificity enables a research design that thoroughly addresses possible explanations and also enables us to draw lessons that are relevant to other market-oriented reforms and other policies broadly speaking. The politics of pension privatization can teach us about the politics of market-oriented reform and policymaking in a wide variety of areas. Specifically, pension privatization gives us insight into how time horizons can influence a reform's likelihood of survival. Policies with long-term payoffs are only likely to survive if they are supported by short-term interests. Pension reform is an extreme example because the payoff for reforms today can be decades in the making. Most economic reforms, however, entail some lag between the adoption of the reforms and the rewards.

Aging populations and expensive pension systems make it imperative to understand when changes to national pension plans will fail to take hold. The study of pension privatization, an important topic in its own right, lends further insight into the political economy of market-oriented reforms broadly. In searching for the most viable and preferable policies, we must consider which of these options are most likely to take hold and which are unlikely to persist. Using the case of pension privatization, this book seeks to provide a better understanding – though far from the final word – about which reforms would be most likely to survive in the long term.

2

Backtracking on Pension Privatization Around the World

Why has pension privatization been able to take hold and fundamentally alter the social contract on retirement in some countries but not others? A wide variety of possible influences on economic and social reforms indicate why pension privatization may have failed. Depending on the issue at hand, the pitfalls of economic reforms may include many sources, such as public backlash, demands from interest groups, short-sighted politicians, fiscal pressures, the advice or requirements from international organizations, legislative politics, domestic coalitions, or some combination thereof. By focusing on the reversal of one policy, we can more precisely theorize about why economic reforms are abandoned and develop expectations that can be tested and modified in other areas.

Academic scholars and policy experts have long identified the danger of frequent reversals in major economic policies and sought to explain them.

Reversals in pension policy are of particular concern because pension policies are targeted at long-term planning. In a World Bank report, Schwarz et al. (2014) conclude that

This constant shifting of policy has been unfavorable in a variety of contexts, but it has been particularly harmful in regard to pension policy. Pensions represent a long-term contract between workers and the government. While it is acceptable that some parameters might need to change over the length of the contract in response to economic and demographic developments, huge and frequent policy shifts lead to worker perceptions that the government is not really providing any old-age security. This in turn undermines workers' willingness to contribute their limited earnings to such a system. (p. 257)

Particularly in the arena of retirement savings, stability may be more important than choosing what may be considered the optimal policy *ex ante*. In some countries the goal of pension privatization was to improve tax collection in part by giving workers an incentive to pay taxes on their official salary instead of accepting unofficial payment on which employers could avoid payroll contributions. This goal of improved tax collection is undermined by policy vacillations. To some degree, workers must buy into the new system for the new system to work.

Stability in national retirement policy matters because individuals plan their savings and retirement strategies based on national policies. Large, frequent shifts in pension policy make it difficult, if not impossible, for citizens to plan effectively. One of the hopes for pension privatization was that it would inspire citizens to plan for their own retirement. By establishing individual mandatory accounts, an ownership society would be created in which individuals would take greater responsibility for their own old age and would closely follow developments in the market and the returns to their own savings. This was a particular draw for developing countries making the transition to a market-based economy in which there were concerns that citizens did not support market-oriented reforms.

I begin by discussing why pension privatization was adopted. I then consider why the trends among reversals are especially puzzling, given our expectations about policy stability. Arguments about policy stability can be interpreted to explain why we should generally expect pension privatization to survive or fail, but they do not provide a very clear expectation for why we observe variation in the reversal of pension privatization. I next discuss the variation in reversals of pension privatization, including where and how they occurred. Many of the commonly given explanations for backtracking are insufficient to explain the trends we observe. Next, I turn to two major areas of reform – the politics of economic reform and the welfare state – to consider a better set of explanations for reversal. Research on the politics of economic reform and work on the welfare state identify the important actors and processes by which policy decisions are made, but ultimately provide an incomplete explanation for backtracking on pension privatization. In part, this is because much existing literature focuses on packages of reform instead of considering the politics surrounding particular measures.

The Adoption of Pension Privatization around the World

Pension privatization directs mandatory social security contributions to individual accounts which are privately managed and invested. The first pension privatization system was implemented in Chile in 1981. Chile's early success with introducing private funded pension funds prompted other Latin American countries to adopt similar measures including Argentina, Bolivia, Chile, Colombia, the Dominican Republic, El Salvador, Mexico, Peru, and Uruguay (Queisser 1998). A handful of West European countries adopted the reform in the 1980s and 1990s, including the United Kingdom, Denmark, the Netherlands, Sweden, and Switzerland. In the late 1990s and early 2000s, several post-communist countries in Europe and Central Asia adopted pension privatization, including Bulgaria, Croatia, Estonia, Hungary, Kazakhstan, Latvia, Lithuania, Macedonia, Poland, Romania, Russia, and Slovakia.

The concentration of pension privatization among post-communist countries in these regions was not coincidental. Indeed, these countries faced similar demographic and fiscal challenges in maintaining state-funded communist-era retirement policies (Augusztinovics 1999; DeCastello 1998; Schwarz 2011; Velculescu 2011). Additionally, the World Bank was providing similar reform advice and offering assistance to these government for adopting reforms (Holzmann and Hinz 2005). Appel and Orenstein (2013) have noted the remarkable convergence on neoliberal economic policies like pension privatization and a flat tax that emerged in this post-communist region. Politicians and policymakers learned from each other and frequently took similar, if not identical, approaches to economic and social policies.

The impetus for pension privatization included social, fiscal, and macroeconomic goals. The World Bank promoted pension privatization as a means of improving long-term planning for retirement systems. In *Averting the Old-Age Crisis: Policies to Protect the Old <u>and</u> Promote Growth*, the World Bank (1994) detailed the benefits of this kind of funded pension system. Unlike a defined benefits system in which retirees receive a guaranteed amount of support, pension privatization is a defined contribution system in which benefits are determined by the returns to individual savings. The idea was that pension privatization would shift the fiscal burden for providing for citizens in their old age away from the state and that citizens would think more about their own retirement. Pension privatization would also bolster domestic savings and thereby improve macroeconomic performance.

Advocates of pension privatization argued that this would help address the rising deficits incurred by PAYG pension systems along with a host of other benefits. The 1994 World Bank report explains that

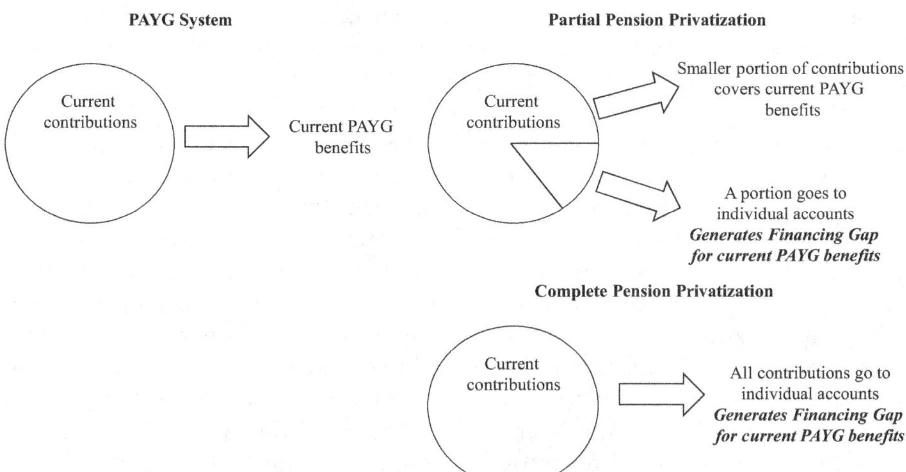

FIGURE 2.1 Pension Privatization and the Financing Gap
Note: Pension privatization was typically implemented as part of a multi-pillar reform in which the first pillar was the PAYG system, the second pillar entailed the privatized accounts, and the third pillar included voluntary retirement savings. Only two countries – Chile and Kazakhstan – pursued complete pension privatization. The size of the financing gap depended on how much money was diverted to individual accounts. Many countries with PAYG systems already ran deficits meaning that they were collecting less in current contributions than their PAYG system required them to pay in current benefits.

The advantages of a mandatory (defined contribution) saving scheme – which requires people to save when they are young so that they will have adequate income when they are old – are that coverage can be broad and benefits are fully portable... A mandatory savings scheme can be part of a national policy to develop new financial institutions, deepen capital markets, mobilize saving, and allocate it to the most productive uses, including uses in the private sector. It also allows workers to increase their return and insure against political or other country-specific risks through international diversification of investments. (p. 244)

The World Bank's advocacy played an important part in the spread of pension privatization. Transnational actors – of which the World Bank was foremost – promoted pension privatization, providing aid and technical assistance, organizing conferences, and arranging for delegations to advise governments considering the reform (Orenstein 2008). Pension privatization was not adopted because of domestic pressures, but instead was inspired by these outside actors who pushed the reform.

Despite the many touted benefits, whether or not pension privatization was adopted depended on a country's particular fiscal situation. In shifting from a PAYG to a funded pension privatization system, governments faced a financing gap. Figure 2.1 demonstrates how this financing gap works.

Brooks (2009) demonstrated that countries faced a double-bind when considering pension privatization. Governments facing the highest implicit pension debt had the greatest need for structural pension reforms, but were least able to afford to cover the financing gap. The financing gap is typically financed by deficit spending. Governments with a large implicit pension debt face negative reactions from investors and international organizations if they increased deficit spending in the short run to finance the switch to pension privatization. Implicit pension debt had a curvilinear effect on the adoption of pension privatization; countries in the mid-range had both the motivation to privatize pensions and could afford to do so. Likewise, because of the cost, of the countries that privatized pensions those with higher levels of implicit pension debt privatized less extensively than those with lower levels of implicit pension debt.

Skeptics of pension privatization have noted that there are other pension policy alternatives. Barr and Diamond (2008) detail the options for parametric reforms which would focus on changing the parameters of a PAYG system (rather than an overhaul like pension privatization). Parametric reforms include reducing the retirement age, decreasing benefits, and eliminating special categories of retirees.

Policy diffusion played an important role too in that countries were learning from each other. Brooks (2007) shows that policy diffusion via learning took place for pension privatization, but not for the adoption of notional defined contributions (NDC). Because pension privatization was more costly to implement and thought to be harder to reverse, governments were more concerned with learning from the experiences of others.

The cost of PAYG systems and the advice of the World Bank promoted pension privatization as an option; domestic political battles determined whether pension privatization was a viable option. On the side of pension privatization were ministries of finance who emphasized cutting the governments' costs. Corporate lobbying by private pension funds and the larger financial conglomerates who owned them also spurred the adoption of pension privatization (Madrid 2003; Williamson et al. 2006; Wilson Sokhey 2010). Politicians and bureaucrats favoring the adoption of pension privatization sometimes allied with the private sector in developing and promoting their proposals. Opponents of pension privatization included ministries of welfare who sought to maintain their hold on power. Cook (2007) details the role of these "statist stakeholders" as a significant hurdle to overcome for those wishing to privatize pensions.

For countries that adopted pension privatization, the shift was enormous and a path departure from PAYG systems. Minns (2001) characterizes this as a "cold war in welfare" that pits "stock markets versus pensions." Brooks (2009) describes this as "a shift from programs that pool risks, bind fates, and join disparate citizens in a common social project of insuring against poverty in old age, toward institutions through which individuals by themselves bear increasing responsibility for protection against the risk of old age poverty" (p. 4). We can see that political behavior did indeed change because of pension privatization. Kerner finds that voters in Latin American countries where pension privatization occurred held politicians responsible for the performance of the stock market.

Given the magnitude of the shift from PAYG to a privatized system, backtracking is all the more remarkable. Backtracking on pension privatization means that in countries that underwent a massive overhaul of social security, politicians later chose – sometimes a few years later, sometimes more than a decade later – to abandon these measures and return to the previous system despite the costs of having privatized pensions, the potential risks of reversal, and continuing challenges in alleviating the fiscal strain and potentially poor benefits generated by PAYG systems.

Should Pension Privatization Survive or Fail?

A great deal has been written about path dependency in the welfare state, particularly in the area of pensions which makes up the single largest social expenditure in most developed countries. Path dependency arguments, however, provide conflicting expectations as to whether pension privatization will survive or fail. Path dependency literature suggests that policy change is rare and difficult particularly in the arena of the welfare state and pensions. On the one hand, this could mean that pension privatization creates a new set of rules that would be difficult to reverse. On the other hand, path dependency arguments also suggest that PAYG systems should be highly resilient to change so that pension privatization would be unlikely to survive. Arguments on both sides provide limited insight into why there has been *variation* in the reversal of pension privatization.

Reasons Why Pension Privatization Should Have Usually Survived

Pension privatization was intended to be a major policy departure that would rewrite the social contract. From this perspective, if politicians were able to adopt and implement such a radical shift, the political system should have been altered in such a way that it would have made pension privatization very difficult to derail. Path dependency theories lay out a number of reasons policies are generally likely to survive: positive feedback loops perpetuate interest group support; policies are often designed to be difficult to change; the supporters of a policy may be able to mobilize more easily than its opponents; and the sheer administrative and bureaucratic effort required to abandon policies make it too difficult to attempt. Rose (1990), for instance, argues that inherited policies create a great deal of institutional inertia, as evidenced by the remarkable staying power of expenditures in the United Kingdom. Change does occur, but Rose argues that it occurs because of the unforeseen consequences of past policy choices.

In *Dismantling the Welfare State? Reagan, Thatcher, and the Politics of Retrenchment*, Pierson (1994) describes the shift to the new politics of the welfare state as one in which countries would be locked in a permanent political battle over austerity measures. This has proven to be largely true in that governments in developed countries are continually trying to address the fiscal burden of expensive PAYG pension systems. Nonetheless, Pierson's theoretical argument about the difficulty of retrenchment suggests that pension privatization – as a path-departing change that fundamentally overhauls the expectations set up by a PAYG system – should be very difficult to get adopted and, if adopted, unlikely to be reversed precisely because it would create a new set of rules that would become self-reinforcing. Myles and Pierson (2001) make a similar claim in noting that "pension policy is a *locus classicus* for the study of path-dependent changes, processes in which choices made in the past systematically constrain the choices open in the future" (p. 306).

Policies determine the context in which political battles occur by changing the preferences of voters and groups and altering the rules of the game (i.e., the legislative outcomes) (Hacker and Pierson 2014). In addition to creating a new self-reinforcing set of rules, there are several reasons that pension privatization should have been especially likely to survive if it was adopted.

First, pension privatization had the potential to fundamentally alter the nature of interest groups, even if it was only partially implemented. Citizens ushered into the new, privatized system would begin to think about their retirement savings under the new rules of the game. Proponents of pension privatization hoped that this reform would go so far as to promote an ownership society in which citizens took greater responsibility for their own retirement savings and cared more about macroeconomic development and stock market performance, which would determine the returns to their investments. Some American commentators have placed a particular emphasis on the argument that pension privatization could promote such a fundamental shift to an ownership society (Nadler 2000). Kerner finds evidence that pension privatization has shaped political behavior. In Latin American countries that adopted pension privatization, he finds that voters rewarded politicians who were in power when the stock market performed well and that the effect of stock market performance on incumbents' electoral success had little influence in countries that had not privatized pensions. Kerner's findings suggest that the reform did indeed alter how citizens think about politics.

Second, pension privatization created another potentially influential interest group in favor of its survival: firms operating in the private pension market. Specifically, private pension funds and investment companies operating in the newly created market of mandatory individual accounts profited from the system's introduction. The logic of collective action suggests that firms operating in the private pension sector should be especially well positioned to influence the political process because they were relatively better organized than other groups (Olson 1965). In the post-communist context, however, we might be more skeptical about applying the Olsonian explanation of interest groups without qualification. Gehlbach (2008) shows that in post-communist politics groups may not be able to credibly offer politicians much in return for favorable policies so that politicians may ultimately favor groups which happen to be politically valuable in some other way such as being more easily taxable.

Third, pension privatization should have been likely to survive because it was adopted with a consideration for its macroeconomic benefits and the signal being sent to investors. The macroeconomic incentives to adopt pension privatization include increasing domestic savings and attracting foreign investment. These potential benefits were arguably even more important after a financial crisis when stimulating the economy is a priority. Reversing pension privatization risked sending a negative signal to investors who might perceive this as a move away from neoliberal reforms that would decrease domestic savings and exacerbate already high deficits. The Argentinean stock market did in fact react negatively to reversals, although these dips were short-lived.[1]

Finally, bureaucratic interests were invested in the survival of pension privatization. The battle over the introduction of pension privatization often occurred among bureaucratic actors who favored or opposed the reform (Ministries of Finance versus Ministries of Welfare). Once one side won – in the case of pension privatization this was often the Ministry of Finance – for reasons of ideology and potentially for reasons related to enhancing its own bureaucratic power that side would not want to surrender its victory. The bureaucratic stakes over pension policy were quite high. National retirement savings are typically one of the largest single categories of government spending. The right to manage that money lends a bureaucracy significant power for which it should fight.

Given public, private, and bureaucratic interests created by the implementation of pension privatization, we should not have expected pension privatization to be abandoned. Path dependency arguments tell us that these groups should have fought for the survival of a policy to which they had become accustomed and depended on for support (citizens), from which they profited (private pension funds, and from which they derived power (bureaucracies).

Reasons Why Pension Privatization Should Have Usually Failed

PAYG social security systems were expected to be highly resilient to change, suggesting that pension privatization reforms would fail to take hold. Citizens who depended on the PAYG system, which offered guaranteed benefits without the risk of market failures, might be unlikely to easily accept new rules under which their future benefits are based on the returns to individual contributions. Indeed, PAYG retirement systems have been cited as one of the classic examples of systems that are likely to become entrenched and will be difficult to change. In the American context, for instance, Campbell (2003) details how Social Security empowered retirees and ensured the program's long-term survival.

There are several specific causal mechanisms that make PAYG systems self-reinforcing and the failure of pension privatization more likely. First,

---

[1] Alexei Barrionuevo, "Argentina Nationalizes $30 Billion in Private Pensions," *New York Times*, October 21, 2008.

a public backlash to losing defined benefits guaranteed by the state is one of the strongest reasons for expecting that pension privatization would be difficult to pursue. Pension privatization shifts the burden from the state onto the shoulders of workers. In many countries, citizens did oppose pension privatization, although the presence and extent of opposition varied from country to country. Any challenges with implementation or poor returns to private pension funds – which was a major issue after the recession that began in 2008 – should have only strengthened citizens' complaints and their demands to return to a PAYG system. The extent of potential public opposition to shifting to a more privatized pension system cannot be overstated. In many of these countries, for decades citizens had planned their retirement around guaranteed benefits from the government.

Second, major bureaucracies also had a vested interest in the PAYG pension systems that were wholly or partially replaced by pension privatization. Although we might expect the bureaucratic winners from pension privatization to help secure its survival, the bureaucratic losers have an incentive to regularly challenge and hinder the new rules of the game in hopes of a reversal. The passage of a major reform might only be the beginning of a bureaucratic power struggle. Major legislation is not the only way that significant policy changes can occur. Rather, very fundamental reorientations of social policies can occur through incremental and poorly publicized changes (Hacker 2008; Jenkins and Patashnik 2012). This suggests that bureaucratic battles over pension policy could play out through competition over regulation and management. Bureaucratic and policy battles can also benefit from a lack of public awareness, which allows them to appropriate influence (DeCanio 2015; Culpepper 2010). Pension reforms are often highly technical making it difficult for citizens to follow debates about changes.

Third, the cost of transitioning from a PAYG to a wholly or partially privatized pension system may have negatively influenced the reform's survival even before its adoption. Nonetheless, the financing gap generated by pension privatization suggests a reason that the cost of reform might undermine itself. More extensive pension privatization translates into a larger financing gap, suggesting that countries with more extensive pension privatization would be the most likely to curtail it.

Finally, a PAYG system typically remained alongside the privatized portion. Returning to an entirely PAYG-based system after instituting pension privatization would certainly be a major turn-about. Doing so, however, was not logistically complicated. Pension privatization did not entail the privatization of physical property; a reversal simply required that existing contributions be redirected back to the PAYG system.

Reasons for Variation in Reversals

Variation was the norm: pension privatization took hold in some countries but not others. Theories provide conflicting expectations about when and why a policy like pension privatization should have survived. Either the old policy is so strong that attempts to overhaul it will fail, or the new policy, once enacted, will create a new political dynamic with new interest groups, making its survival likely.

Both expectations are correct. Major reforms will not always stick so we must identify *when* and *why* change is possible. Research has identified a number of important factors shaping policy stability and change, including the nature of coalitions, how policies shape political behavior, and the effect of policies on power politics and redistribution (Maltzman and Shipan 2008; Mettler and Soss 2004; Moe 1990, 2005; Skowronek 1995). Work in this vein has also focused on stability and change in the welfare state. Hacker (2008) argues that social security and healthcare in the United States have undergone a fundamental shift to more privatized systems, not through large pieces of groundbreaking legislation, but instead through incremental changes. Campbell (2003) examines how social security laws altered the American political terrain, transforming retirees into one of the most influential interest groups (and ensuring the survival of the social security system). These works highlight which actors are most likely to be influential (bureaucrats and the public) and the mechanisms by which they will shape politics (lobbying, popular mobilization, and voting).

Baumgartner and Jones (1993) develop the idea of punctuated equilibrium, in which major policy changes are rare and occur at critical junctures via the development of new issues, new solutions, and agenda-setting. According to Baumgartner and Jones, there is only an illusion of policy equilibrium. In reality, policies are constantly evolving. Punctuated equilibrium might provide us some insight into why pension privatization fails: when problems and challenges with the functioning of pension privatization arise, politicians and interest groups have different ideas about the best solution. Baumgartner and Jones's argument rests on disagreement about the best way forward. This is not a particularly compelling explanation in the case of backtracking on pension privatization. Disagreements about whether and how to pursue pension privatization and about whether the short- and long-term benefits were real preceded its introduction. The financial crisis that began in 2008 may have sparked the battle about what to do but did not introduce fundamentally new ideas. A deeper explanation of how external changes like financial crises lead to major policy shifts allows us to incorporate some of the theoretical arguments discussed here, while adding a clearer explanation of variation in reversals.

Although little research has directly taken up the issue of reversals of major policy reforms, Patashnik (2008) draws on path dependency ideas, arguing that the reforms that survive are those that are supported by political structures; generate "creative destruction," which replaces old coalitions with new ones; and win the support of interest groups. Welfare state reforms, like the Employee Retirement Income Security Act (ERISA), were able to survive because they garnered the support of an interest group, including workers with ERISA-governed retirements who were invested in its survival. Another example includes the New Deal. Hacker and Pierson (2014) cite the example of Eisenhower's acknowledgment of the durability of the New Deal; a durable coalition in support of these changes to the welfare state had been made, and backtracking was politically unthinkable. The Medicare Catastrophic Coverage Act (MCCA), however, is among one of the shortest-lived social reforms ever enacted. Because of a public backlash, Congress reversed the measures, ending plans to cover Medicare expenses with premiums instead of with current contributions. New public policies create new political battles that sometimes result in a policy's survival and other times in its failure.

If a policy's survival depends on disrupting existing coalitional patterns, then the logical next step is determining when these existing patterns can in fact be interrupted. Theories of reversal should consider the conditions under which reforms are able to generate a "new politics" – to borrow Schattschneider's phrase – in which interests and institutions will support a policy's survival. This is precisely the task I undertake by offering a novel argument that combines politicians' incentives to reverse and the strength of potential opposition stakeholders.

Much research focuses on policies that are intended to improve the general welfare of the public over the demands of particularistic interests. Pension privatization is a case in which its intention and the nature of the subsequent beneficiaries are contested. Proponents of pension privatization argue that it improves general welfare by promoting domestic savings and boosting retirement benefits in a sustainable way. Opponents maintain that pension privatization perpetuates inequality and is a reform designed for the benefit of the financial sector, rather than society at large. Depending on how pension privatization was designed and implemented, there is some support for both the proponents and opponents of pension privatization. As a result, pension privatization provides an interesting case in which the new reform may generate popular support or may gain the attention of special interest groups (like private pension funds). There is no guarantee, however, that pension privatization will necessarily secure support from any group.

The trends in reversals of pension privatization raise important questions about work on policy stability and change. To better understand reversals in pension privatization, we must explore the roles played by bureaucracies, citizens, private pension funds, and, last but not least, politicians. Exogenous factors like financial crises are surely an important part of the story. Finally, we must consider how groups and financial crises differ across countries. Change is possible, but how and why will it occur?

Trends in the Reversal of Pension Privatization

The countries that have privatized pensions are to be found in Latin America, Europe, Central Asia, and Australia. These states vary with regard to a range of potential factors influencing both adoption and reversal. Privatizing countries include the following (with reversing countries bolded and italicized):

Argentina, Australia, Bolivia, Bulgaria, Chile, Colombia, Costa Rica, Croatia, *the Czech Republic*, Denmark, Dominican Republic, El Salvador, *Estonia*, *Hungary*, *Kazakhstan*, *Latvia*, *Lithuania*, Macedonia, Mexico, the Netherlands, Peru, *Poland*, *Romania*, *Russia*, *Slovakia*, Sweden, Switzerland, *the United Kingdom*, and Uruguay

Pension privatization has been curtailed in twelve of the twenty-nine countries in which it was adopted, yet reversals were not an inevitable choice for countries that experienced challenges in implementation or public complaints about the new system. Despite initial challenges in the implementation and coverage of privatized pension systems, a number of countries have engaged in a second round of reforms intended to improve the performance of privatized pension systems (Hujo and Rulli 2014; Kritzer 2008; Kritzer et al. 2011). This second round of reforms has included measures intended to address a wide range of issues, such as the coverage provided (including gender disparities), competition amongst private pension funds, investment regulations, payout options, and individual behavior (including voluntary savings patterns).

Writing about the Chilean reforms, Kritzer (2008) explains that "The International Monetary Fund supports these changes because they strive to retain the basic features of the individual account system and, at the same time, address its major shortcomings" (p. 81). Her comments underscore that problems with implementation necessitate adjustment not reversal. Nonetheless, several governments chose to cut back, in whole or part, the extent to which their national retirement systems relied on pension privatization. Table 2.1 summarizes global trends in the reversal of pension privatization measures. These reversals share an important similarity: they cut back on contributions to the second, privatized tier of pensions. Reversals differ from changing the parameters of a privatized system.

Theoretically, variation in the survival of pension privatization is interesting and puzzling. Countries that have long been labeled as devoted to market-oriented reforms – such as Poland, Estonia, Hungary, and Russia – have curtailed or abandoned pension privatization. Conversely, countries long labeled as laggards in economic reforms (although in some cases they have now caught up), like Bulgaria, have adopted and maintained pension privatization.

Reversals of pension privatization have also varied on several important dimensions highlighted in Table 2.1 and include whether the reversal was made in a single piece of legislation or whether it was spread over several measures, the extent of the reversal, and whether or not the reversal was temporary or permanent. Some countries, like Argentina, reversed the system in one step; the Argentine government announced a renationalization of the pension funds in 2008, which ended the privatized pension system introduced fourteen years earlier. The Hungarian government abandoned pension privatization in a single legislative decree in 2010 (although some additional specifications about the

TABLE 2.1 *Reversals in Pension Privatization*

	Year of reform	Partisanship in year of adoption	Year(s) of reversal	Partisanship in year of reversal	Multi-step or one time	Extent of reversal	Temporary or permanent
Argentina	1994	Right *Justicialist Party*	2008	Left *Civic Coalition*	One time	Complete	Permanent
Czech Rep.*	2011	Right *Civic Democratic Party*	2014	Left *Social Democrats*	One time	Complete	Permanent
Estonia	2002	Right *Estonian Reform Party*	2009, 2010	Right *Estonian Reform Party*	Multi-step	Partial	Temporary & permanent
Hungary	1998	Left *Socialists (MSzP)*	2010	Right *Fidesz*	One time	Complete	Permanent
Kazakhstan	1998	Personalist Authoritarian *No dominant party*	2013–2015	Party of Power *Nur Otan*	Multi-step	Complete	Permanent
Latvia	2001	Right *Latvian Way*	2009, 2010	Right *New Era Party*	Multi-step	Partial	Temporary & permanent
Lithuania	2002	Left *Social Democratic Party*	2009, 2010	Right *Homeland Christian Dem. Union*	Multi-step	Partial	Temporary & permanent
Poland	1999	Left *Solidarity Electoral Action*	2011, 2013	Right *Civic Platform*	One time	Partial	Temporary & permanent
Romania	2004	Left *Social Democratic Party*	2009	Right *Liberal Democratic Party*	One time	Partial	Temporary
Russia	2001	Right *Unity*	2012, 2013	Center Right/ Party of Power *United Russia*	Multi-step	Complete	Temporary & permanent
Slovakia	2005	Left *Movement Dem. Slovakia*	2006, 2007	Left *Smer-SMD*	Multi-step	Partial	Permanent
UK	1988	Right *Conservative Party*	2013	Right *Conservative Party*	One time	Complete	Permanent

Sources: Égert (2012 p. 8); Kay (2009); Orenstein (2008); Schwarz (2011, pp. 18–19); Whitehouse (2011); Department for Work & Pensions (UK), White Paper, "The single-tier pension: a simple foundation for saving," January 2013 (available at www.dwp.gov.uk/single-tier-pension, accessed February 27, 2014); IMF Country Report No.14/258. *The Czech government adopted a form of limited pension privatization in 2011 which was implemented in 2013. At the beginning of 2014, the newly elected Social Democratic government announced a reversal to take effect in 2016.

terms of the reversal were subsequently announced). In Russia, the government announced its reversal in two steps, curtailing the privatized tier in December 2012 and again in December 2013 and nearly completely eliminating the second tier.

The extent to which governments abandoned pension privatization also varied. Most reversals were partial and cut contributions to the second, privatized tier of pensions rather than eliminating the system altogether. Only two countries – Argentina and Hungary – chose to completely abandon the policy of pension privatization. The Russian government also chose to abandon pension privatization wholesale, but it has done this in a staggered manner. The British government announced in 2013 that it would be moving to a system based on a flat benefit rate. This could be evidence both of the resiliency of the PAYG system – which, for various reasons, would be resistant to change – and of the resiliency of the new privatized pension system, which was difficult to abandon even after a relatively short period of time.

Finally, governments have chosen to pursue temporary and permanent reversal measures. The Estonian government chose to reduce contributions temporarily, specifying that contributions would return to their previous rates in two years. Temporary measures constitute a less extreme type of backtracking, but a step that could lead to a permanent alteration. Choosing to temporarily curtail pension privatization may reflect a different political logic than a one-time permanent step to cut the system altogether. As with a partial reversal, a decision to cut pension privatization temporarily may reflect an initial test of reactions to pension privatization or may indicate that pension privatization took hold but not as strongly as in countries in which it remained completely intact.

The variation in reversals in pension privatization and the ways in which they have been pursued are separate but closely related questions. This variation provides an empirically rich context in which to examine important theoretical questions about the politics of market-oriented reforms and the welfare state.

Fiscal, Political, and Social Pressures to Reverse Pension Privatization

Financial crisis, partisan politics, advice from international organizations, and post-communist trajectories on economic reform influenced the trend in reversals of pension privatization. These factors provide the starting point for helping us understand why the social contract on retirement could be altered in some countries but not in others.

Reversals in pension privatization have occurred in the aftermath of the financial crises beginning in 2008. This is consistent with work showing that financial crisis can change coalitions and undermine support for particular policies. In *Politics in Hard Times: Comparative Responses to International Crises*, Gourevitch (1986) demonstrates how recessions can alter the nature of coalitions, resulting in major policy changes. Changes in coalitions can bring together unexpected allies who enable new policies to be pursued. In keeping with Gourevitch's expectations, financial crisis undermined support for diverting revenue to individual accounts in some countries. The effect of the financial crisis depended on how severely a country was impacted and the fiscal benefit of reversing pension privatization.

International organizations have been shown to influence the spread of particular policies around the world, particularly regarding economic and social policies. The World Bank was especially instrumental in promoting pension privatization as a way to address aging populations and expensive PAYG retirement systems. Orenstein (2008) details how transnational policy actors – in particular, the World Bank – aided in the policy development, transfer, and implementation of pension privatization. The spread of pension privatization was very much shaped by a process of international policy diffusion.

Because international organizations like the World Bank played such an important role in promoting pension privatization and assisting in its adoption, one speculation has been that reversals were instigated by a shift in the position of the World Bank and other organizations. Orenstein (2011) argues that the 2008 financial crisis led to a rethinking about pension reform and changed attitudes in support of policy solutions that favored the use of financial markets. He further notes a shift in the pension reforms promoted by the World Bank beginning in the late 1990s and early 2000s. The financial crisis provided a final death knell for pension privatization advocacy by empowering its critics at the domestic and international levels.

International organizations were instrumental in the adoption of market-oriented reforms like in the area of pensions. Appel (2011), for instance, explains how global economic integration led East European governments to converge on many tax policies, particularly in the area of corporate taxation, in order to attract foreign capital. In their quest to attract investment, countries that differed on a number of different dimensions adopted strikingly similar packages of tax laws. Personal income taxes were one area in which domestic factors did have significant influence, but this was the exception to the general trend. What is especially striking about post-communist tax laws is that the Central and Eastern European governments went beyond more industrialized countries in establishing these systems. Similarly to tax policy, international organizations have played an important role in influencing pension reform around the world. Indeed, the post-communist countries have adopted similar paths in pursuing radical, neoliberal reforms in terms of both taxation and the spread of pension privatization (Appel and Orenstein 2013).

Although the World Bank has moderated its promotion of the adoption of pension privatization, the World Bank and the international community have *not* supported the reversal of pension privatization. Even opponents of pension privatization argue that its reversal is reactionary and short-sighted (Simonovits 2011). A 2008 World Bank report argued that parametric and structural reforms had not gone far enough. It urged governments to increase the retirement age, strengthen the connection between contributions and benefits, and improve the second, privatized tier by taking steps such as encouraging competition amongst private funds (Kasek et al. 2008). The report urged the post-communist countries to follow the Latin American model in improving fund performance and oversight.

Amidst debates about maintaining Russia's privatized system in Fall 2012, the World Bank's Russian director, Mikhail Rutkovsky, publicly but unsuccessfully urged the government to maintain the 2002 pension reforms.[2] Reversal, then, was not the only obvious solution to criticisms of pension privatization. Indeed, some experts believed that challenges associated with pension privatization warranted further structural measures. The softening of the World Bank's position on pension privatization has corresponded with problems relating to the implementation and functioning of privatized pension systems around the world. This makes it difficult to claim that the shift in the World Bank's position caused the revision or reversal of privatized pension systems. It is equally likely that the World Bank maintained its modified position because these problems emerged and because there was a growing trend in governments making serious parametric and structural changes to pension privatization.

The shift in the World Bank's promotion of pension reform provides a better explanation for why countries around the world have not continued to adopt pension privatization than for why governments chose to backtrack on previously adopted reforms. (In fact, the Czech Republic partially privatized its pension system in 2011 after the shift in the World Bank's stance and following the financial crisis.) This is not to deny that transnational actors have played – and are playing – an important role in spreading information about pension reform. Rather, the role of transnational actors appears to be significantly mediated by domestic conditions. As such, the decline in strong advocacy for pension privatization may be better viewed as a permissive condition that enabled – but did not ensure – that pension privatization could be reversed.

Another potential explanation is that governments of opposite partisan ideology reverse the measures of previous governments. Right-wing governments justified reversals of pension privatization as a means of avoiding increases in taxes and deficits. Of course, although most reversals have been under right-wing governments, if we consider countries over time, 65 percent of the country-year observations in which reversals *did not occur* were also under right-wing governments. Right-wing explanations only take us so far.

Table 2.1 points out that eight of the twelve reversing countries have had right-wing governments, thereby highlighting one possible explanation for reversals: right-wing governments reverse pension privatization. Here too we find that this explanation only goes so far. Hellman (1998) demonstrates that alternations in power often do not lead to reversals in market-oriented reforms (despite fears to the contrary). Indeed, Table 2.1 reveals mixed results regarding

---

[2] *RIA Novosti*, October 9, 2012.

partisanship, alternations in power, and reversals of pension privatization. In Argentina, a right-wing government adopted the reform and a left-wing government reversed it. In Hungary, Poland, and Lithuania, a left-wing government adopted the reform which was later curtailed by a right-wing government. In Latvia, right-wing governments (although comprised of different specific parties) both adopted and reversed pension privatization. In Russia, the same center-right party of power – United Russia – was responsible for the introduction and reversal of pension privatization. Likewise, in Kazakhstan, the same political leadership – although different parties of power – backed both the introduction and reversal of pension privatization. In the United Kingdom and Estonia, the same party also introduced and later reversed pension privatization.

The Hungarian case, however, reveals why partisanship may still play an important part of a complete explanation of reversal, even if partisan politics played a distinct role in different countries. The Hungarian Socialist Party (MSzP) introduced pension privatization in 1998, which was subsequently reversed by the right-wing Fidesz government elected in 2010. Fidesz had expressed concerns about the financing gap generated by pension privatization since the adoption of the policy and justified its dismantling by arguing that they wanted to avoid higher taxation and curb rising deficits (Fultz 2012). Although partisan preferences clearly motivated the reversal, fiscal costs and pressure from the European Union (EU) also played an important role in the policy turnabout. After winning the election in Summer 2010, the new Fidesz prime minister, Viktor Orbán, requested that the EU increase its maximum allowed deficit from 3.5 to 7.5 percent of GDP. He specifically asked the European Commission to take into account the effect of pension privatization on Hungary's deficits (Simonovits 2011). This suggests the Hungarian government may have wanted to avoid a reversal if possible. Indeed, previous Fidesz governments had revised the pension privatization reforms, but they had not sought to eliminate the system altogether. The EU refused Orbán's request, and in Fall 2010 the Hungarian government announced a temporary suspension of payments to the second, privatized pillar of pensions (this would quickly become a permanent reversal of Hungary's 1998 reform) (Égert, 2012). Thus, it appears to be a combination of fiscal pressures and domestic political factors, including partisan policy goals, which explain the Hungarian reversal.

Reversals in pension privatization are largely a post-communist phenomenon, with the exceptions of just two countries: Argentina and the UK. Why, then, are reversals concentrated among the post-communist countries? One possible explanation is a standard communist legacy argument: these countries used to be communist countries, underwent a difficult transition to the market, and found a lack of public support for radical reforms such as pension privatization. Appel and Orenstein (2013) explain why economic reforms have followed a remarkably similar path in Central and Eastern Europe, indicating that global forces have had a common impact on these countries. Although the residual influence of communism on public opinion and its ability to hamper reform was a serious concern in the early 1990s, this explanation is particularly weak. First, those countries that have been the most radical economic reformers did not face a public backlash that resulted in large-scale reversals. On the contrary, countries that instituted the most dramatic market-oriented reforms saw political turnover but not reversals in economic reforms (Hellman 1998). Public opinion has been influential on policymaking, including in social areas such as housing, education, and pensions (Roberts 2010), but has not eroded market-oriented reforms wholesale.

Furthermore, some of the post-communist countries that adopted pension privatization reversed it while others did not; the communist legacy argument has difficulty explaining this variation. There are arguments about differences in the communist legacies (Kitschelt et al. 1999; Grzymała-Busse 2002), but none of these can really be linked directly to why there would be more or less support for pension privatization. Grzymała-Busse (2002), for instance, argues that the nature of the Communist Party during the communist era determined its ability to reinvent itself and successfully compete in elections, or not. Communist parties with legacies of reform, like the Hungarian Workers' Party, were able to more effectively recreate their party and win elections. Ultimately, the argument that the communist legacy undermined support in pension privatization is not a plausible explanation for the variation in reversals of pension privatization that we observe.

Another possible explanation is that many of the post-communist countries in Central and Eastern Europe are members of the EU. The EU set deficit guidelines that made maintaining pension privatization more difficult. Specifically, the EU enforces deficit guidelines which require governments to avoid taking on too much debt (Barr and Rutkowski 2005; Ferge and Juhasz 2004). Several of the post-communist countries that privatized pensions petitioned the EU to make exceptions to the maximum allowed debt levels to account for their pension privatization reforms which had increased borrowing in the short term. The EU initially agreed, but later declined thus putting more pressure on these countries to cut pension privatization (Casey 2012). The other members of the EU – which were also not post-communist countries – mostly did not privatize pensions (with the exception of Sweden and the United Kingdom). Therefore, a reason for reversals being concentrated among the post-communist countries could be that they were EU members and were the countries that had privatized pensions. As a result, what looks like a post-communist phenomenon is really more an EU phenomenon.

As with the communist legacy argument, however, two EU post-communist countries that privatized pensions did not reverse: Bulgaria and Croatia. Russia is a post-communist country that has abandoned its pension privatization reforms but is not an EU member country. Additionally, there is significant variation in the nature and degree of reversals. Although the EU's deficit requirements may have pressured governments to consider curtailing pension privatization, this does not appear to be the only factor explaining reversals.

TABLE 2.2 *Factors Influencing the Reversal of Pension Privatization*

	Influence on reversing pension privatization
Financial crisis	Triggered discussions of reversal, filtered through domestic politics
Partisan politics	Politicians of the right and left both have incentives to reverse pension privatization
International organizations	Shift in advice was permissive condition for reversals, not causal
Post-communist politics	Reforms weren't uniquely unpopular in post-communist countries

Remaining Questions. The factors discussed here are summarized in Table 2.2. The financial crisis of 2008 undeniably sparked debates about pension privatization in some countries, partisan battles culminated in debates about social security reform in some countries, the shift in the World Bank's stance led some politicians to reconsider, and the EU's deficit guidelines prompted structural changes to social security in some places. None of these factors, however, offer a definitive causal explanation for why financial crisis, partisan battles, the World Bank's stance and the EU resulted in reversals in some places but not others.

The degree of financial crisis – one of the most likely instigators – does not directly correlate with reversals of pension privatization. The World Bank's shift in its policy stance is more accurately seen as a permissive condition which made reversal possible, but did not provide an independent motivation to backtrack. Partisan battles certainly mattered, but they do not map onto our standard expectations: right-wing governments were the ones most likely to reverse this market-oriented reform. The EU's deficit guidelines certainly spurred governments to consider reversing, but not all EU members that privatized pensions have also reversed. Finally, although reversals were concentrated among the post-communist countries, there is divergence in their pension privatization trajectories. Pension privatization was adopted by some post-communist countries but not others and was reversed by some reformers and not others.

Ways Forward: Theories of Market-Oriented Reform and the Welfare State

Limited work directly addresses the issue of backtracking and has often done so with a consideration of packages of reform rather than specific measures. Scholars have correctly argued, however, that we can adapt overly deterministic path dependency theories to explain institutional change (Ebbinghaus 2005). Moving beyond commonly given explanations, two areas of research are most relevant to our understanding of why pension privatization might be reversed: (1) the politics of market-oriented reforms; and (2) comparative research on the welfare state, including why pension privatization was adopted in the first place. Neither body of literature fully explains why pension privatization was reversed, but both provide an important starting point.

The Politics of Economic Reform

Transitions to democracy and the market in the 1980s and 1990s – including the fall of communism in Europe, the Caucasus, and Central Asia – sparked renewed research around which policies were best for economic growth and which political systems were most likely to adopt better policies. Poor economic policies – and possibly reversals – could be the result of a range of factors: the wrong political institutions; public opposition; lobbying by special interest groups; or political polarization.

Democratic institutions are determinants of economic growth in part because democracies are thought to make better policy choices (e.g., North 1990; Rodrik 1991). This is because in democracies, politicians have the right incentives to accomplish better outcomes. Democratic institutions are also thought to facilitate trust and economic interactions. Przeworski (1991), however, challenges the idea that democracies are better at economic reform. He describes a J-curve which represents the dip in consumption and economic performance resulting from the introduction of market-oriented reforms. These reforms are characterized by short-term costs with long-term and uncertain benefits, and such measures are "driven by desperation and hope, not by reliable blueprints" (p. 189). The problem lies in part with the incongruence between the time necessary to realize the benefits of market-oriented reforms and when politicians face reelection. Even if politicians are able to adopt painful but necessary reforms, those same politicians are likely to face public backlash and be voted out of office in favor of politicians who will reverse course.

Przeworski provides a clear expectation for why market-oriented reforms might be reversed: the public backlash against the short-term costs may not allow the transition to a market-based system to progress. Przeworski (1991) writes that

…[I]n the face of political reactions, governments are likely to vacillate between the technocratic political style inherent in market-oriented reforms and the participatory style required to maintain consensus. They abandon or postpone some reforms, only to try them again later. And each new time they encounter a smaller stock of initial confidence. Ultimately, the vacillations of financially bankrupt governments become politically destabilizing. (p. 189)

As politicians alternate between reform and reversal, the public has less and less confidence in the reforms, making progress even more difficult. For the post-communist European countries, Przeworski thought that geography was one reason to be cautiously optimistic about breaking this cycle.

In contrast to Przeworski, Hellman (1998) made the compelling argument that democracy had actually promoted progress on economic reforms by curtailing the influence of special interest groups. According to Hellman, special business interests – rather than the average citizen – will block progress on economic reforms. Hellman notes that democratic and economic reforms were correlated among the post-communist countries. The countries that had experienced the most turnover in free and fair elections had also made the most progress on economic reforms.

Democracy and the market go together, argues Hellman, because democracy curbs the influence of short-term winners of economic reform. In the post-communist countries (as well as other regions), the short-term winners were wealthy businesspeople who profited from early privatization deals and market-oriented reforms. Where the political system is not very democratic, these short-term winners have a greater influence on the content of economic reforms. The worst possible outcome is a partial reform equilibrium in which some market-oriented reform had been adopted, but in which there were many loopholes – such as tax breaks and special subsidies – that empowered the short-term winners, that is, the wealthy businesspeople, enabling them to profit from partial reform.

Where the political system is more democratic, politicians are less inclined to use their resources to give powerful businesspeople the special breaks that undermined overall progress on economic reform. Therefore, even when the public objected to the short-term costs of market-oriented reforms and voted politicians out of office, subsequent political leaders did not abandon the course of reform. Poland is a good example of the political logic described by Hellman. In the early 1990s, the country's Solidarity-led government, led by Lech Wałeşa, adopted a number of important market-oriented reforms. Upon facing reelection as president in 1995, however, Wałeşa lost, and the Solidarity party subsequently lost power. Although the Polish government adopted a number of social reforms intended to offset the costs of the transition for the public, Polish leaders never significantly backtracked on these early market-oriented reforms.

Others have confirmed Hellman's insight that powerful special interest groups – particularly wealthy businesspeople – can have a disproportionate influence on political systems and promote corruption (e.g., Barnes 2003, 2006; Ganev 2007; Murphy et al. 1992; Rutland 2000). Wealthy businesspeople can use a variety of means to exercise undue influence on the government. Businesses can lobby the government through either official or unofficial channels. They can mobilize citizens to back particular proposals and pieces of legislation (Walker 1991), though this has been a less common tactic in the post-communist world. Finally, businesses can exert structural leverage on governments that fear a loss of investment (Przeworski 2008). This final tactic is a classic means of business influence that is captured by the exit, voice, or loyalty game in which the mere threat of exit is sufficient to sway the government's policy position (Hirschman 1970). Lindblom (1982) echoes this concern in his discussion of how implicit threats from businesses could corrode democratic politics. In summary, private businesses have been identified as influential interest groups, often with the potential to influence economic policy, and their role in the reversal of pension privatization should be seriously considered.

Other work clarifies the circumstances under which democracy is most likely to promote stable market-oriented reforms, thereby providing more nuance to our understanding of the connection between democracy and the market. Frye (2010) argues that democracy promotes economic reform and development, but only when there is a low level of political polarization. Evidence from the post-communist countries confirms that polarization mediates the effect of democracy on reform. The Bulgarian case epitomizes how political polarization hampers progress on important market-oriented reform. Alternations in power between the Bulgarian Socialist Party (BSP) and various parties and alliances of non-BSP parties resulted in inconsistent progress on market-oriented reforms in the 1990s. At the other end of the spectrum, the Polish case exemplifies why democracy can promote progress on economic reform. Finally, Russia pursued inconsistent reforms under a polarized democracy in the 1990s, before the rise of autocracy in the 2000s resulted in stalled economic reforms. Although the partisanship of the government fails to offer a complete explanation for backtracking, political polarization may contribute to reversals of market-oriented reforms.

Gehlbach and Malesky (2010) find that the presence of more veto players promotes the adoption of market-oriented reforms and helps prevent reversals by weakening the power of special interest groups that oppose these measures. In a similar vein, Nooruddin (2011) finds that institutionalized gridlock can result in more stable economic growth by making policy change harder and more predictable. These findings are consistent with Hellman's argument that the concern should be less about public backlash – as Przeworski's characterization of reform suggests – and more about neutralizing the influence of potentially powerful special interest groups.

Instead of considering overall progress on reform, I focus on the political economy of reversing one specific reform: pension privatization. Additionally, only limited research addresses reversals. Many of the factors that influence the adoption of reforms are also likely to play a role in whether or not these reforms survive. As stated in this chapter's opening quote from Schattschneider (1935), new policies create "a new politics." Once policies are adopted, new interest groups develop and favor the survival of the reform. International pressures, which may have been present when considering the adoption of reforms, will also change once a reform has been adopted. Because frequent shifts in pension policy are widely considered to be ill-advised, even experts who opposed the introduction of pension privatization might not back its reversal. In short, we must draw on existing theories to develop a clearer idea of how the influential factors and actors identified in the broader literature help explain reversals generally and reversal in pension privatization in particular.

When reversals are addressed, the emphasis is usually on packages of reform (as in Frye 2010, Gehlbach and Malesky 2010, and Nooruddin 2011). As a result, our theories are based on general trends, not battles over specific pieces of legislation. For instance, democratic governments with low political polarization have been shown to make more progress on market-oriented reforms and to be less likely to backtrack. Does this mean that the reversal of pension privatization is less likely in democratic regimes with a lower level of polarization? Perhaps, but establishing this would require us, at a minimum, to theorize more about the link between regime type and the dynamics of pension privatization. Regime type might influence the reversal of pension privatization because politicians respond to different demands in different regimes or because different regimes empower some groups relative to others. If politicians are not responding to popular demands, however, then regime type is likely to have limited influence. By examining a specific reform, we can also reduce the level of abstraction when we consider packages of reform.

Second, much – though not all – of the research on the politics of economic reform points to the role of public backlash, partisan politics, and interest groups in determining the course of reforms. These common explanations are insufficient to fully explain the reversal of pension privatization. We must theorize more precisely about how and why public opinion, partisan politics, and domestic politics influenced the reversal of pension privatization.

Welfare State Politics

Research on broad trends in the development of welfare state policy tends to emphasize several major factors: historical legacies, coalition politics, institutional factors, and economic crises. Historical legacies can matter in a variety of ways, but one of the primary means by which history matters is in defining the current set of policy choices. In their comprehensive survey of social policy changes in Latin America, East Asia, and Eastern Europe, Haggard and Kaufman (2008) highlight the importance of coalitions, economics, and institutions that have independent and interactive influences on the development of the welfare state. They trace the development of initial social welfare policies through major periods of global and regional change to better explain how and why welfare states evolved as they did.

In a similar vein, Hemerjick (2012) emphasizes the importance of historical factors in explaining the divergent paths of welfare state reform across EU member countries. He argues that welfare policies are not just a combination of ad hoc measures lacking foresight, as they are often characterized; rather, policymakers mix and match old and new policies to adapt to changing situations. According to his estimation, we should not be so pessimistic about the trajectories of welfare states, which are more responsive than often thought. This provides a useful framework in which to consider how historical factors lead to combinations of old and new policies, possibly including PAYG pension systems and elements of privatized pension systems. It provides little clarity, however, regarding when pension privatization will play a smaller or bigger role in national retirement policy.

Indeed, Hemerjick notes that "Welfare state change is work in progress, leading to patchwork mixes of old and new policies and institutions, on the lookout perhaps for more coherence" (p. 14). In short, what we call the "welfare state" is a combination of very different policies which may – or, more likely, may not – be coherently connected. Precisely because the policies that constitute welfare states are so different and can be dictated by different socioeconomic, fiscal, and political concerns, we should consider studying specific policies individually, rather than attempting to lump together very different policies under the heading of the welfare state.

Economic crises have also been identified as an important determinant of changes in welfare state policies. Gourevitch (1986) explored the ways in which economic crises affect policymaking. He notes that countries' policy responses to the same stimulus – economic crisis – differ for four main reasons: the mechanisms of representation (political parties and interest groups); the organization of the state; actors' ideology; and coalition politics. Gourevitch considers whether and why countries maintained free trade or pursued protectionism after several major economic crises. In particular, Gourevitch notes that economic crisis can spur change by causing a shift in the coalitions built across social groups.

The scope of Gourevitch's question – whether countries respond to financial crises with free trade or protectionism over time – is broad. By his own admission, the broad scope of his question makes it difficult to assess competing explanations. He writes that it is "difficult to judge among alternative explanations of why these bargains occurred rather than some others and of the status of various factors in explaining the different bargains" (p. 33). The methodological problem is further complicated by the fact that, "the relationship of economic situations to mediating institutions and ideologies does not appear constant" (p. 33). By focusing on one policy area over a much shorter time period (i.e., the reversal of pension privatization), we can much better assess which explanations are best.

More recently, Häuserman (2010) examines pension policy in France, Germany, and Switzerland in the period between 1970 and 2004. Like Gourevitch, she emphasizes the importance of coalitions – specifically cross-class coalitions – in building support for major pension reforms. Häuserman argues that sociostructural shifts enabled far-reaching changes. This argument, however, is particularly difficult to apply to the case of reversals in pension privatization. The changes to which Häuserman refers occurred slowly over decades and introduced fundamental, if not always structural, changes to the pension policies in these three countries. By contrast, pension privatization was in place for less than a decade in many countries in which it was introduced. The types of socio-structural changes to which she refers did not occur in this relatively short time period between the introduction and reversal of pension privatization. The question about reversing pension privatization, then, is different from why the reforms were adopted in the first place.

Other research on specific reforms confirms the importance of coalitions and crises as explanations and addresses in greater depth who the most important actors are. In particular, the wave of pension privatization around the world spurred research on its adoption, although few predicted that, or why, there would be a counter-wave of reversals. Cook (2007) writes about the pursuit of welfare reforms in post-communist politics, identifying, in part, the importance of statist stakeholders in the process. Chandler (2004) also provides an in-depth analysis of Russia's pension reforms over time, focusing on changes in legislative power and bureaucratic actors. These works identify who the most important actors are likely to be, but do not provide us with clear expectations about whether or not these actors may undertake the decision to reverse previously adopted measures. Finally, in the vast majority of welfare state research, the questions are about the adoption of policies rather than the reversal of specific measures. Work on retrenchment addresses a kind of reversal, but focuses on parametric changes – reductions in an existing policy – rather than structural changes such as reversals in pension privatization. More research is needed, then, to understand when a fundamental structural change can and will be abandoned.

One area in which research on the welfare state has given us less insight than might be expected is when and why major policy changes will be able to successfully alter the social contract. Certainly, coalitions and crises instigate change, and statist stakeholders and public opinion play a central role. But when will a major shift be locked in or reversed? Research on the welfare state suggests that if and when politics fundamentally alter coalitions, and do so in a durable way, the policy is more likely to stick (Gourevitch 1986 is just one example). This is consistent with work on policy stability (i.e., Patashnik 2008; Hacker and Pierson 2014), which also emphasizes the political significance of how policies do (and do not) change coalitions. The key component of this explanation, then, is the scope of the conditions: when and why will domestic politics shift in favor of reversals? Furthermore, if a politician has her own incentive to reverse – which was the case regarding pension privatization, where reversing meant freeing up short-term revenue – then identifying when and how domestic politics will facilitate or hamper reversal initiatives is also central to explaining why backtracking occurs.

Conclusion

Theories of reversals and the welfare state are currently missing a full explanation for why a policy like pension privatization would be reversed. There are conflicting theoretical expectations about whether pension privatization should have survived: either the PAYG pension systems should be so entrenched that pension privatization should have generally failed, or pension privatization should have become entrenched as the new rules of the game went into effect. Commonly given explanations in academic and policy circles for the reversal of pension privatization highlight important factors, but do not offer a full causal explanation for the variation in backtracking that has occurred. The 2008 financial crisis starkly emphasized the significant fiscal costs generated by pension privatization and led to a modification in the advice from the World Bank which began advocating a range of possible pension reforms instead of advocating pension privatization as strongly. Both of these factors, however, influenced all of the countries that had privatized pensions, albeit to varying degrees. It is also not the case that only right or left-wing governments engaged in reversals, nor is there a clear pattern of alternations in power resulting in reversals.

Research on market-oriented reforms and the welfare state has been more focused on packages of reform and on identifying broad policy trends than on explaining why any particular policy would succeed or fail. There are theoretical and methodological advantages to focusing on a particular policy area. While broad characterizations of trends in welfare state regimes tend to be more descriptive in nature and characterize the larger political debates, because of their large scope, they are not ideal for testing specific explanations. Such works often have a take-away point that democracy, institutional design, and history matter in complicated and interrelated ways. These are valuable contributions, but serve a different role than mine. By focusing on a specific empirical trend, we can come to a clear conclusion about which factors matter, and how, in political debates over economic and social policy. This is not to argue that the findings from a particular policy area are not relevant for an understanding of other policies (but instead that testing them simultaneously poses methodological problems). Rather, we must consider how different policies are similar and distinct both in developing and testing theories.

Different policies spark different political debates and influence different groups. Geddes (2003) warns against a research design that compares the influence of a single group across policy areas; different policies – even within the arena of the welfare state – are influenced by different factors. In testing particular explanations, however, it is theoretically and methodologically simpler to focus on a single policy area. A comparison of reforms in healthcare and pension privatization would raise complications in explaining how the different timelines for planning shaped politicians' incentives and interest groups' sway. Differences in financial sector interests between healthcare and pensions would further complicate the comparison. Comparing pension privatization and the privatization of state-owned enterprises would also be problematic; pension privatization entails a recurring financing gap, while the cost of privatizing property is largely one-time.

Important theoretical and methodological challenges can be addressed by focusing on the reversal of a particular reform such as pension privatization. Pension privatization as a reform also presents some unique characteristics that allow us to assess possible explanations of reversal. It was promoted as a social reform, but one with a number of financial and macroeconomic benefits.

Pension privatization was supposed to promote domestic savings, encourage the development of the financial sector, attract foreign investment, and boost growth. In considering why this policy was curtailed, we can evaluate how the financial and social consequences either bolstered or undermined its survival. Finally, pension privatization posed a challenge for politicians facing tighter fiscal constraints, since it diverted current contributions away from covering the payment of current benefits.

Although pension privatization is unique, answering this specific empirical puzzle can provide generalizable findings relevant to several areas of research. Pension privatization is a market-oriented and welfare reform and can provide insight into both areas. Politicians and policymakers often attempt change, but are not always successful in their efforts. When and why did governments choose to reverse pension privatization?

3

A Theory of Policy Reversal

To understand why a major potentially path-departing change does not survive, we must consider the nature of the policy that was adopted, including the cost of implementing and maintaining it and its effect on domestic groups. The degree of pension privatization varies significantly across the countries that pursued this reform and influences two factors which determine the likelihood of its survival: the financing gap generated by pension privatization and the extent to which various domestic stakeholders support keeping pension privatization. More extensive pension privatization translates into a larger pot of money that politicians can access to obtain short-term revenue. More extensive pension privatization also means that citizens depend more on the new retirement system for security in old age and that private pension funds and investment companies enjoy greater profits from managing and investing retirement savings. Private pension funds will lobby politicians to maintain pension privatization and citizens may vote against politicians who reduce or eliminate mandatory contributions to the individual retirement accounts to which citizens have become accustomed. Furthermore, more extensive pension privatization could create more entrenched bureaucratic interests with a stake in seeing the continuation of pension privatization. The effect of more extensive pension privatization, then, generates countervailing pressures: fiscal incentives to reverse and domestic political incentives to maintain.

Because of these countervailing pressures, I argue that adopting a moderate degree of pension privatization made pension privatization more easily reversible. This challenges the conventional wisdom that it is primarily more extensive reforms that are more difficult to change. Financial crisis prompts politicians to consider sources of short-term revenue to shore up government services and, possibly, prevent increases in taxes. Following the financial crisis of 2008, politicians have been most likely to backtrack on pension privatization in conditions where the fiscal benefits are large but citizens and private pension funds are not strongly supportive of the new system. Moderate pension privatization results in a significant amount of money being diverted from current costs while simultaneously failing to generate significant support for the reform among public and private interests. A lesser degree of pension privatization entails little fiscal benefit in reversing; a large degree of pension privatization generates much greater support among citizens and private pension funds who would fight for its survival, even though politicians could gain short-term revenue by backtracking.

Politicians were eager to learn from other countries' experiences, particularly those that had pursued a similar degree of pension privatization. Pension privatization – like many economic reforms – was adopted and reversed in cross-national waves in which governments observed and learned from each other's experiences. The World Bank played an instrumental role in promoting the benefits of pension privatization and providing assistance in designing and implementing such reforms. In considering reversals, governments could observe the reaction from investors in other countries, the public, and international organizations.

My argument about the effect of fiscal pressures is inspired directly by the findings in Brooks (2009). Brooks finds that the implicit pension debt of the PAYG pension system had a curvilinear effect on the adoption and degree of pension privatization. The countries that were most likely to privatize pensions had mid-range levels of implicit pension debt which generated a fiscal incentive to reform and meant governments could still afford to do so. Countries with little implicit pension debt faced little pressure to reform; those with large implicit pension debt could not afford the cost of diverting mandatory contributions to individual accounts nor could they risk the consequences of high deficits in the short term to cover the resultant financing gap.

My argument is distinct from previous accounts, including Brooks (2009), in several ways. First, and perhaps somewhat obviously, I am addressing a different empirical question – reversals not adoption. Adoption and reversal are related, but distinct issues. We must consider how the factors that prompt the adoption of a policy may or may not be responsible for its reversal. Second, I focus on initial conditions, specifically how the nature of the reform adopted influences fiscal costs and the nature of potential domestic stakeholders and how external factors like financial crisis will prompt reversal for some reforms – like a moderate degree of pension privatization – and not others. Finally, I consider why we would observe variation in how reversals are pursued in different countries. The approach to backtracking affirms how and why moderate reforms were most susceptible to reversal when financial crisis struck and domestic political conditions made reversal both politically desirable and feasible.

Low levels of opposition from the public and fiscal pressures on the government created conditions that were conducive to reversing. Domestic politics then determined whether or not pension privatization was reversed. Due to a variety of factors different governments have different preferences over how to distribute and redistribute pensions. Domestic political conditions including partisan political battles and policy goals played a central role in determining when these permissive conditions – limited domestic opposition and fiscal pressures – resulted in a reversal of pension privatization, i.e., a reduction or elimination of contributions to individual accounts established by these second-pillar reforms. All of the countries studied here did, of course, face greater fiscal pressures after the 2008 recession. Ultimately, the political battles which determined the future of pension privatization were influenced – to varying degrees – by a wide range of actors, including Ministries of Finance, Ministries of Welfare, state Pension Funds, private pension funds, business associations, international organizations like the World Bank and IMF, and individual experts and leaders. To offer a complete explanation of reversals, I incorporate an understanding of fiscal pressures and the initial reform design filtered through domestic political conditions to result in reversals.

A link exists between the conditions resulting in a certain type of reform being adopted, the resulting risk of reversal, and how that reversal is likely to take place. In the case of pension privatization, moderate pension privatization was a distinct kind of pension privatization which made reversal more likely and, depending on domestic conditions, was more likely to be either wholesale or mediated through partial, temporary, and staggered measures.

In this chapter, I offer a new understanding of how the degree of reform influences the ability to successfully maintain new policies and alter the social contract, or not. Unlike other theories, I emphasize the opposing pressures generated by the extent to which politicians pursued reform initially. Other work – including studies of packages of reforms – has identified a tension between politicians' fiscal motivations and citizens' opposition to measures that gain short-term revenue. Przeworski (1991) explains the logic by which politicians' desire for long-term growth might be hampered by citizens' short-term concern with falling consumption. My argument reverses this logic: when pension privatization has been pursued to a moderate degree and fiscal pressures arise, it is the politicians seeking short-term benefits who will undermine market-oriented reforms and citizens (and other private actors) whose support can facilitate the survival of costly but necessary measures.

Politicians' Incentives to Reverse or Maintain Pension Privatization, and to Reverse in Different Ways

I assume that politicians are primarily office-seeking in nature. Although politicians can and do have other motivations besides winning elections, successful politicians will have to concern themselves primarily with staying in office. In order to win and retain office, politicians are served well by finding sources of revenue which they can spend on the policies their supporters care about. Politicians therefore respond to business lobbyists – like private pension funds – for a variety of reasons related to winning elections. Businesses can provide them with campaign donations, can rally the public, and can provide important information. Politicians are also, of course, concerned with the preferences of citizens who can vote them out of office.

Pension privatization, in particular, poses a challenge for politicians in terms of short- and long-term planning. Short-term resources must be diverted to allow for long-term fiscally sustainable planning. Private pension funds profit from this system – in direct proportion to the extent to which it was pursued. Citizens should come to expect their own retirement security to depend on the existence and performance of individual retirement accounts in direct proportion to the extent that pension privatization was pursued.

I address these pressures on politicians in turn: politicians' fiscal and political incentives to reverse pension privatization, pressure from potential domestic stakeholders to maintain pension privatization, and the nature of policy diffusion. The observable implications of my theory are that we are more likely to observe reversals of pension privatization during periods when a new budget is being debated (and fiscal constraints are more pressing and salient), during or in the aftermath of a financial crisis, and just after elections have been held (when a public backlash would be less consequential for politicians in office).

Pension policy – like many policy areas – is influenced by a wide range of domestic and international actors. In the domestic arena, the relevant groups include those in the public sector such as government bureaucracies and agencies, political parties, and individual politicians and those in the private sector, including private pension funds and business associations. Citizens also matter although the specific groups of citizens who are most relevant depends on to which groups leaders care about appealing. Here, for instance, current retirees and future retirees have distinct preferences regarding pension policy. In the international arena, actors like the World Bank and the IMF regularly publish and advise governments on pension policy. In developing a full explanation of reversals, I take into account the role of these varied groups.

Finally, my theoretical expectations also have implications for how – and to what degree – politicians are likely to pursue reversals. When the domestic situation puts a country under an especially high degree of fiscal strain, the government is likely to completely abandon contributions to the second privatized tier. When potential domestic stakeholders are a greater concern for politicians – either because the reform was extensive or because of the nature of domestic political competition – then we are more likely to observe reversals that are moderated by being partial, temporary, and staggered.

Politicians' Incentives to Reverse Pension Privatization

Pension privatization diverts money into individual accounts; this money could otherwise be used to cover pensions for current retirees, or it could be spent in other areas (see Figure 2.1 in Chapter 2). The financing gap generated by pension privatization proved to be a major strain on governments' finances

(Bielecki 2011). The extent to which pensions were privatized determined the size of the pot of money at stake. Critically, the annual recurring costs of pension privatization are not sunk costs, i.e., they ae not one-time costs paid when the policy is adopted or implemented. With pension privatization, the cost of transferring all citizens to the new, privatized system is incurred annually over a period of several decades. Even after all citizens have been switched over to the privatized system (reforms are typically phased in excluding those over a certain age), money directed to individual accounts continues to be a potential source of revenue to be accessed by the government for other purposes. Because of the recurring costs, pension privatization was an especially tempting source of short-term revenue. In every election and every budgetary cycle, politicians had a source of revenue being tied up in individual accounts.

Debates about backtracking on pension privatization should be most likely at times of fiscal duress. Politicians should be especially likely to look for short-term revenue when a financial crisis occurs which reduces the government's tax revenue and spending power. We have long known that financial crisis sparks new political debates. Gourevitch (1986) details how crisis can result in shifting political coalitions which, in turn, alter economic policies. More immediately, financial crisis can spark debate about what the government spends on and how to get short-term revenue. At the very time that the government coffers are less full, therefore, financial crisis may also spark increased public demands for more spending in areas such as unemployment benefits and other forms of social assistance.

Financial crisis should be a prime trigger for discussions of reversing pension privatization. As the government has less income, more demands are being made. Raising taxes or decreasing spending are particularly unappealing options during a financial crisis. The money being diverted to individual accounts – a seemingly responsible long-term policy adopted in better times – suddenly seems unsustainable and like a convenient source of short-term revenue. Whether financial crisis actually results in reversals, however, should depend on how much money is being diverted to individual accounts and whether citizens and private pension funds were likely to object. Financial crisis triggers politicians to consider reversals; reversal only happens if the fiscal incentive is large enough and domestic stakeholders do not block doing so.

Reversing pension privatization is not, of course, the only way in which politicians might gain access to short-term revenue, but financial crisis made alternate options undesirable. Pension privatization was an especially vulnerable target because the amount of money being diverted for future retirees was easily identifiable and quantifiable; the increasing value of those individual accounts was a tempting source of revenue. Why would politicians choose to reverse pension privatization instead of increasing revenue by cutting spending in another area, increasing deficits, or raising taxes? In part, the financial crisis that began in 2007 made the options of increasing deficits or raising taxes especially undesirable. Long time horizons and individuals' general tendency to undervalue saving in the present further made individual pension accounts an easier target than other areas of spending like healthcare, unemployment, infrastructure, and many other areas.

Pension privatization is similar to other market-oriented reforms as a policy choice for which there are short-term costs and long-term benefits. Indeed, the idea of the J-curve – as described by Przeworski in *Democracy and the Market* – is based on the assumption that market-oriented reforms would cause increases in inflation and unemployment from which economies would recover at some uncertain future time and with some uncertainty about the future benefits. This is partially why Przeworski (1991) characterizes market-oriented reforms as "a plunge into the unknown, a risky historical experiment born out of desperation and driven by hope, not by justifiable benefits" (pp. 138–9). Roland (2000) echoes this concern by advocating on behalf of more small-scale policy experimentation rather than radical policies that may be more difficult to abandon. The short-term costs and uncertain long-term benefits of pension privatization are similar to other market-oriented reforms in this regard. Whenever politicians are weighing decisions where there are short-term sacrifices in exchange for uncertain, future benefits, we would expect there to be a similar motivation for politicians to abandon reforms to access short-term revenue.

Critically, this discussion emphasizes why pension privatization is different from other market-oriented reforms: the costs are more easily identifiable and quantifiable in individual accounts and the costs recur for a longer period of several decades as opposed to one-time costs. Consider the major categories of market-oriented reforms described by the European Bank for Reconstruction and Development (EBRD), which tracks the progress of post-communist countries on market-oriented reforms. The market-oriented reforms tracked by the EBRD include privatization, enterprise restructuring, price liberalization, trade and foreign exchange systems, competition policy, banking reform and interest rate liberalization, and securities markets and non-bank financial institutions. Privatization of state-owned enterprises, like pension privatization, required some short-term costs. The state gained revenue from the sale of state-owned enterprises, but consequently lost the annual revenue that could be gained by continuing to own and operate large industrial firms. The lost revenue from selling state-owned property, however, is not as clearly evident or accessible as the money being diverted to individual accounts. Furthermore, renationalizing private property is arguably more challenging than redirecting mandatory retirement contributions to the PAYG portion of pension savings. Likewise, backtracking on liberalization or banking reforms might gain the state some short-term fiscal advantages.

From a politician's perspective, the cost of reversing would also influence his or her decision. Indeed, the anticipated cost of reversal will influence the extent of reform adopted in the first place. Roland (2000) argues that more radical reforms are more likely when reversal costs are lower, because a mistake can be more easily corrected; when there are no reversal costs, "the big bang will always dominate" (p. 41). In considering reversals, then, the money to be gained by reversing may not be outweighed by the expense of doing so. In the case of pension privatization, the direct fiscal cost associated with backtracking was relatively minimal and mostly administrative; existing mandatory contributions would simply have to be diverted back to the PAYG portion of pensions. Thus, pension privatization is a reform that incurs significant, annually-recurring, costs and for which reversal would not cost the government much money.

The fiscal incentive to gain short-term revenue applies regardless of partisanship. Politicians of all ideologies should want to access the money diverted by pension privatization, albeit for different reasons. According to traditional ideological norms, right-wing politicians would want to eliminate pension privatization to avoid raising taxes or deficits, and left-wing politicians would want to eliminate pension privatization as a means of finding funding for additional areas of spending. To date, eight of the eleven countries in which reversals occurred did so under right-wing governments. These right-wing governments cited an explicit desire to avoid raising taxes and higher deficits in doing so. This does not preclude, however, that left-wing governments also have reasons to backtrack on pension privatization.

Politicians' incentive to eliminate the recurring financing gap generated by pension privatization suggests a linear effect on the likelihood of reversals: as the extent of pension privatization grows, so does the pot of money that politicians can access by reversing pension privatization and, therefore, politicians' likelihood of reversing. Again, these are not sunk costs which cannot be recovered. Rather, politicians have a recurring incentive to access the money being tied up by switching to a privatized system. From a fiscal perspective, it is surprising that politicians ever had the self-control to maintain pension privatization, although they have, to date, in about two-thirds of the countries in which it was adopted.

Politicians' Incentive to Maintain Pension Privatization

Although politicians have a clear fiscal motivation to abandon pension privatization, groups in the public and private spheres have the potential to be domestic stakeholders, making the reversal of pension privatization politically infeasible. Domestic stakeholders encompass a wide range of groups, including private pension funds, business associations, citizens with contributions invested in the second pillar, and various government bureaucracies including Ministries of Finance, Ministries of Welfare, and state Pension Funds.

Domestic stakeholders have been thought to play an important role in maintaining policies, particularly in the area of the welfare state and regarding pensions. Pierson (2000) details how increasing returns to particular groups from status quo policies can generate path dependence, making change particularly unlikely. Specifically, interest groups' support for social policies makes changes in areas like pensions generally unlikely. Pierson (1998), for instance, writes that

Especially with large, complex, and deeply institutionalized programs like health care and pensions, social actors are likely to place a high value on predictability and continuity in policy. Reform is not enough; powerful interests seek reasonable assurance that the new policies can be sustained. (p. 555)

By this reasoning, both the adoption and reversal of pension privatization is difficult to explain. As mentioned in the previous chapter, Pierson specifically cites PAYG pension systems as an example of a highly resilient public policy that is resistant to change in part because current workers should be unlikely to accept the double burden of paying for the previous generation's retirement while simultaneously saving for their own (Pierson 1998, p. 553). Policies that provide benefits to which citizens feel entitled are very difficult to abandon. But this also suggests that workers who have become used to a new privatized system should also value predictability and continuity and resist a sudden turnabout in their retirement expectations; a reversal undermines their current savings strategies.

In the public and private spheres, there were two major sources of potential opposition to the reversal of pension privatization – citizens whose contributions were invested in the second pillar and private pension funds who were investing them. I focus on these two groups here not because they are the only relevant domestic stakeholders, but rather because they were the most likely to pose a political hurdle for politicians who wanted to reverse pension privatization. Citizens and managers of private pension funds were likely to seek some assurance from politicians that pension privatization was not a temporary experiment when it was introduced or, at the very least, to have believed that such a major shift was not a brief diversion from the PAYG system. Pierson (2000) explains that one reason path dependency creates such powerful resistance to change is because policies are designed to be difficult to alter. One central concern of politicians in adopting pension privatization was in gauging the potential reaction of investors and the public (Brooks 2009). Indeed, the heads of corporate pension firms were instrumental in pushing for its adoption (Naczyk and Palier 2014). In part, politicians were concerned about the effect of rising deficits on investment. Politicians sought to reassure the public and investors that this was an important and viable market-oriented reform with myriad benefits. Pension privatization is a prime example of how path dependency could work: politicians design programs to make them difficult to reverse or, in this case, to reassure others that the policy will last.

Although interest group support helps explain why policies are likely to stay in place, variation in domestic stakeholders can also help us understand why a policy may be reversed. Interest groups vary both in terms of their support for policies and also in their level of political influence. If domestic stakeholders either only weakly support a policy or are not politically influential, then they are unlikely to help ensure a policy's survival. In other words, the extent to which a policy defines the social contract between politicians and citizens will influence how entrenched citizens are in its survival. This builds on work that suggests that politicians do not simply respond to public opinion. Rather, parties are likely to respond to interest groups and activists with more intensely held preferences (e.g., Bawn et al. 2012). As such, the extent to which interests groups care about a policy is part of what determines whether that group will be influential on an issue.

Interests clearly vary in the degree to which they support status quo policies. A group may have a strongly held interest in the continuation of certain benefits or not. Consider tax policy as an example. A very large tax break, even for a very small group, may result in sustained and significant political action on the part of its beneficiaries to maintain it. Smaller tax advantages, however, are not likely to engender the same level of activism on the part of recipients. Bawn et al. (2012) argue that in the United States activists were responsible for the Democratic Party taking up the issue of civil rights (for which the party previously had little support) and for the development of the Republican pro-life versus Democratic pro-choice stances on abortion. In both cases, it was an active and vocal minority (in these cases heavily influencing the parties' respective nomination processes) that resulted in policy changes. The extent to which groups care about an issue should partially determine their political influence.

Groups may care about keeping pension privatization, but will vary in the extent to which they are politically influential. This goes back to Mancur Olson's foundational work – *The Logic of Collective Action* (1965) – in which he argues that a group's size and organization determine its ability to influence the political system. For example, citizens as a whole are a large and diverse group that will have more difficulty in organizing. All of the citizens included in a country's privatized pension system will face significant challenges in coordinating on particular political action, even if they agree about the best course of action. Conversely, firms in the private pension sector can more easily organize because their group is smaller and has more resources with which to lobby politicians.

The type of group will shape how the group attempts to influence the government. Citizens might be the most influential through voting, while firms will attempt to influence the government through lobbying. In the private sector, interest groups enjoy political influence due to their structural importance to the economy, rather than direct lobbying. Groups of firms that are important for the economy may, as a result, enjoy favorable government policies because the government wants them to do well. Conversely, firms that are not structurally important would be able to curry little favor with the government.

Across countries, variation in the groups favoring pension privatization can be traced back to the extent to which pension privatization was pursued. The degree of pension privatization will influence both the extent to which interests are strongly held and, in some cases, whether they will be influential. Regarding pension privatization, there are two potential domestic stakeholders that might block the reversal of pension privatization: the private pension sector and citizens. Interest groups in the private and public sectors will vary, however, in the extent to which they support status quo policies and their ability to be politically influential. Critically, the extent of pension privatization will influence the extent to which interest groups support status quo and, in part, the extent to which they will be politically influential.

Private pension funds and investment companies investing in pensions profited from the continuation of pension privatization. These firms served as a potentially influential force lobbying against reversal. The extent to which private pension funds and investment companies became influential domestic stakeholders in pension privatization, however, varied depending on the extent of pension privatization adopted in a country. In countries where more money had been invested with private pension funds from mandatory contributions, the funds would have greater lobbying capacity and would be more structurally important to the economy.

The size of the private pension sector varies widely across countries that privatized pensions. For instance, the private pension sector in Chile – the first country in the world to adopt pension privatization – is much larger than the private pension sector in Bulgaria, which adopted a relatively limited degree of pension privatization. In Chile, 100 percent of a person's future retirement savings depend on her contributions and the returns to the investment of those contributions. In Bulgaria, only 37 percent of a person's future retirement savings depend on the same contributions (Brooks 2009). It is difficult to imagine, then, that a citizen in Bulgaria would be as concerned about the functioning of the privatized pension system (or whether it exists at all) as a citizen in Chile. The logic about more extensive reforms creating more entrenched policies can also be seen in the privatization of state-owned enterprises. Scholars argued that more rapid and more extensive privatization of state-owned enterprises would help to create an ownership society and keep privatization in place. In part, this is because the market is embedded in non-market institutions as Polanyi (1944) emphasizes. In this case, where the privatization of property was more extensive, property owners were a larger group with more resources and greater potential to influence the government. Renationalization seems especially unlikely in countries like Poland, Hungary, or the Czech Republic in the 1990s, when a large amount of state property was transferred to private ownership. Rodrik (1991) echoes the importance of institutional reform which protects the market when he describes "institutions for high-quality growth"; he emphasizes that non-market institutions must protect the ability of the market to function. Where reforms go further, they are more likely to be entrenched and longer lasting.

Similar arguments have been made about pension privatization. Pension privatization was also expected to promote an ownership society, not only encouraging citizens to think about their retirement savings in a different way but to think of themselves as owners with vested interests in the stock market (Kerner). For advocates of pension privatization, the hope was that citizens would care about macroeconomic policies that promoted growth and would hold politicians accountable accordingly. Once again, we see that more extensive reform should result in stronger and more influential domestic stakeholders.

Furthermore, governments engaged in major public campaigns to gain public support, or to at least mitigate any potential public opposition to the switch to a more privatized system (Müller 2001). There is a similarity here in the adoption and reversal of pension privatization in that neither was instigated by public demand. Although pension privatization was not necessarily wildly popular in countries in which it was adopted, there is evidence that citizens were somewhat supportive of it or at least found it preferable to previous systems that were perceived to be broken (Müller 2001). Even citizens who were opposed to the introduction of pension privatization might not support its reversal. Once their retirement contributions were being paid into the privatized system, a switch back to a PAYG system might mean a loss of future benefits, depending on the returns their contributions had been earning.

In summary, more extensive pension privatization should create stronger domestic stakeholders in the private pension sector and the public. In countries where a large proportion of future retirement benefits would be based on individual accounts, citizens were more likely to be invested in its long-term survival. In these cases, we should see clearly at work the feedback loops about which Pierson and others write. Citizens had adapted to new rules of the game, made their retirement and savings decisions based on these rules, and were invested in seeing returns to the individual accounts to which they had contributed. Were the government to nationalize these accounts or otherwise change the rules in a way that risked losses, citizens would likely object.

Additionally, where pension privatization was implemented more extensively, private pension funds would be structurally more important to the financial sector of the economy and would enjoy more resources with which to influence the political system. Citizens in more extensively privatized systems would also have a greater interest in the survival of pension privatization and would, in turn, more vocally oppose its reversal. Thus, as the pot of money gets larger, politicians simultaneously have a greater fiscal interest in reversing pension privatization to gain short-term revenue, but face greater opposition to reversal from citizens and private pension funds.

Politicians' electoral timeline provides an observable implication of the fiscal incentives to reverse. Elections force politicians and parties to consider public opinion and lobbying demands. Roberts (2010) notes that the timing of debates about housing, education, and pension policy in the post-communist

TABLE 3.1 *Degree of Pension Privatization and Likelihood of Reversal under Financial Crisis*

Degree of reform	Political implications	Likelihood of reversal
Limited	Smaller pot of money, interest groups weakly support pension privatization	Unlikely
Moderate	Larger pot of money, interest groups moderately support pension privatization	Most Likely
Extensive	Largest pot of money, interest groups strongly support pension privatization	Unlikely

European countries is evidence of a relatively high quality of democracy in the region. If reversals of pension privatization are the result of a public backlash to the reform, then we are likely to see incumbents legislating reversals shortly *before* elections are held. In this case, we should also see campaign debates about the issue of pension privatization. Conversely, if politicians are reversing pension privatization to access short-term revenue but are concerned about public opposition to the reversal, then we are likely to see reversals debated and adopted just *after* elections have been held.

Reversal Most Likely when Degree of Pension Privatization is Moderate

The annual recurring financing gap created by pension privatization creates countervailing pressures: when pension privatization has been more extensive, politicians are more tempted to cut pension privatization to access short-term revenue; however, simultaneously more extensive pension privatization means citizens and private pension funds are domestic stakeholders who are more opposed to reversal. Financial crisis creates a fiscal imperative to find short-term revenue. Reversal will occur when a large fiscal incentive exists to do so (because of the amount of money being diverted to individual accounts) and when domestic interest groups do not strongly support pension privatization and do not block backtracking. Table 3.1 summarizes my expectations about the degree of reform and the likelihood of reversal.

Limited Pension Privatization. Where pension privatization was limited, there is less of a fiscal incentive for politicians to reverse pension privatization. Domestic stakeholders in the public and private spheres will be weaker, suggesting that, if politicians wanted to, a reversal would be more politically feasible. But because the pot of money is smaller, politicians are less likely to be tempted to access this source of short-term revenue.

Extensive Pension Privatization. Where pension privatization was extensive, politicians are likely to be the most tempted to reverse the policy. Politicians will be countered, however, by domestic stakeholders in the public and private spheres. High costs will be associated with the most extensive pension privatization, in which citizens have been incorporated more fully into the privatized system. Additionally, private pension funds and investment companies will have the most money at stake in systems where the costs of pension privatization are highest. Therefore, a reversal of pension privatization should be less likely when reform was extensive.

Moderate Pension Privatization. A reversal of pension privatization should be most likely when pension privatization was pursued to a moderate degree. Where pension privatization was moderate, politicians are more tempted to reverse pension privatization for short-term fiscal gains (than they would be under low costs) and are less constrained by domestic stakeholders (than they would be under high costs). Thus, combining the expectations under limited and extensive pension privatization, we can see that it is when reforms were moderate that we should be most likely to see reversals when financial crisis hits.

The political and fiscal incentives created by the degree of reform – both in regards to politicians' desire to find short-term revenue and to accommodate domestic stakeholders – also explains why politicians would choose to reverse pension privatization instead of revising the system to function better. Popular complaints about privatized pension systems have included the decline of their value after the financial crisis, a lack of choice between funds, limited transparency, high administrative costs, and a lack of competition amongst funds (Drahokoupil and Domonkos 2012; Ebbinghaus et al. 2012). Others note that pension privatization perpetuates inequality by rewarding most those who already earn more and therefore contribute more to individual accounts (Baker 2009; Remington 2011). If politicians' primary concern was addressing the public's concerns about low returns to individual pension accounts or complaints about administrative fees and other regulatory problems, then the reversal of pension privatization would be unnecessary. Instead, politicians could address the specific criticisms by improving the regulation of private pension funds, limiting administrative fees, and encouraging competition. To address concerns about inequality, governments could also pass complementary policies designed to provide additional retirement support for those in the lower income brackets.

Revisions to pension privatization that were intended to bolster its survival and improve performance would not, however, gain politicians access to short-term revenue. In countries where pension privatization was extensively pursued – including Chile, Colombia, El Salvador, and Peru – politicians may have very much wanted to regain access to the mandatory contributions being diverted to individual accounts. Working against reversal in these four countries was that nearly all of their citizens' pensions came from individual accounts. Citizens expected and planned their retirements based on individual accounts. The private pension sector in these countries has also grown tremendously since reforms were introduced (Tapia 2008). As such, politicians facing complaints about pension privatization were much more likely to revise the privatized pension system than to scrap it.

Politicians' Incentives to Pursue Reversals of Pension Privatization in Different Ways

The nature of reversals of pension privatization varies on three important dimensions – whether reversals were one-time or multi-step, the degree of reversal, and whether reversals were temporary or permanent (see Table 2.1 in Chapter 2).

Reversals of pension privatization that are modified in any of these ways have important implications for the political process. First, any of these three measures – temporary or partial reversals or spreading out reversals over several pieces of legislation – suggest that politicians are learning about the consequences of doing so and that they are minimizing or avoiding public reactions. Politicians interested in avoiding objections from the private or public sector should also pay attention to electoral timelines. If politicians are concerned about making unpopular moves, then legislation to reverse pension privatization should be observed just after elections have taken place (including by incumbents returning to power) and discussions about reversing pension privatization should be downplayed during campaigns.

Second, these modified reversals also indicate that the main instigators of reversals are politicians seeking short-term fiscal resources and trying to avoid opposition to doing so. It is much less likely that temporary, partial, or staggered reversals would be a response to public demands to reverse pension privatization. If there was public demand for eliminating pension privatization, we would be more likely to see reversals happening as a one-time piece of legislation promoted during campaigns and either adopted just before elections by incumbents or just after a new party had been voted into power.

The theory presented here is a very different kind of political story about hurdles to market-oriented reforms as compared to commonplace ones. In this case, it is not constraints from interest group politics or public reactions keeping politicians from being foresighted, but it is politicians' own desire to spend in other areas or avoid raising taxes in other areas preventing progress. The mediated nature of reversals suggests that, regarding pension privatization, it was politicians themselves who had the main incentive to see pension privatization curtailed and they sometimes did so in ways that mitigated potential negative reactions.

Finally, qualifying reversals by taking intermediary legislative steps provides another reason to think that partisanship is not the whole story. Eight of the eleven countries that reversed pension privatization did so under right-wing governments and did so in various ways. There must be something besides partisan ideology, then, that explains why governments varied in their approach to pension privatization. The two countries that reversed under left-wing governments – Argentina and Slovakia – did so in distinct ways. There does not appear to be a "right-wing" type of reversal and a "left-wing" type of reversal.

TABLE 3.2 *Expectations about Variation in Types of Reversals*

	Political implications	When likely
Temporary reversal	Tool to learn about reactions from private investors and citizens	More likely in the immediate aftermath of financial crisis when investment has dropped
Multi-step reversal	Tool to learn about reactions from private investors and citizens	More likely when same party that adopted pension privatization is spearheading the reversal
Partial reversal	Reveals stronger interest group support for pension privatization & stronger resistance to reversal	More likely at higher end of moderate pension privatization

The logic underlying different types of reversals bolsters the arguments about why reversals occur at all and demonstrates how differences in these pressures across countries result in different political strategies for backtracking. Table 3.2 summarizes my expectations regarding different types of reversals and when such measures are most likely.

Temporary, multi-step, and partial reversals all suggest that politicians want to learn about the consequences of reversals and may be concerned about a backlash from private investors, private pension funds and citizens. These different modified reversals also have distinct implications which make them more likely under certain circumstances.

Temporary reversals in contributions should be most likely when politicians are concerned about the potential reaction of investors or the public. This is particularly likely in the immediate aftermath of a financial crisis for countries that depend heavily on foreign investment. Temporary measures should be more likely depending on the fiscal and electoral situation. Regarding the fiscal situation, a temporary measure suggests a knee-jerk reaction to the immediate circumstances. Temporary measures are most likely to be a quick reaction to financial crisis and worsening government revenue. Politicians want short-term revenue quickly, but do not want to commit to backtracking as a long-term policy course.

Temporary measures may minimize a negative reaction from investors by providing a reassurance to private investors that the move is not permanent. Likewise, citizens may see a temporary measures as a necessary short-term change which will not permanently influence their retirement savings. Although some experts have noted that temporary measures can in fact have long-term and permanent consequences (Égert 2012), citizens may be easily convinced (or not realize) what the long-term consequences will be. Temporary measures should be the least politically controversial precisely because they are explicitly designed to expire; the default is going back to the privatized system put in place.

Multi-step reversals also suggest that politicians are engaging in a learning process. Unlike temporary measures, however, a multi-step reversal suggests concern with a backlash from the public or private investors. Politicians may choose to pursue an initial curtailment, gauge the reaction, and then proceed with additional measures to reverse. Multi-step reversals may also indicate that politicians are attempting to build political coalitions which will support a greater degree of backtracking. At the very least, a multi-step reversal indicates that there is not political support for entirely abandoning pension privatization in a single move.

Partial reversals may be most likely at the higher end of moderate pension privatization. In countries where interests in the public and private sectors are more successful in opposing proposals to reverse pension privatization, politicians will be more likely to seek partial reversals as a compromise. A partial reversal allows politicians to gain some access to short-term revenue without suffering the same political losses due to a backlash from groups that support pension privatization. A partial reversal is also more likely to be the result of a compromise in which politicians have floated the idea of a reversal and met some resistance to doing so.

Degree of Reversal. A final note is necessary about variation in the extent to which governments chose to eliminate pension privatization. The degree of reversal is also relevant although there is limited variation on this. Half of the countries that abandoned pension privatization did so completely. The other half chose partial reductions to the second privatized tier of individual accounts. There is really only one important distinction in the degree of reversal: partial or complete. Given the limited basis on which to develop or test a theoretical argument, I do not focus on the degree to which politicians backtracked. Nonetheless, a complete reversal suggests politicians faced a worse fiscal situation which prompted them to permanently abandon the previous reform in a single piece of legislation.

Critically, observing the nature and degree of reversals confirms the logic for why reversals are more likely when moderate reforms were adopted. The key is that moderate pension privatization generated significant short- and medium-term fiscal costs for politicians, but failed to create a new deal that was embedded in domestic stakeholders. If politicians pursue partial or temporary reversals under the circumstances discussed and stagger reforms to mitigate a potential backlash, then this provides evidence that the political concerns identified in my theory are in fact politicians' primary considerations.

Bureaucratic Stakeholders

Bureaucratic politics played an important role in debates over the adoption of pension privatization. Bureaucracies were also sometimes the source of proposals for reversing and revising pension privatization. Cook (2007) discusses the central role played by "statist stakeholders" in debates over pension reforms in post-communist countries, including Russia. Ministries of welfare tended to oppose pension privatization, whereas finance and economic ministries supported its passage. More extensive pension privatization might make bureaucratic interests more committed to the survival of pension privatization. However, the role played by the bureaucracy in setting policy will vary tremendously by country. In some cases, the heads of important ministries were replaced to allow pension privatization to be passed and implemented more easily (Müller 2001).

Bureaucracies can, in theory, play an important role in promoting certain policies, particularly when the policies enhance the organization's own bureaucratic power. For instance, bureaucracies played an important role in the adoption and implementation of pension privatization. Certainly, welfare ministries had reasons to be concerned about the direction of new policies that might strengthen or weaken their own power. In other policy areas, we have seen that bureaucracies can play an independent role in providing expertise and pursuing their own bureaucratic interests. Bureaucracies can indeed become influential policymakers, although this may require a very particular set of circumstances, i.e., a bureaucracy with unique goals and officials who can develop ties with a wide-ranging coalition in order to provide unique services. Carpenter (2001) describes an instance of this kind of bureaucratic expansion in the development of the US postal system. Similarly, it might be possible for those running private pension funds to advance their own goals of earning profits and align themselves with citizens who see their own retirement benefits as tied to the performance of private pension funds.

In some cases, bureaucracies' own policymaking powers may in fact lead to their functioning as a "second set of veto players," with the ability to comment on and alter the nature of legislation. Cook (2007) describes how Russia's state Pension Fund during the 1990s enjoyed extensive policymaking powers. The power and influence of bureaucracies should be considered in their particular domestic contexts. In the realm of social reforms, welfare and finance ministries may or may not play an influential role.

Bureaucratic powers like welfare ministries may be the most influential if they ally themselves with social interests or political parties advancing a particular agenda. For instance, in the case of the adoption of pension privatization, economic and finance ministries drew on the expertise from private pension funds and investment companies in pushing their proposals. As such, we may observe ministries latching onto existing political and social positions on pensions, rather than developing or pursuing unique agendas.

Despite the potential for bureaucratic influence, welfare policies – and pension privatization in particular – form an important part of the social contract between the state and citizens. As a result, bureaucracies may be more likely to serve as an intermediary between politicians and citizens, but ultimately the decision rests with politicians who are responding to fiscal and electoral pressures. Even if bureaucracies draft legislation, they are likely to do so at the behest of politicians. Given the conditions under which reversals of pension privatization should be most likely to occur – including the financial crisis and when there is a large financing gap but a lack of domestic opposition – bureaucratic politics would be likely to play a smaller role in reversals than in the adoption of pension privatization.

Policy Diffusion and Politicians' Incentives to Reverse Pension Privatization

The diffusion of reversals is also an important influence that links back to the extent of pension privatization and the risk of reversal. In particular, countries would be most likely to learn from and imitate other countries that adopted a similar degree of pension privatization and faced a similar situation in terms of their implicit pension debt and government finances. Economic policies have often been found to spread in waves, particularly in recent times. For instance, the extent of variation in capital account openness declined by more than half in the 1980s and 1990s due to policy diffusion (Simmons et al. 2008). Similarly, perhaps, pension reforms might spread in waves around the world.

Policy diffusion can occur in a variety of ways, including imitation, economic competition, coercion, and learning (Shipan and Volden 2008; Simmons et al. 2008). Governments may imitate each other, relying on a simple heuristic logic to simplify which policy choices they make. Governments may also compete, with each adopting similar policies in order to pursue shared goals like attracting or keeping investors. Persuasion from an outside force – such as an international organization – may also be responsible for the spread of policies. Learning is also an important aspect of policy diffusion; politicians and policymakers rely on the experiences of other countries in order to understand whether these policies are successful and how groups – including citizens, firms, and investors – will respond to policies.

Policy diffusion via learning is also important for citizens, especially in democratic countries. Linos (2013) explains how politicians use the experiences of other countries to reduce voters' uncertainty about the consequences of reforms in health, family, and employment laws. Citizens are best persuaded by the example of countries that are considered comparable to their own. Politicians seeking to sell the public on a particular course of action are most likely to highlight the experiences of countries comparable to their own.

We are especially likely to observe countries learning from each other when a reform requires a large and potentially expensive shift in policy. Brooks (2007), for instance, shows that diffusion processes were more likely in the spread of pension privatization than in the adoption of notional defined contribution (NDC) pension systems. NDC reforms credited individual contributions with notional rates of return which determined future benefits. Brooks explains that pension privatization entailed a larger and more costly shift, making governments more likely to look to the experiences of other countries in order to determine if it was appropriate for them. Because the cost of reform has been linked to whether countries seek to learn from others' experiences, it is likely that governments considering reversing pension privatization would also look to countries that pursued a similar degree of reform. In cases in which countries have similar costs, the parameters surrounding reversal may also be similar.

Governments would also look to countries that pursued a similar degree of reform and faced similar circumstances because these countries' experiences provide useful shortcuts for figuring out what policy options are possible and what the consequences of those options might be. The notion of learning by shortcut draws on the idea of bounded learning, in which policymakers rely on cognitive shortcuts. Weyland (2006) writes that,

> ... [R]ationality is distinctly bounded as hard-pressed decision-makers regularly and automatically rely on heuristics that facilitate the complicated process of making choices, but that can also cause biases. (p. 5)

Weyland notes that even the most informed policymakers who are best poised to engage in systematic cost–benefit analyses will be overwhelmed with the amount of information available and need to rely on easier ways of coming to conclusions. In particular, policymakers will be drawn to highly publicized success cases and, possibly, to the experiences of other countries in the region. Chile, for instance, grabbed the attention of other Latin American governments with its radical, new option for pension privatization.

The mediating effect of the degree of reform on diffusion is consistent with evidence that international influences are channelled through domestic processes. Stroup (2012), for instance, finds that the behavior of international NGOs is influenced by their country of origin. Rather than globalization leading international NGOs to converge on best practices, their operations continue to reflect the nature of domestic politics. The degree to which the reform was pursued in the first place should determine the nature of debates about reversals. Learning from other countries' experiences should occur as a means of figuring out how to respond to the challenges posed by a recurring financing gap.

Historically, politicians have learned from both the economic and political consequences of other countries' actions. Meseguer (2004) notes that the attractiveness of privatization as a policy option can be attributed to how it improved Margaret Thatcher's political fortunes, rather than its potential economic benefits. Furthermore, because democratic leaders come to office through competitive elections, they cannot afford to be as ideological as doing so might alienate voters on whom they depend for reelection (Meseguer and Escribà-Folch 2011). Relatedly, economic crises are likely to lead to learning about what does work in a variety of ways, including means of gaining short-term revenue.

Politicians deciding whether to reverse pension privatization have at least two major concerns, though they can learn from other countries' experiences. One concern is public backlash. Any policy decision in a country with competitive elections should make politicians concerned about the public's reaction.

A reversal in particular, however, raises concerns about whether those favoring the policy will oppose backtracking on it. As a result, politicians will want to see how citizens in other countries respond to a reversal of the same policy.

Another concern regarding the reversal of pension privatization was the potential response from investors. The international investment community had expressed concern at demographic trends in the region along with the trajectory of pension reform. Standard & Poor's published a report calling for governments to avoid pursuing pension reforms that would denigrate their fiscal situation in the long run. More broadly, in the aftermath of the 2008 financial crisis, politicians might have been particularly concerned about policies perceived to be anti-market. Many East European governments had already lost significant foreign investment because of the crisis and would therefore be especially keen not to discourage any remaining or potential new investors. Observing how investors responded to the reversal of pension privatization in other countries would be especially useful to these governments.

Drawing on Linos' argument again about how policy diffusion works across democracies, politicians may justify a reversal – whether temporary or permanent – by pointing out that countries with similar systems had done the same thing. This is also a form of policy learning. For instance, in 2009 the Baltic countries of Estonia, Latvia, and Lithuania all adopted a combination of temporary and permanent measures reversing pension privatization. The governments of Russia, Hungary, and Poland observed this backtracking and noted that that there was limited negative reaction from the public and investors, meaning they could reasonably draw on the Baltic examples to justify their own moves. In contrast, none of the countries with the most extensive pension privatization mentioned above (Chile, Colombia, El Salvador, and Peru; see Brooks 2009), reversed pension privatization; drawing on each other's experiences, they were more likely not to see reversal as a viable option.

Market-oriented reforms have often occurred in waves, suggesting that learning may be present. Meseguer (2005) notes, though, that policy diffusion by learning can look very similar to policy diffusion that occurs merely by emulation. In many cases, she argues, there is strong evidence that governments are emulating each other's market-oriented reforms in order to send a positive signal about their commitment or credibility in promoting growth. Distinguishing between learning and emulation is particularly challenging. To establish that learning is occurring, Meseguer (2005) explains that we must observe that politicians are obtaining information purposively and that they are gaining a better understanding of causal relationships from doing so.

In the case of pension privatization, the motivation to learn about potential reactions from the public and investors makes it especially likely that politicians would intentionally seek information in order to gain a better understanding of the consequences of particular choices. In other words, the context of pension privatization makes it likely that learning – and not just emulation – occurred. Reversing pension privatization risked sending a negative, rather than a positive, signal, making it unlikely that governments were trying to send a positive signal to investors by copying each other's reversals. Furthermore, diffusion by competition for investors' money – also referred to as a "race to the bottom" in areas like regulatory and tax policy (Meseguer and Gilardi 2009) – is unlikely here. The concern was that reversals might deter investment, rather than spur it.

Cross-national evidence can provide proof that is consistent with learning, but an in-depth examination of the politics of reversing pension privatization can more fully establish that it was learning – which was purposive and focused on enhancing policymakers' causal knowledge – that was in fact taking place. Simmons and Elkins (2004) argue that finding evidence that countries model their behavior on their sociocultural peers demonstrates learning from other countries' relevant experiences. As such, if there is evidence that countries that privatized pensions are learning from those with comparable degrees of reform, this would provide additional support to the idea that learning, and not emulation, is occurring.

The spread of reversals in pension privatization can also be linked with European Union (EU) membership. Many of the countries that reversed pension privatization were members of the EU. The organization played an important role in influencing pension policy, albeit somewhat indirectly. In general, the EU provides only broad guidelines for pension policy rather than strict prescriptions (European Commission 2012) and some have criticized the EU for being inconsistent in the legislation addressing pensions that does exist (Guardiancich 2013). The European Union does, however, set deficit guidelines that made it more difficult for countries to maintain pension privatization, a policy that often raises deficits in the short to medium term (Casey 2012). Therefore, countries that faced similar pressures from the European Union could learn from each other about ways to keep their deficits within the guidelines, as well as from the EU's reaction to how they chose to keep deficits in check.

EU countries consult regularly about policy issues, making learning across the region especially likely. The EU does not provide strict guidelines about the type of pension system a country should adopt. Instead, the EU limits its pension policy guidelines to encouraging countries to develop fiscally sustainable and adequate pension coverage for its citizens. The EU member countries that privatized pensions petitioned the EU to allow for higher deficits due to their pension reforms. The petitions were ultimately denied (Casey 2012). EU member countries therefore faced similar pressures to keep their deficits in check. This also suggests, of course, that the EU had a direct effect – independent of diffusion by learning – on pension policy. The deficit guidelines faced by EU member countries simply made it difficult to maintain pension privatization. Not all EU members, however, reversed pension privatization, meaning that EU membership alone is only a partial explanation.

The World Bank also has the potential to influence the diffusion of reversals across countries. The previous chapter addressed the role of the World Bank in promoting the adoption of market-oriented pension reforms, including pension privatization. Although some have noted that the World Bank played a central role in promoting pension privatization (Orenstein 2008), others have argued that countries were not responding to pressure from international organizations, which instead were responsible for disseminating information but not the content of reforms (Weyland 2006). I noted in particular that the World Bank did not endorse backtracking on pension privatization. Although World Bank experts modified their recommendations about adopting pension privatization, recommending that some countries consider other measures like NDC reforms, they publicly opposed moves to cut or eliminate contributions to the second tier of pensions. Nonetheless, countries receiving assistance from the World Bank could, in principle, be more likely to model their policies on each other. The reason might be that they are more likely to learn from other countries that also receive World Bank loans. In this case, governments may have been looking to learn more information about how the World Bank would react to a reversal in pension privatization. Another argument is that the World Bank creates policy norms that spread across countries, but the World Bank did not endorse reversals which makes this argument less persuasive.

The World Bank's influence on the diffusion of *reversals* in pension privatization is possible, but less likely than EU influence. Of the 23 countries that received more than four pension-related loans from the World Bank, only 13 pursued multi-pillar reforms like pension privatization (Andrews 2006). Additionally, there were no stipulations made with World Bank loans that financial assistance would be withdrawn if pension privatization was not maintained or even if pension privatization was never implemented. The Georgian government accepted loans to establish a multi-pillar system and never did so with no apparent consequences regarding its loan (Andrews 2006). Indeed, although the World Bank did not endorse backtracking on pension privatization, it had modified its policy advice to less enthusiastically promote it. In the context of the 2008 financial crisis, it probably would have seemed unlikely even to politicians at the time that the World Bank would retaliate because of a turn away from pension privatization.

Lastly, the World Bank as an international organization encompasses many more countries than the European Union and has less direct influence on many of those countries than the European Union. The World Bank and EU are, of course, fundamentally different kinds of international organizations, with the former being an international lending organization and the latter being a unique geopolitical organization designed to support economic growth and trade among member nations. Accepting loans from the World Bank is largely voluntary (although some might argue that developing countries that lack alternative sources of revenue also lack a true choice about accepting loans), while EU member countries are largely obligated to follow EU directions (unless they choose to leave the union). We should expect, therefore, that the EU plays a much more central role in the pension politics of its member countries than the World Bank.

In summary, because the reversals of pension privatization occurred in waves, this suggests that countries were either influenced by the same external pressures, emulating each other, learning from each other, or some combination thereof. Theoretical arguments about how policy diffusion works make it likely that a learning process, rather than emulation, was indeed taking place. Combined with a consideration of the influence of the degree of reform, there should be a connection between diffusion and costs: countries should be most likely to learn from those with similar policy designs, in this case meaning those with a comparable degree of reform. In this way, the theoretical expectations here reveal how domestic conditions – specifically the extent to which pension privatization was adopted in the first place – shapes policy diffusion.

Theoretical Significance of the Argument

I have developed theoretical expectations that highlight politicians' simultaneous incentives to reverse reforms (to gain short-term revenue) and to maintain reforms (due to domestic stakeholders). In doing so, I incorporate the role of a number of important actors, including certain groups of citizens (those with contributions in the privatized second pillar), private pension funds and their business associations, the potential role of bureaucratic actors, and international organizations. In the previous chapter, I further considered the role that political parties and partisan goals play in shaping pension policy.

My theoretical expectations here also incorporate an understanding of differences in the degree of pension privatization. The degree of pension privatization increased politicians' incentive to use reversal as a way to gain short-term revenue, while also creating domestic stakeholders in pension privatization. I further link politicians' incentives to reverse and to maintain reforms with learning from the experiences of other countries. Considerations about the reversal of pension privatization are linked to domestic conditions and are especially likely to inspire learning about the political and economic consequences of doing so. Politicians, however, are most likely to learn from other countries with a similar degree of pension privatization, as their experiences are the most relevant.

This theoretical explanation is novel and modifies our understanding of how the extent of reform influences a policy's survival. First, my theory of reversal is grounded in the design of the policy initially adopted. This is critical because it suggests that economic reforms should be adopted with more consideration of whether they are designed to last. Acemoglu and Robinson (2013) write that "Economic reforms implemented without an understanding of their political consequences, rather than promoting economic efficiency, can significantly reduce it" (p. 21). Pension privatization was adopted with a clear understanding that there would be recurring costs associated with the degree of pension privatization pursued. Despite *ex ante* knowledge of the costs, these costs play a critical role in whether pension privatization survives.

This also allows us to link the reversal of pension privatization with longer-term trends in the welfare state and policymaking. Initial conditions – including demographic conditions, the cost of the PAYG system, and deficits – influence whether and to what degree pension privatization was adopted, which in turn influence the likelihood of reversal. In principle, we might have been able to predict which countries would adopt pension privatization and where it was most likely to be abandoned; in other words, we could identify where PAYG systems were the most likely to endure or fail.

Second, my theory modifies our understanding of how more radical and extensive reforms will influence their durability. Some experts advocated on behalf of more radical market-oriented reforms, particularly for the post-communist countries, because they were thought to be more likely to stick. More radical reforms, however, may only be likely to stick if they are extensive enough to truly renegotiate the social contract and create private and public interests that can and will successfully fight for their survival, even if the short-term costs are high. Critically, however, these domestic stakeholders must be more powerful than politicians' fiscal incentives to access short-term revenue to spend in a variety of areas or to avoid raising taxes or deficits. Regarding pension privatization, countries should be the least likely to be stuck in the middle. Governments, then, might consider minimal reforms that allow them to test-run policies without a risk of turnaround, or very extensive reforms, which make sure that policy volatility will be low and the new system has a real chance to succeed.

Third, I emphasize the importance of the short-term gains from reversing despite the potential costs of doing so. Roland (2000) argues that a "big bang" approach is more likely when reversal costs are low. This would suggest that countries privatized pensions most extensively when they anticipated that it was easy to later abandon the reforms. Roland's expectation is especially unlikely in the case of pension privatization: it does not seem especially likely that the countries that privatized most extensively did so because they believed a reversal would be easy. Indeed, Brooks (2007) argues that learning by diffusion mattered more for structural reforms like pension privatization because politicians thought it would be harder to reverse. Furthermore, politicians would have been well aware of the recurring costs of pension privatization and that these costs would be higher if more extensive pension privatization was pursued. If politicians overcame the political and fiscal hurdles to initiate pension privatization, reversals should have been unlikely.

The argument developed here explains why the partisanship of the government and legislative politics may be less important factors in the survival of certain policies. Indeed, the costs of the policy may have such a large and central influence that it matters little whether the party in power is left or right wing and the type of opposition it faces. Rather, in this case at least, partisanship may be more accurately viewed as a permissive or contributing condition. Most reversals (eight out of ten) occurred under a right-wing government, but many right-wing governments did not abandon pension privatization.

My theoretical argument can also inform theories of policy stability and change. Explanations of policy change have often centered on why rare policy changes do occur. Pension privatization, however, is a good example of how policy is continually in flux and under negotiation. This is not a case of "punctuated equilibrium," in which a seemingly stable equilibrium was interrupted by a new issue or change in agenda setting (Baumgartner and Jones 1993). Instead, politicians should be most likely to access the revenue tied up by pension privatization when domestic stakeholders fail to block them.

Finally, my expectations have implications beyond the specific area of pension privatization. As noted above, many market-oriented reforms are characterized by short-term costs and long-term benefits. Pension privatization is certainly unique in several ways, which, as previously discussed, help explain why politicians would hone in on reversing pension privatization as a means of gaining short-term revenue instead of using other options. Nonetheless, almost all market-oriented reforms require short-term costs, which are argued to bring longer-term gains. As such, we should see a similar dynamic in which the development of domestic stakeholders in the new policy plays an important role in discouraging politicians from reversing to avoid short-term costs or to gain short-term advantages.

An important practical lesson of this theoretical argument is that policymakers need to more seriously consider how policies do, or do not, alter the short-term interests of affected groups. Because there is a time inconsistency problem – in which short-term sacrifices must be made for long-term gains – there should be domestic stakeholders in the short term if the policy is to survive. The parameters of this theory may change depending on the circumstances – i.e., how large the short-term costs are compared to long-term gains and why groups will support a reform or not – but the same idea holds across policy areas. Long-term benefits may be insufficient to secure a policy's survival if groups do not support its continuation in the short term.

The argument here is different from existing concerns about why market-oriented reforms might be abandoned; other explanations focus on how public opinion and interest group lobbying will block necessary economic reforms. The argument here highlights that politicians' short-term fiscal incentives will undermine reform if domestic groups do not support the measures and pressure politicians to keep reforms in place. If we want policies to survive, we should take the support of domestic groups seriously. Here, the extent of reform should create domestic stakeholders who are more politically influential. It may often be the case that more extensive reforms in other areas would have the same effect.

In the subsequent empirical chapters, I test my theoretical expectations about the influence of the degree of pension privatization on the likelihood of reversals in pension privatization and the role of policy diffusion. I also assess the role of legislative politics, which I find to have a limited effect on the likelihood of reversing pension privatization. The quantitative and qualitative analysis shows that the degree of pension privatization has a curvilinear effect and that policy diffusion plays some role. The advantage of taking a multi-method approach allows me to identify the evidence for broad, cross-national trends, while also taking a closer look at the political processes and causal mechanisms at play in the reversal of pension privatization. The consequences of varying degrees of pension privatization connect how politicians, public and private interest groups, and learning across countries shaped reversals as suggested in the theoretical expectations presented in this chapter.

GLOBAL TRENDS IN PENSION PRIVATIZATION REVERSAL

4

Evidence on Pension Policy Reversal from the Around the World

The map in Figure 4.1 shows the countries that privatized pensions and those which subsequently reversed pension privatization. We can see that the adoption of pension privatization has been heavily concentrated in the countries of Latin America and Europe. Reversals have overwhelmingly occurred among the post-communist countries of Eastern Europe. Argentina and the United Kingdom are the two countries outside this region that have reversed pension privatization.

Figure 4.2 shows that reversals have indeed been concentrated overwhelmingly among countries in the mid-range of pension privatization, a category which heavily overlaps with the post-communist countries of Central and Eastern Europe. The dashed reference line indicates the average degree of pension privatization at 60 percent of an individual's future pension. The solid lines indicate 1 standard deviation above and below the mean. Data are taken from Brooks (2009) and supplemented with other sources (see the data appendix to the chapter).

Global trends suggest that the post-communist countries may be special or unique in some way that explains the regional concentration of reversals. There is an obvious difference between the mostly Latin American reformers on the far right of Figure 4.2, who extensively pursued pension privatization and kept these systems in place. Kazakhstan is the notable exception in having adopted extensive pension privatization and subsequently having reversed the policy. On the far left are countries that adopted only a very minimal degree of pension privatization and have also not reversed course for the most part.

An examination of the countries in question as described in Figures 4.1 and 4.2 suggests that the extent of reform did mold politicians' fiscal incentives and domestic ability to consider reversing pension privatization. The cross-national trends offer further illumination of why this was a regional trend. Particularly

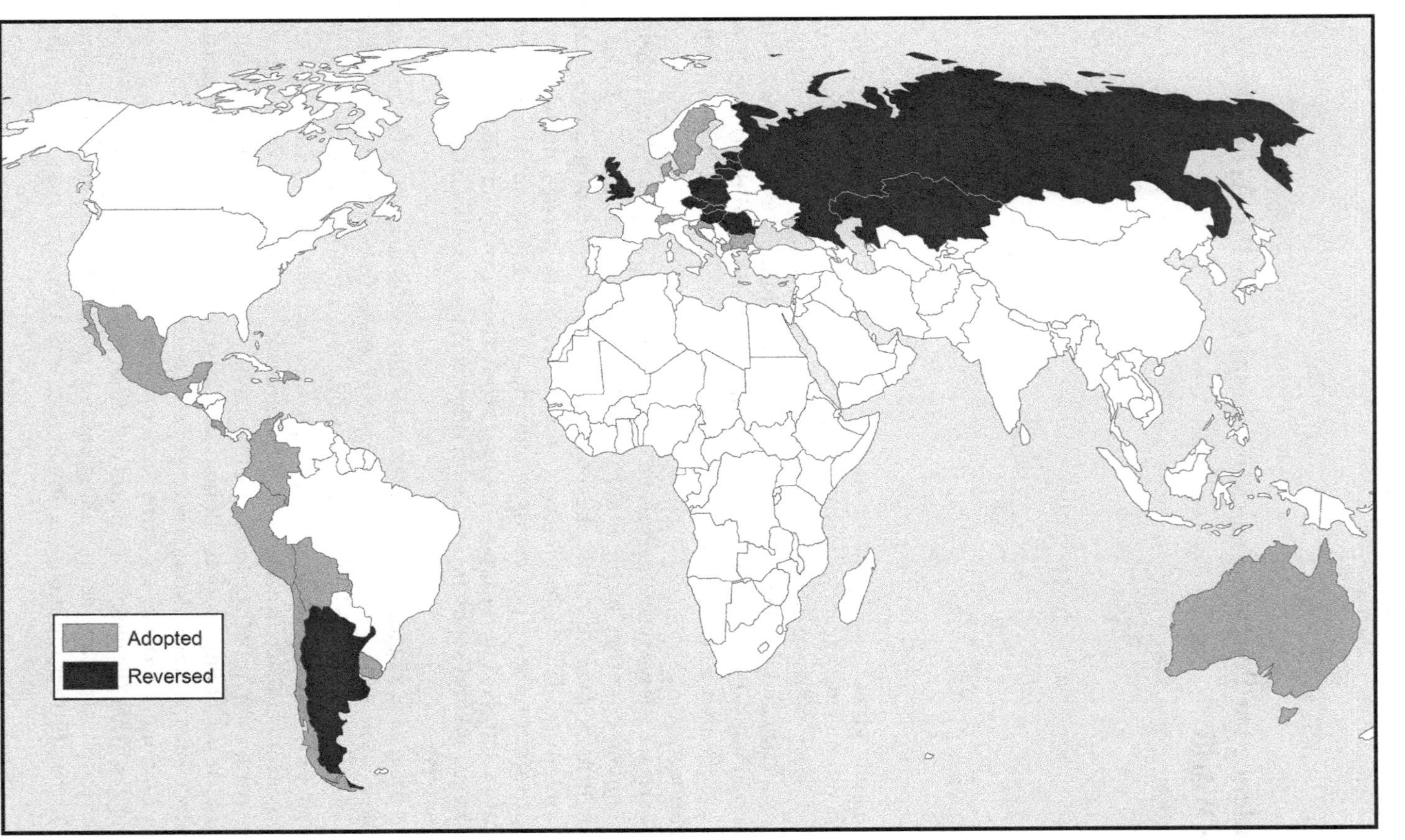

FIGURE 4.1 Pension Privatization and Its Reversal Around the World

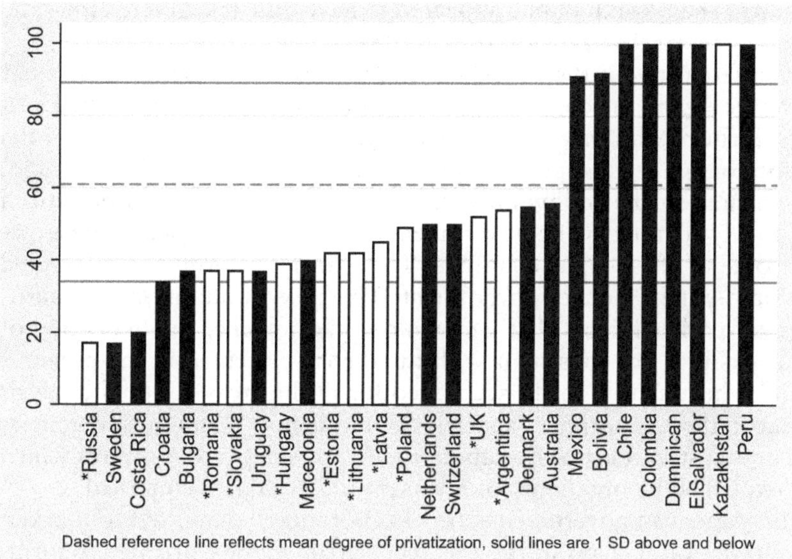

FIGURE 4.2 Degree of Pension Privatization & Reversal
(reversing countries indicated by white bars and starred country names)

telling is that one government that bucked regional trends by adopting less extensive pension privatization than was typical for the region – Argentina – conforms to my theoretical expectations about reversal.

The post-communist countries do have unique political legacies under communism and underwent a transition to a market-oriented economy at roughly the same time while experiencing many similar – if not identical – pressures from the European Union and the international community. In the case of pension privatization, the post-communist countries also share similarities in the cost of their PAYG systems which translated into the degree to which they pursued pension privatization. In other words, the post-communist countries are unique here because of the theoretical reasons described in the previous chapter – the degree of pension privatization. This also explains why reversals of pension privatization have been concentrated among these post-communist countries.

Figure 4.2 also clearly emphasizes that there are a group of eight countries – mostly Latin American countries plus Kazakhstan – which nearly or completely privatized their entire national retirement systems. Only one of these extensive reformers – Kazakhstan – has backtracked. Kazakhstan is an extremely authoritarian regime which has been ruled by the same president, Nursultan Nazarbayev, since the fall of communism likely explaining why even extensive pension privatization could not secure the reform's survival by altering the social contract. The Kazakh public appeared to have little reaction to either the introduction or reversal of pension privatization.

What is different about the overwhelming majority of these countries that did not reverse? Again, the degree of reform is the critical difference. The Latin American reformers who privatized extensively did so at the beginning of the wave of adoptions of pension privatization. Chile was the first to adopt in 1980, with implementation the following year. Right-wing governments privatized more extensively than left-wing governments and this also explains the experiences of some of these eight countries. The Chilean reforms were adopted under the right-wing Pinochet government. The time of adoption and partisanship are two other factors that we would think influence the likelihood of reversal, factors that are consistent with the theory presented in the previous chapter, and which can be easily accounted for in the cross-national analysis below. In short, there is nothing "special" about the post-communist countries of Central and Eastern Europe nor about the Latin American reformers which cannot be explained by my theory of reversals and evaluated empirically.

The Latin American governments are also not more committed to market-oriented reforms or less prone to the reversal of market-oriented reforms than other governments in other regions. Despite the adoption of extensive market-oriented reforms in many Latin American countries in the 1980s and 1990s, progress on reforms has been inconsistent and more subject to reversal than reforms in other regions, including Asia (Singh and Cerisola 2006). Macroeconomic policy volatility has been identified as a major hindrance to growth (Sahay and Goyal 2006). Based on regional trends, Latin American politicians are not more invested in pro-market policies. If anything, Latin American politicians as a group are less inclined to maintain market-oriented policies.

A wave of left-wing victories between 1998 and 2008 has further driven a move toward less market-oriented policies in some countries (Flores-Macías 2012). Notably, the wave of left-wing victories, including Chile in 2000 with the election of Ricardo Lagos as president and Bolivia in 2005 with the election of Evo Morales as president. Chile and Bolivia adopted an extensive degree of pension privatization (100 percent in Chile and about 90 percent in Bolivia as shown in Figure 4.2) and in neither country have there been serious discussions about reversing of pension privatization. The question for countries like this – with left-wing executives and facing financial crises – is not about why market-oriented reforms would be abandoned, but *which* market-oriented reforms would be abandoned. Because pension privatization had been so extensive, my argument suggests that domestic stakeholders blocked its reversal as a viable option, even if left-wing politicians were looking for a source of short-term revenue or opposed the policy for partisan reasons. For instance, we can compare Chile to Argentina. When the financial crisis hit, Chile passed provision to bolster the state-provided social security benefits for those with the lowest incomes. By contrast, a moderate degree of pension privatization had been adopted in Argentina and the government chose to abruptly and completely end pension privatization in 2008.

Furthermore, certain countries did not follow the regional trend – i.e., they pursued a more or less extensive degree of pension privatization than was typical of the region – and we see that these cases conform to my theoretical expectations about reversal. For instance, Croatia pursued much less privatization than other post-communist reformers and has also not backtracked to date. The one Latin American country that has backtracked – Argentina – also adopted a moderate degree of pension privatization.

The most limited pension privatization reformers include Russia, Sweden, Costa Rica, and Croatia. Given the limited number of countries, this suggests that there may be a curvilinear relationship in which the least and most extensive reformers were the least likely to reverse, but it is possible that there are primarily two groups: extensive reformers and everyone else. As Chapters 5 and 6 will address, Russia has reversed pension privatization and its political battles follow the logic of a moderate reformer, although it falls among the least extensive reformers. The statistical analysis below suggests that there is indeed a curvilinear relationship, but the curvilinear effect should be interpreted with some caution given the limited number of countries. Regardless, the cross-national empirical trends and duration analysis indicate that moderate reformers were the most likely to backtrack, thereby confirming my theoretical expectations that the degree of reform influenced politicians' fiscal incentives and the role of potential domestic stakeholders. In countries like Sweden and Costa Rica which are among the more limited reformers, there have not been serious debates about reversing pension privatization and – if my theory is correct – we should not observe serious reversal discussion because there should not be strong fiscal pressure to reverse. Nonetheless, even if we consider moderate reformers to be all of those who did not extensively privatize pensions, the same political logic holds.

Explaining the Degree of Pension Privatization

The reasons for the adoption of pension privatization include a combination of fiscal pressures, international pressures (including World Bank advocacy), and domestic conditions which made pension privatization a desirable policy option and one that was politically feasible to pursue.

Countries varied widely in how extensively they pursued pension privatization. The degree of pension privatization adopted in a country is closely related to the size of implicit pension debt before pension privatization was adopted. This has been emphasized in current explanations of the adoption of pension privatization, notably including the work of Brooks (2009). The higher the cost of the PAYG pension systems (measured by implicit pension debt) the greater the fiscal pressure to reform and, simultaneously, the more expensive doing so would be. Therefore, it was countries with mid-range levels of implicit pension

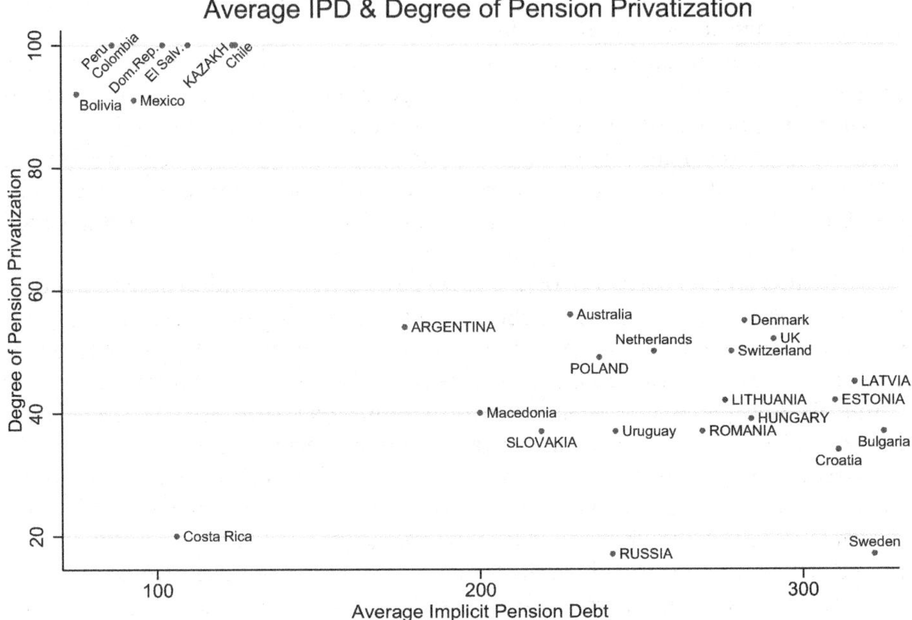

FIGURE 4.3 Average Implicit Pension Debt and Degree of Pension Privatization
Note: Countries in ALL CAPITALS are those that reversed pension privatization.

debt which were the most likely to adopt pension privatization: they felt the pressure to do so and could afford the cost of switching over.

Implicit pension debt does indeed predict a large percentage of variation in the degree of pension privatization. In a bivariate regression, implicit pension debt explains 62 percent of the variation in the degree of pension privatization. Countries with very large implicit pension debt were only able to afford to privatize pensions to a limited degree. Figure 4.3 demonstrates this relationship.

In thinking about selection effects on the adoption and reversal of pension privatization, one of the biggest differences between reformers and non-reformers – which also predicts reversal – is implicit pension debt.

Once pension privatization has been adopted, however, the question is about variation among privatizing countries, not the differences between privatizing and non-privatizing countries. There are strong theoretical reasons to think that implicit pension debt and the degree of pension privatization should have a different influence on the risk of reversing pension privatization. Implicit pension debt should have a positive and linear effect on the risk of reversal. The degree of pension privatization should have a curvilinear risk, as explained above. This is confirmed by looking at the correlation between implicit pension debt, pension privatization, and reversal. A pairwise correlation between implicit pension debt and reversal reveals a positive and significant relationship. A pairwise correlation between the degree of pension privatization and reversal reveals a negative and significant relationship. These correlations help to confirm that these two variables – implicit pension debt and the degree of pension privatization – must be included as separate independent variables in the model in order for the model to be correctly specified and that a selection model would not be appropriate.

A Duration Model of Pension Privatization Reversal

The degree of reform, policy diffusion effects, and domestic economic and political conditions are factors that change over time. The question, then, is not limited to 29 countries of which 12 reversed, but involves 29 countries over time. In particular, *changes* in global trends and domestic circumstances are likely to prompt reversal. If the initial conditions under which reforms are adopted remain in place, we might think backtracking would be much less likely in general. Something must change to prompt backtracking. And, although certain trends may appear evident among the reversing countries, these may simply be correlation or coincidence. As such, duration analysis can shed light on *when* and *why* countries are most likely to experience reversals in pension privatization.

My central inquiry – when will market-oriented reforms survive? – considers the timing of reversals so that an event history model is most appropriate. I do not, however, have any theoretical expectation about whether the likelihood of reversals will increase or decrease over time. As such, the Cox proportional hazard model is best because it does not require any assumption about the likelihood of the event increasing or decreasing over time (Box-Steffensmeier and Jones 2004).

I examine the twenty-nine countries that have implemented pension privatization around the world from 1980 when pension privatization was first adopted in Chile through 2012 which was the most recent year of data available at the time of analysis. Countries enter the dataset in the year in which the country privatized pensions; countries only exit the dataset in the event that a complete and permanent reversal was legislated (this applies to Argentina and Hungary). In the case of a complete and permanent reversal, the country is no longer a relevant observation as reversal cannot occur. Twelve countries have pursued reversals with several pursuing reversals in multiple years (see Table 2.1 in Chapter 2). The countries in question include (reversing countries are bolded and italicized):

Argentina, Australia, Bolivia, Bulgaria, Chile, Colombia, Costa Rica, Croatia, ***Czech Republic***, Denmark, Dominican Republic, El Salvador, ***Estonia***, ***Hungary***, ***Kazakhstan***, ***Latvia***, ***Lithuania***, Macedonia, Mexico, Netherlands, Peru, ***Poland***, ***Romania***, ***Russia***, ***Slovakia***, Sweden, Switzerland, ***UK***, Uruguay

The dependent variable is a binary variable capturing whether a reversal was legislated in a given year; a country receives a "0" in each year in which pension privatization existed but no reversal occurred and a "1" in each year in which a reversal was legislated. A reversal is classified as legislation that cuts or eliminates contributions to the privatized pension tier in a given country-year. There are 13 instances of reversal out of 442 observations.[1]

I do not have sufficient observations of reversals to estimate models in which the dependent variable is either the nature or degree of reversals; variation on these dimensions is addressed in the case studies. Nonetheless, this cross-national statistical test provides an initial test of the argument that a reversal of pension privatization is most likely when there is a moderate degree of pension privatization.

Independent Variables

Implicit Pension Debt. Implicit pension debt (IPD) is the government's current set of obligations to pensioners under the PAYG system. IPD data are obtained by using existing data on IPD to impute IPD data across the countries and years under study.[2] Following the method used in James and Brooks (2001) and Brooks (2009), I regress the available data on IPD on the percentage of the population over the age of 65 (one of the main predictors of the size of a country's pension debt). I then use the resulting equation to calculate IPD values for other country-years based on data for the percentage of the population over the age of 65.

Degree of Pension Privatization. Data for the degree of pension privatization are taken from Brooks (2009: 59–61). Brooks provides a valuable tool to scholars seeking to better understand the nature of pension reform and pension privatization, in particular, by quantifying the extent to which pension privatization was pursued taking into consideration the parameters of the country in which reforms were adopted. There are no comparable data that systematically quantify this major difference in pension privatization.

The measure I use from Brooks (2009) is the percentage of future pensions that come from the individual privatized account. The degree of pension privatization influences the extent to which interests in the public and private sector will be entrenched and will be politically influential. The degree of pension privatization is the percent of an individual's future pension that will come from the individual account. The estimates are based on simulations that account for the size of contributions to individual accounts and assume thirty-five years of payroll contributions, a 4.5 percent annual rate of return on investments, a 2 percent yearly growth in wages, and twenty years of retirement. Changing the assumptions would, of course, change the percentage of privatization. The

---

[1] Three countries' reversals are excluded from the quantitative analysis because they had occurred too recently at the time of analysis to include them in the dataset: the Czech Republic (2014), Kazakhstan (2013–2015), and the United Kingdom (2013).

[2] The equation I use to calculate implicit pension data is: IPD = $-7.3 + 18.64*$ Age over 65. For existing data on IPD, see: Holzmann, Palacios, and Zviniene (2004), Kane and Palacios (1996), Palacios and Pallarès-Miralles (2000), and Van de Noord and Herd (1993).

simulations are useful not because they represent the only possible outcome, but because they provide a reliable comparison of the extent of privatization across countries.

Brooks' simulation requires "the legislated contribution rate to the mandatory pension systems that can be allocated to the private component of the reformed system" (p. 59). For a few cases – Lithuania, Macedonia, Romania, Russia, and Slovakia – this percentage is not easily identifiable and simulations cannot be conducted. For these cases, I have drawn on additional sources to supplement Brooks' data. More information on addressing these missing data on the degree of pension privatization is provided in the data appendix to this chapter. Because these pension reforms have been described extensively in a variety of sources, we can provide reasonable estimates by pairing the five countries with missing data to countries for which there are data.

Policy Diffusion. The potential presence of policy diffusion effects as mediated by reform circumstances and EU membership necessitates the inclusion of a spatial lag term. Here, the influence of countries on one another is not conceptualized in terms of space. Countries may have a similar degree of reform, but be located far apart geographically. Being an EU member does denote some geographic proximity, but there is no reason to think that EU countries that are more physically proximate are more likely to influence one other. A country's position in a network and its economic similarity to other countries – things which come with membership – may be more influential in decisions about economic policy than geography per se (Cao 2010).

In this case – as in many political economy examples – the spatial lag model (also known as a spatial autoregressive model) is most appropriate. Unlike the spatially lagged error model, the spatial lag model does not confine the effect of "space" (or proximity based on specified characteristics) to the error term, but rather includes the effect of space in the substance of the model (Beck et al. 2006, p. 30). Substantively modeling spatial dependence is preferable to a model that treats this type of dependence merely as a nuisance in the error term (Franzese and Hays 2007).

The spatial lag term is preferable because it allows the direct modeling of the diffusion effects based on the degree of reform and EU membership.[3] For each country-year observation, the spatial lag denotes a sum of the dependent variable of neighboring countries' policies (reversals), weighted by how connected a country and each neighboring country are (Drukker et al. 2012; Haining 2003, pp. 81–84).[4] Spatial lag terms can be easily included in Cox proportional

---

[3] Recent work confirms that diffusion effects are best captured by the inclusion of a spatial lag term. For example, Linos (2013) demonstrates policy diffusion effects for welfare state policies among OECD countries using spatial lag terms (see especially pp. 89–92).

[4] I use an inverse-distance spatial weighting matrix from the specified coordinates (EU and degree of reform), and apply a Euclidean distance measure. An inverse-distance matrix is most appropriate because it allows for all observations to influence each other (within the parameters of the specified spatial weights matrix) (Drukker 2009).

hazard models (for just one recent example, see Crabtree, Darmofal, and Kern 2015; see also Darmofal 2015).

What constitutes a neighboring country is determined by how the weights matrix has been specified. Here, I specify the spatial weights matrix by shared EU membership and by comparable country circumstances. Based on the politics of pension reform and the most likely diffusion process to be happening here (as discussed in Chapter 3), I expect that countries are most likely to be influenced by other countries with comparable circumstances, including the degree of pension privatization, the level of implicit pension debt, and government finances. I conduct principal component analysis on three variables – the degree of pension privatization, implicit pension debt, and deficit – and use the resulting component score to define the spatial lag along with EU membership.

Additional Independent Variables. Other independent variables capture the fiscal, political, and legislative context. Political variables on partisanship and opposition fractionalization are taken from the Database of Political Indicators (DPI) (Beck et al. 2001). Left is a binary variable in which a country is coded as "1" if the largest party in parliament is left-wing (and "0" otherwise). In a small percentage of observations (about 10 percent or 43 out of 442 observations), the DPI has omitted partisanship data; it appears that this is because the winning party was ambiguously named. For instance, the Movement for Bulgaria won in 2005 and was a left-wing coalition led by the Bulgaria socialist party. Missing data on partisanship has been replaced using the same coding rules as the DPI.[5] Majority captures the number of seats held by the government; it is also taken from the DPI. Left Majority is the size of the government's majority when a left-wing government is in power.

I use the Freedom House measure of political rights as an indicator of democracy, rescaled so that higher numbers indicate more democratic systems (Freedom House 2013). Freedom House is preferable to other measures like Polity and binary measures used by Przeworski et al. (2000) which omit meaningful variation (Herrera and Kapur 2007). EU membership is a cross-sectional binary variable with the relevant countries coded as "1."

Data on GDP growth and deficits are taken from the 2013 edition of the World Development Indicators (WDI). The deficit variable is revenue minus expenses minus net acquisition of non-financial assets and is measured as a percentage of GDP. The deficit variable is critical in capturing the fiscal situation faced by countries. There are missing data, however, in 136 of the 442 observations (about 31 percent of cases). To be sure that these missing data are not producing incorrect estimates, I use multiple imputation to address these missing data (Honaker, King, and Blackwell 2011). The results presented in the data appendix are those based on the original dataset with no imputed

---

[5] More information on replacing the data for this small percentage of cases can be found in the Appendix to this chapter.

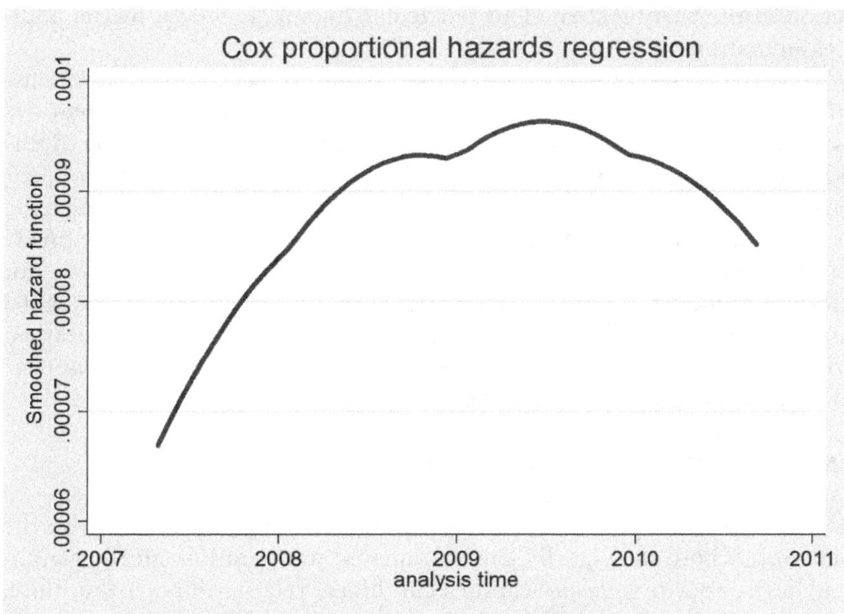

FIGURE 4.4 Baseline Hazard of Reversing Pension Privatization

data, the results using five datasets of imputed data, and the results using ten datasets of imputed data. The substantive results remain the same across the models.

Risk of Reversing Pension Privatization Around the World

A Cox proportional hazard analysis reveals that countries with a moderate degree of reform were indeed the most likely to reverse pension privatization. The full regression results are available in the Appendix to this chapter. The baseline hazard confirms that a Cox model is appropriate because the risk is nonmonotonic over time; the risk increases until 2009, decreases, then increases again before subsequently declining once more.

The proportional hazard model shows that several factors played an important role, including the degree of pension privatization, opposition fractionalization, and GDP growth. GDP growth is just outside the bounds of traditional statistical significance. The results, however, indicate a relationship in the expected direction in which higher levels of growth are correlated with a lower risk of reversing pension privatization.

Opposition fractionalization is based on a Herfindahl index of opposition parties in the government. A higher value indicates a less fractionalized system. The results indicate that the less fractionalized a political system, the more likely a reversal will be. The reason for this may be that in systems with less fractionalized opposition, there are fewer sources of potential political opposition in the party system. This particular finding, however, merits additional examination.

Several variables that are not statistically significant merit additional discussion. Implicit pension debt – the cost of the former PAYG pension system – is not a statistically significant predictor of reversing pension privatization in this analysis. This may be because implicit pension debt predicts the degree of pension privatization so strongly. Once pension privatization has been adopted, the results here suggest that it is the degree of reform and not the cost of the PAYG system that predicts reversal. Finally, the size of the left-wing majority is not statistically significant. As with any statistical analysis, the results are not the last word on the causal effect of any of the variables considered here. Rather, these results are indicative that the degree of pension privatization does appear to play a causal role in the manner indicated.

The Effect of the Degree of Pension Privatization on the Risk of Reversal

The degree of pension privatization has a statistically significant effect on the risk of reversal; both the variable and its squared term are statistically significant and have opposite signs indicating a curvilinear relationship. Furthermore, these results indicate that the risk of reversal is greatest for moderate reformers. This evidence suggests that there are more than two relevant groups – more extensive reformers and all others – and instead suggests that there is a curvilinear relationship between the degree of reform and the risk of reversal.

The results are consistent with the explanation that governments facing limited pension privatization feel less fiscal pressure to reverse while politicians facing extensive privatization may want to gain short-term revenue by reversing but are blocked by domestic stakeholders. The analysis is based on a sample of 29 countries over time (with a total of 443 observations) so this should be interpreted with some caution given the relatively limited number of countries and the limitations of confining our study to the time period of 1981 to 2012. Nonetheless, the results are strongly suggestive that the degree of pension privatization influences the risk of reversal and that there is a difference between limited, moderate, and extensive reformers.

Figure 4.5 shows the size of the effect based on calculations of the change in the hazard rate.[6] Comparing the mean degree of pension privatization (60 percent) to one standard deviation below the mean (38 percent) decreases the risk of reversal by nearly 60 percent. Comparing the mean to the minimum value of 17 percent decreases the risk by 253 percent. Conversely, comparing the mean to a standard deviation above the mean (88 percent pension

---

[6] The equation for calculating the effect of a covariate on increasing or decreasing the hazard rate is: $\%\Delta h(t) = [e^{\wedge}\beta\,(x_i = X_1) - e^{\wedge}\beta\,(x_i = X_2)\,/e^{\wedge}\beta\,(x_i = X_2)] * 100$ where $\beta =$ coefficient, $x_i =$ covariate, and X_1 and $X_2 =$ different values of the covariate; see Box-Steffensmeier and Jones (2004), p. 60.

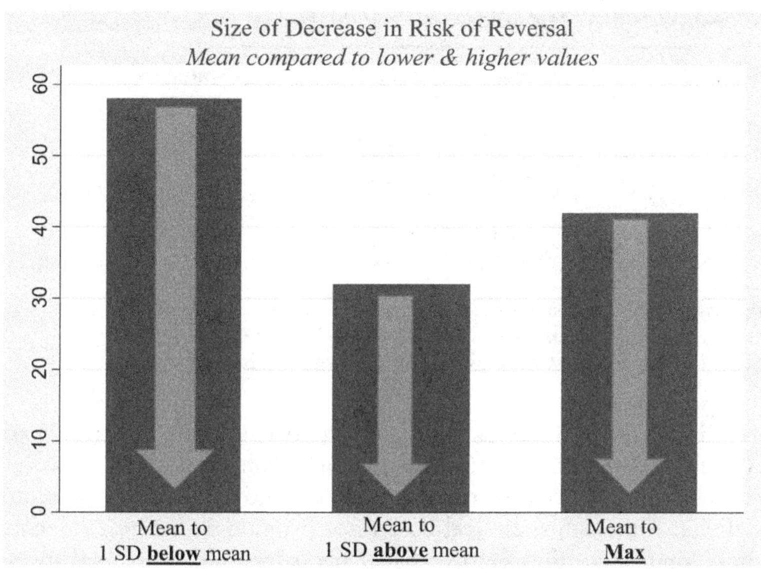

FIGURE 4.5 Comparing Average Pension Privatization to More or Less Extensive Reform *Decreases* Risk of Reversal

privatization) or the maximum value (100 percent privatization) decreases the risk of reversal by 30 or 40 percent, respectively. These results hold even when taking into account other major theoretical explanations for reversals. As such, the cross-national trends provide a compelling support for the argument that the extent of reform is an influential part of the political story of reversals.

Fiscal Pressure and the Risk of Reversal

I argue that the intensity of fiscal pressure was an important part of the impetus to consider reversing pension privatization. All countries face fiscal pressures, albeit to varying degrees at different times. Depending on domestic political conditions and the degree of pension privatization, a reversal in pension privatization would occur. My argument is probabilistic in that I would suspect that greater fiscal pressure makes a reversal more likely although it certainly does not guarantee that a reversal will occur.

The results of my analysis of cross-national trends suggests that more fiscal pressure is associated with a greater risk of reversal. Specifically, higher deficits and poorer GDP growth are associated with a greater risk of overturning pension privatization although the coefficients are not statistically significant in these models. Because fiscal pressure is such a central part of the story, in addition to the Cox proportional hazard model, I also present a t-test comparing deficits and GDP growth in reversing and non-reversing countries. Table 4.1 be presents the result of an independent sample t-test comparing the mean deficit and GDP growth in countries that did and did not reverse pension privatization.

TABLE 4.1 *Comparing Fiscal Pressures across Countries*

Variable	N	Mean	Stan. Dev.	P-value
Deficit				
Non-reversing	294	−1.31	3.24	.00
Reversing	12	−4.10	3.58	
GDP growth				
Non-reversing	429	3.61	3.54	.00
Reversing	13	−1.19	9.28	

Note: These results are based on an independent sample t-test assuming equal variances across groups. The results are the same for an independent sample t-test assuming unequal variances. The p-value is based on a two-tailed test.

As shown in Table 4.1, countries that reversed pension privatization had larger deficits than non-reversing countries and a decline in GDP. Countries that did not reverse pension privatization on average enjoyed GDP growth and had smaller deficits. Although these trends do not provide definitive evidence, they are strongly suggestive that greater fiscal pressure makes reversal more likely.

Critical to understanding reversals, however, is examining how fiscal pressures are filtered through the political system. The case study chapters examine in depth how these fiscal pressures influenced domestic political debates.

Other Explanations for Post-Communist Reversals

The evidence above is consistent with the expectation that a reversal of pension privatization is most likely when there has been a moderate degree of pension privatization. We still might be concerned, however, that this is picking up on some other underlying reason that the post-communist countries both adopted less extensive pension privatization than many (though not all) Latin American reformers and subsequently reversed. Two of the most cited reasons for post-communist reversals – which have already been mentioned in Chapter 2 – are the role of the European Union and the role of the World Bank. Another explanation has been that the spread of certain ideas about economic reform has been regionally based.

An oft-cited reason for post-communist reversals is that the European Union created fiscal pressures with its deficit guidelines which made the financing gap generated by pension privatization impossible to sustain (Casey 2012). The statistical analysis above includes a control for EU membership, which could have created additional fiscal pressures on countries to reverse. The variable for EU membership is not significant, although that does not eliminate the possibility that EU deficit guidelines heightened the fiscal pressures on governments. After all, politicians had ways to reduce deficits other than backtracking on pension privatization. Moreover, the Latin American reformers who adopted extensive pension privatization and kept the reform also faced strong fiscal pressures to keep deficits in check. Indeed, a common argument has been that governments are already limited in their deficit spending because of concerns about how investors will react.

There is also the consideration of the role of the World Bank and its shift in advocacy for pension privatization which I discussed in Chapter 2. Orenstein (2008) details how a shift in the World Bank's proposals regarding pension privatization preceded subsequent changes in global trends on pension reform. Theoretically, the change in the World Bank's advice can be seen as a permissive condition that made reversing more likely to be considered by politicians, but did not itself motivate the reversal or explain why some countries reversed and others did not. Arguing that the World Bank's less enthusiastic and more qualified support for pension privatization is primarily responsible for reversals is not especially compelling given the theoretical reasons discussed in Chapter 2 that pension privatization was supposed to be a radical revolution in the social contract on retirement. Once adopted, all of the reasons that pension privatization should have become entrenched are relevant regardless of the stance of the World Bank. The World Bank's change in stance is a better explanation for why countries stopped adopting pension privatization than why countries reversed. The case studies in subsequent chapters also help establish that the World Bank's change in advocacy was, at best, only a partial consideration.

The influence of the change in the World Bank's advice is difficult to quantify and therefore to evaluate with statistical analysis. We can, though, consider the timing of the change in World Bank advice and the correlation with reversals. We can also look at changes in the baseline hazard over time to see whether the baseline risk of reversal rises markedly before and after the shift in World Bank advice. The shift in advice can be dated to a conference held by the economist Joseph Stiglitz in 1999, which challenged many of the positive claims made by World Bank reports about pension privatization; Orzsag and Stiglitz (2001) subsequently published an article entitled "Ten Myths about Social Security Reform." The first reversal was not until nearly a decade later in Argentina in 2008. This would be consistent with the explanation that the change in the World Bank's position was a permissive condition that made backtracking possible. Figure 4.4 shows that the baseline hazard increases markedly around 2008 and 2009 (when the first reversals were happening) and peaks around 2010 before declining again. This would also be consistent with the argument that the World Bank's change in advice made reversing pension privatization a viable option so that when financial crisis struck the baseline risk increased.

Ideas, particularly ones that took hold among the post-communist countries, are also important. Appel and Orenstein (2013) demonstrate how ideas propagated the spread of pension privatization and the flat tax among Central and East European post-communist countries even when these ideas were not backed by international organizations providing significant resources.

Perhaps, then, the idea of reversing pension privatization simply took hold as had previous reforms.

The spatial lag included in the analysis above partially addresses the possibility of regional diffusion. In this model, the spatial lag is not significant. The full results of the model are available in the Appendix to this chapter. In the analysis presented here, the spatial lag defines neighbors based on EU membership and whether a country faced a similar reform context (including the degree of pension privatization, implicit pension debt, and the national deficit); the explanation is that countries with a similar reform context and similar pressures from the EU will be more likely to emulate each other's policy choices. All of the post-communist countries in the analysis (except Russia and Kazakhstan) are EU members; Macedonia is a candidate EU country. Although there are accounts indicating the politicians in post-communist countries were observing and learning from each other's choices, what may have appeared to be learning in fact could have been politicians using other countries experiences to justify their actions. As mentioned at the beginning of the chapter, there are cases like Croatia in which the government did not follow regional trends (they pursued less pension privatization than was typical for a post-communist country) and have not, to date, reversed. Likewise, Argentina pursued less extensive pension privatization than its Latin American neighbors and has reversed. These cases are especially suggestive that the degree of reform was a central factor in determining the risk of reversal.

The case studies in following chapters suggest that policy diffusion via learning actually was occurring across the region which should make us hesitant to dismiss the possibility that diffusion was an important factor. Furthermore, the case studies suggest that the EU's deficit guidelines did figure into politicians' calculations about whether to retain pension privatization so that we should not dismiss this possibility on these results alone. The results here are instructive in showing that the degree of reform matters for the risk of reversal, but should be evaluated in the context of countries' real-world experiences with reversal and are not a basis on which to dismiss complementary explanations.

Conclusion

Trends in the reversal of pension privatization around the world suggest the degree to which pension privatization was pursued played an important role in shaping the landscape of political battles that determined its survival. These patterns in social security reform around the world allow us to connect why pension privatization reforms were adopted in the first place and why they ultimately survived or not. Examining cross-national trends, therefore, gets us a step closer to evaluating why this particular reform was more likely to endure.

Cross-national trends alone, however, are limited in what they can tell us about some of the important causal mechanisms linking reform design and reversal or about variation in the types of reversal. The analysis here tells us nothing about how governments enacted reversals and whether they did so in a single piece of legislation or phased in the reversal. We also know nothing about the extent to which governments backtracked. Both the means and degree of reversal, however, are theoretically significant. Domestic political pressures played a critical role in how quickly and how extensively governments pull back on pension privatization. The consequences of doing so are significant as well. Economists and policymakers predicted different long-term consequences would be associated with partial and complete reversals.

We also have little information from these global trends about public opinion or the role of important interest groups, including private pension funds. For a reform like pension privatization which was designed to fundamentally alter the social contract, public opinion is a vital issue to address. Furthermore, the statistical analysis cannot lend any clear insight into the role of lobbying by private pension funds. Given the amount of money to be gained by private pension funds who could manage and invest mandatory social security contributions, it is simply not plausible that private pension fund managers and professional associations did not at least attempt to play a role in the design of pension reforms even if their efforts were not successful.

I address these issues in the following chapters by leveraging the details of pension privatization reversals in Russia, Hungary, and Poland. Taken together, the cross-national evidence and the case studies provide a fuller picture of how, why, and to what extent governments failed to alter the social contract on retirement using pension privatization.

                                            Evidence on Pension Policy Reversal

Data Appendix to Chapter 4

Cox Proportional Hazard Models Predicting Reversal of Pension Privatization

	Model 1 No imputed Data	Model 2 5 imputed datasets	Model 3 10 imputed datasets
Degree of pension privatization	.41 (.18)**	.37 (.18)**	.38 (.17)**
Degree of pension privatization squared	−.006 (.003)**	−.006 (.003)**	−.005 (.002)**
Implicit pension debt	.002 (.01)	.0008 (.01)	.0007 (.01)
Opposition fractionalization	−3.72 (1.55)**	−4.06 (2.03)**	−4.17 (2.06)**
Left-wing majority	−.93 (1.48)	−.68 (1.51)	−.80 (1.50)
Deficit	−.16 (.19)	−.19 (.16)	−.18 (.16)
EU membership	−.06 (1.29)	.85 (.20)	.74 (1.17)
Democracy	−.11 (.39)	−.27 (.35)	−.25 (.34)
GDP growth	−.07 (.05)	−.05 (.04)	−.05 (.04)
Spatial lag	−.00002 (.00003)	−.0002 (.0002)	−.0002 (.0002)
Number of reversals	12	13	13
Number of countries	28	28	28
Observations	298	399	399
Model significance	.0000	.0000	.0000

Standard errors in parentheses

$* p < 0.10$, $** p < 0.05$, $*** p < 0.01$

Note: The number of reversals does not indicate the number of reversing countries. Rather, reversals are country-year and some countries have multi-year reversals. See Figure 2.1 for a summary of reversal cases. There is one additional reversal case – Argentina 2010 – which can be included with the imputed data because the imputed data addresses missing deficit data.

Countries Included in the Analysis

The countries included in the analysis are the following (with reversing countries bolded and italicized): ***Argentina***, Australia, Bolivia, Bulgaria, Chile, Colombia, Costa Rica, Croatia, ***Czech Republic***, Denmark, Dominican Republic, El Salvador, ***Estonia, Hungary, Kazakhstan, Latvia, Lithuania***, Macedonia, Mexico, Netherlands, Peru, ***Poland, Romania, Russia, Slovakia***, Sweden, Switzerland, ***the United Kingdom***, and Uruguay.

Three countries that passed pension privatization legislation are not included in the statistical analysis – the Czech Republic, Kosovo, and Ukraine. The Czech government adopted a law in 2011 regarding partial pension privatization measures and a law in 2014 legislating reversals, making its reform too recent to be included at the time of analysis. Kosovo is excluded due to missing data. The Ukrainian government adopted pension privatization measures intended to create a second tier in 2003, but has not implemented them to date (Betliy and Giucci 2011).

The British reversal (in 2013) and the Czech reversal (in 2014) occurred too recently at the time of analysis to include in the observations of reversals. There are several interesting cases of reform that include measures similar to pension privatization, but are excluded here because they are not national reforms. India adopted a defined contribution scheme, including private investment for all government workers (voluntary for all other citizens) in 2004 (Dave 2006). Nigeria also adopted a Chilean-style reform in 2004, but only for federal government workers (Casey and Dostal 2008). In Panama, contributions to the second tier are restricted to higher-income individuals (Mesa-Lago 2008). India, Nigeria, and Panama are excluded because their pension privatization reforms were restricted to federal government employees and are not national. Hong Kong and Taiwan have also adopted pension privatization-type reforms, but are excluded because they are not countries.

Missing Data on the Degree of Privatization

Imputation methods are one way to address missing data, but in this case there is a more substantive and appropriate way to handle missing data on the extent of pension privatization. I pair the five countries with missing data on the degree of privatization with their most similar reform counterparts for which data on the degree of privatization are available. Aside from conducting simulations (which is not possible due to missing data for these countries), this is the best way to complete the dataset. Pension privatization in these countries has been extensively analyzed; thus, we can be confident that this provides a reasonable estimation of the degree of privatization and more accurate data than imputation methods.

Countries are paired primarily on two dimensions: the nature of the reform and the size of contributions going to the individual account (see sources listed below). By pairing countries that adopted similar types of reforms and similar degree of contributions, we can be confident that their depth of privatization is similar though not identical. Although the reforms in paired countries are not identical, they are more comparable versus other countries/possible pairings.

The table below summarizes these pairings. Each country was carefully matched based on its similarity with other countries.

Pairing Countries to Address Missing Data on Degree of Privatization

Country with missing data on percent private	Country with similar pension reform	Percent private in Brooks 2009 (for country with similar pension reform)
Lithuania	Estonia	42
Macedonia	Hungary & Estonia	39 & 42
Romania	Bulgaria	37
Russia	Sweden	17
Slovakia	Bulgaria	37

Sources for pairing countries: Immergut and Andersen (2007), Drahokoupil and Domonkos (2012), Müller (2008).

Lithuania: Lithuania and Estonia have a traditional, mandatory PAYG first tier combined. Their second tiers are similar in that the pre-funded component is optional for many citizens (although in Estonia it is mandatory for those up to 18 and in Lithuania it is optional for all insured) (Müller 2008, p. 12). The contribution rates are similar. In Estonia, the total individual contribution rate is 6 percent and in Lithuania 5.5 percent (Drahokoupil and Domonkos 2012; Müller 2008). The difference in the optional nature of the second tier is the largest difference between the two, but they are nonetheless very similar in the depth of privatization, particularly as compared to other countries. For instance, Lithuania is quite different from the Latvian case (with 45 percent private in Brooks 2009) where the individual contribution rate is 10 percent and the first tier is based on notional defined contributions rather than a traditional, mandatory PAYG system (Müller 2008, p. 12).

Macedonia: Macedonia's reforms are most similar to Hungarian and Estonian measures, which have a percentage of private contributions of 39 percent and 42 percent, respectively. I therefore use 40 percent as an approximation for the degree of privatization in Macedonia based on these two values. Macedonia has a mandatory PAYG first tier and a mandatory pre-funded second tier and adopted a similar partial privatization reform like Hungary and Estonia for its second tier (Müller 2008, pp. 12–13).

Romania: Romania and Bulgaria both have a mandatory first tier based on pension points (a way of linking current contributions with future payments). Both have a second, pre-funded tier that is mandatory up to a certain age (42 in Bulgaria and 35 in Romania; in the Romanian system participation in the second tier is optional between the ages of 35 and 44). The individual contributions rate to the second tier is 6 percent in Bulgaria and is planned to increase from 2 percent to 5 percent in Romania.

Russia: Russia adopted a system in which the first tier is based on notional defined contributions and the second, pre-funded tier is mandatory, although citizens had the option to have their second-tier contributions managed by the state bank or individual pension funds. The Russian reforms are similar to Poland with the notable exception that Russia gave citizens a choice about contributing to individual accounts managed by the state bank or by a private pension fund. Additionally, the percentage of wages going to the second tier in Poland was 9 percent compared to 6 percent in Russia. This reflects a deeper degree of pension privatization in Poland than in Russia. The Russian reforms are more akin to the depth of privatization in Sweden, which also combined notional defined contributions in the first, public tier with partial privatization of the second tier (Immergut and Andersen 2007). As such, Russia's degree of privatization is set at 17 percent (the percent of total pensions from private accounts for Sweden according to the simulation in Brooks 2009).

Slovakia: Slovakia and Bulgaria have a mandatory first tier based on pension points and a pre-funded second tier. In Bulgaria, the second tier was implemented as being mandatory for those up to the age of 42 and in Slovakia it was mandatory for all new entrants to the labor market and optional for all others. In Bulgaria, the individual contribution rate to the second tier is 5 percent of wages and in Slovakia it is 9 percent of wages. Although a significant difference, because the reform is mandatory for a larger swath of the population in Slovakia, the degree of privatization is still comparable to Bulgaria.

Replacing Missing DPI Data for Government Partisanship

The partisanship variable comes from the Database of Political Indicators. There are observations with missing data on partisanship in the DPI that are easily replaced following the DPI coding rules given some extra investigation into the partisanship of the government. Because of the relatively small nature of this dataset (there are 28 countries over time), it is feasible to take the extra time to code the partisanship of the government in cases where doing so for the entire (and impressive) DPI dataset might be too time consuming.

The variable of interest is **gov1rlc** in the DPI dataset which captures the partisanship (left-wing, centrist, or right-wing) of the largest party in the legislature. The DPI Handbook indicates that party name is the first indicator used to code partisanship. If the party name does not clearly indicate partisanship (as in Christian Democratic being right-wing, Social Democrat being left-wing, etc.), coders look for a party platform to identify the party's position on economic issues. If no platform is found or the party does not have economic policy as a central issue, partisanship is left as missing.

In most of the cases, it appears that the DPI does not code partisanship for the country-year observations because a party had a name that was ambiguous regarding partisanship. This is often the case for coalition parties formed for particular elections and nationalist parties. Leaving these observations as missing, however, is misleading as it suggests that the government was neither clearly right nor left-wing. In most of these cases, a cursory check of election results reveals the partisanship of the government. For instance, the Bulgarian election in 2005 was overwhelmingly won by the Coalition for Bulgaria – an ambiguous name – which was led by the Bulgarian Socialist Party. This was clearly a left-wing coalition and left-wing government. In the DPI, however, partisanship is missing for these country-years.

In total, I replace 44 missing country-year observations for 13 countries (there are 399 observations in the models estimated in the paper so this constitutes about 11 percent of observations). In my dataset, a "1" indicates a left-wing government in the legislature and a "0" indicates a right-wing government. I use Adam Carr's electoral archive to confirm election results, founded and maintained by Dr. Adam Carr and available at http://psephos.adam-carr .net/.

For the post-communist countries, a good source describing the nature and partisanship of post-communist parties is Ishiyama and Bozóki (2002). For parties created since the publication of this book, I rely on the characterization of the party in the general media to code partisanship.

Only two countries with missing data were not post-communist: Colombia (2011–2012) and Peru (2001). In both cases, it appears that the DPI left the partisanship coding as missing because right-wing parties won who had ambiguous names regarding partisanship and possibly because some people considered the parties to be personalist parties promoting the president's agenda. In Colombia and Peru in these years, however, these are clearly not left-wing parties, which is how the variable is coded. As such, I replace the missing data with a "0."

The only missing partisan data in my dataset that cannot be replaced is for Switzerland for the period 2004–2012. The Swiss People's Party won the most seats in 2003 and 2011 legislative elections; they are generally considered a populist and nationalist party. Economic issues, while part of the party's platform, are not a defining characteristic of the party's agenda. A detailed description of the replacement of missing data for each of the 13 countries is given below:

- Bulgaria (2006–2009): The Movement for Bulgaria won in 2005 and was a left-wing coalition led by the Bulgarian Socialist Party. These country-years are probably missing in the DPI because the coalition is ambiguously named.
- Chile (1980–1989): For Pinochet's time in power, the DPI codes partisanship as missing. Given the DPI's coding rule about focusing on economic policy, however, this would clearly be a right-wing government and is coded as such in the database.
- Colombia (2011–2012): The right-wing Uribe alliance won in 2010. These country-years are probably missing in the DPI because some considered this a personalist party and the name does not clearly indicate partisanship.
- Croatia (2012): This is a left-wing Social Democrat coalition. These country-years may be missing in the DPI because it was a coalition although the coalition was entitled, "Social Democratic Party and allies."
- Estonia (2008–2012): The right-wing Estonian Reform Party won the most seats in the elections in March 2007 and March 2011. These country-years are probably missing in the DPI because "Reform Party" does not clearly denote partisan affiliation.
- Hungary (April 2010): The Fidesz party (right-wing) won the election in April 2010 and subsequently reversed pension privatization. The DPI, however, does not change the coding of partisanship until the following year (2011). This is the general rule followed by the DPI; after an election, the coding of the partisanship of the government changes in the following year. It would, however, be misleading to code this as a "1" which makes it look as if the Socialists reversed pension privatization. Hungary 2010 is coded as a "0" for its right-wing government, which was in power the majority of the year and responsible for the reversal that occurred in Hungary in 2010. This is the only country-year observation in which partisanship changed in the year of the election and there was a reversal by the new party in that year.
- Kazakhstan: DPI codes this as missing likely because Nazarbayev is a personalist dictator whose party has dominated post-communist Kazakh politics in

the post-communist era. His party is clearly not a left-wing party (particularly based on economic policies) and is coded as "0" in the dataset.

- Latvia (October 2010 election, October 2011 election): A center-right Unity Party won most seats in the 2010 election and left-wing Harmony won most seats in 2011, but it was still a right-wing coalition government in 2011 so coded as "0" for 2011 and 2012. The partisanship of the largest governing party is the key.
- Macedonia (2002, 2007–2012): The Internal Macedonian Revolutionary Organization (IMRO) is coded as "0" because it is not a left-wing party. These country-years are probably missing in the DPI because IMRO is considered a nationalist party with a name that does not clearly indicate partisanship.
- Peru (2001): The Peru 2000 movement won. I code this as "0" because it is definitely not a left-wing party as it backed Fujimori and his right-wing economic policies. These country-years are probably missing in the DPI because Peru 2000 was considered by some as a personalist party that was more of a vote for Fujimori than an actual party.
- Poland (2008–2012): These country-year observations are missing in DPI, but Law & Justice and Citizen's Platform are in power – two well-known right-wing parties – so they are coded as right-wing. These country-years are probably missing in the DPI because the party name may not clearly denote partisanship. These are widely considered right-wing parties.
- Romania (2005–2012): In November 2004, a center-left coalition won in both houses (National Unity) so 2005–2008 are coded as left-wing. The 2008 election was complicated, but the result was a right-wing government. The Liberal Democratic (right-wing) party got 115 seats (the largest number of seats) and the Social Democratic Alliance with the Conservative Party (the Social Democrats are left-wing and the Conservatives are right-wing) got 114 seats. The Liberal Democrats (right-wing) and Social Democrats (left-wing) formed a government. The Prime Minister, Emil Boc, from 2008–2012 was from the right-wing Liberal Democrats which won the most seats so I code this as a right-wing government. These country-years may be missing in the DPI because it is a complicated election.
- Slovakia (2005–2006, 2011–2012): Movement for a Democratic Slovakia was elected in September 2002 and was clearly anti-market reform (see Ishiyama and Bozóki 2002). In 2011, the Smer–SMD coalition won power. These country-years may be missing in the DPI because it was a coalition although the coalition was with the Social Democrats and another left-wing party (Smer) making it clearly a left-wing government.

PART III

PENSION PRIVATIZATION REVERSAL UNDER MODERATE REFORM

Overview of Case Studies

My theoretical explanation of reversals focuses on how the degree of pension privatization influences politicians' fiscal incentives to reverse and how the degree of pension privatization is associated with citizens and private actors' benefits from pension privatization. I examine my theory and corresponding hypotheses about variation in the type and degree of reversal by examining three country cases – Russia, Hungary, and Poland.

The case studies provide analytical leverage in three important regards. First, the case studies also allow me to examine causal mechanisms in greater depth than the quantitative analysis. The theoretical expectations laid out in Chapter 3 are based on the argument that politicians are motivated by the desire to access short-term revenue and that domestic stakeholders will be more or less supportive of pension privatization and more or less politically influential depending on how extensive pension privatization was. The quantitative evidence is consistent with this but does not provide direct evidence of actors' motivations which the case studies can do.

Second, the case studies allow me to evaluate hypotheses about the *nature* and *degree* of reversal. In particular, I argue that if reversals pursued in a way that includes temporary measures, partial curtailments, or are staggered over time then this suggests that politicians are trying to learn about the reversal's consequences (specifically about reactions from the public and investors) in order to minimize any potential negative political consequences. In this way, the case studies address a different aspect of the dependent variable by looking at *how* reversals varied. The quantitative analysis established that there is a causal relationship between several factors – including the degree of pension privatization – and reversal. The case studies take the next step in demonstrating the process by which this occurs and the type of backtracking.

Finally, the case studies also contribute a fuller picture of other factors that are addressed only indirectly, or not at all, in the quantitative analysis of reversals in pension privatization. For instance, we can observe in greater depth how public opinion played a role, or did not, in the consideration of these reforms. I am also able to address in greater detail the role of international organizations including the World Bank, the International Labour Organization (ILO), and the Organization for Economic Cooperation and Development (OECD) in policy discussions.

Coverage in Existing Work

A great deal has been written about pension reform in Hungary and Poland, much more than about pension reform in Russia.[1] As such, I contribute an in-depth understanding of the politics of recent Russian pension reforms which is largely not addressed in other works. I then use the Hungarian and Polish cases to complement our understanding of variation in the reversal of pension privatization using a wide variety of secondary sources including accounts from some of those responsible for the pension privatization reforms and some Hungarian and Polish language sources.

As oft-cited examples of post-communist countries pursuing exemplary market-oriented reforms, Hungary and Poland receive a great deal of attention in policy and academic circles. For just a small portion of this body of work about pension reform in Central and Eastern Europe including those with a focus on Hungary and Poland, see: Appel and Orenstein (2013), Aleksandrowicz (2007), Augusztinovics and Martos (1996), Chłoń et al. (1999), Égert (2012), Gessel et al. (1998), Guardiancich (2004), Müller (1999, 2001, 2003, 2008), Naczyk and Domonkos (2014), Nelson (2001), Orenstein (2000, 2008, 2011, 2013), Palacios and Rocha (1998), Palacios and Whitehouse (1998), Rocha and Vittas (2002), and Stanko (2003). A 2012 special issue of *Global Social Policy* was organized around the theme of "Governing pension fund capitalism in times of uncertainty" and focused on the countries of Central and Eastern Europe although with little mention of Russia (Ebbinghaus et al. 2012).

Furthermore, organizations like the World Bank, European Union, and private international insurance companies like the AXA Group and the Dutch-based AEGON regularly produce reports on pension politics in these European countries including the state of private pension funds, but again these typically omit the Russian case. The World Bank has played a more active role in pension reform in Hungary and Poland than in Russia which explains why

---

[1] As a crude measure of this, the results of a search on Google scholar for the term "Russian pension reform" yielded 51 results compared with 196 results for "Hungarian pension reform" and 199 results for "Polish pension reform" (searches conducted on December 1, 2014). By this measure, more than three times the amount of work has been published in English about pension reforms in Hungary or in Poland than about pension reforms in Russia.

there are more reports about Hungarian and Polish reforms than Russian ones. Furthermore, in the cases of Hungary and Poland, the reformers themselves and domestic experts have published detailed accounts of the political deliberations about reform. For examples regarding Poland, see Gronicki and Jankowiak (2013) and Hausner (2001, 2002). Regarding Hungary, see Gál and Tarcali (2003), Gál et al. (2001), and Simonovits (2000, 2002, 2006, 2009, 2011, and 2012).

There has been much less written about the Russian case of pension politics. Chandler (2004), Cook (2007), and Remington (2014b) are notable exceptions in focusing on the case of Russian pension politics. Moreover, Russian reformers have not published as extensively – in English or even in Russian – about the political debates resulting in pension privatization and its reversal. Most analyses of pension reform in Russia focus on the nature of the reform and explaining how the system works not the political dynamics driving reform (for example, see Orlov-Karba 2005 and Solov'ev 2015). The Russian case, therefore, provides an opportunity to learn from the experiences of a country that has been much less studied in regards to the politics of pension reform.

Key Similarities across Russia, Hungary, and Poland

First, all three countries have regular elections and politicians are concerned with responding to public opinion. The Russian political system is less competitive and less transparent than in Hungary or Poland, but politicians nonetheless are concerned with responding to public demands and do so in the context of elections. (I address the difference between Russia's political system and the other countries in greater depth below.) Work on authoritarian regimes confirms that elections in such countries are important even if they lack characteristics of competitive democratic systems (e.g., Blayde's 2011 work on business cycles surrounding Egyptian elections). Because all of the countries have regularly contested elections and politicians are concerned with public opinion, they provide a good basis on which to compare the role played by legislative politics in reversals.

Second, all three cases are post-communist countries making them more similar than other comparisons. This allows me to control for some aspects of the communist legacy and the shared experience of transitioning to a market economy. Communist legacies are not, of course, identical and vary in important and distinctive ways (Grzymała-Busse 2002 is just one example).

The shared communist legacy also allows me to consider how countries with important similarities differed in their transitions to the market. In many ways, the reversal of pension privatization has been a post-communist phenomenon. As stated earlier, only two of the countries that have reversed pension privatization (Argentina and the United Kingdom) were not post-communist. One explanation for this regional trend suggested by the quantitative analysis is that almost all of the post-communist countries pursued moderate degrees of pension privatization. However, we can see variation within post-communist countries with moderate pension privatization suggesting how different degrees of reform lead to a similar outcome (reversal) albeit through different paths. By examining three post-communist cases in greater depth, I can evaluate my theoretical expectations and better examine why these reversals have been a post-communist trend.

Key Differences across Russia, Hungary, and Poland

I selected the cases based on variation on key independent variables: the degree of reform, partisanship, and membership in the European Union. By adopting this approach, I am able to develop rigorous, structured comparisons across the three cases. Structured comparisons are particularly useful when they focus on the effect of the same potential cause across cases (George and McKeown 1985; King, Keohane, and Verba 1994). By focusing specifically on the effect of the degree of pension privatization, legislative politics, and EU membership, I can partially avoid the "too few cases, too many variables" problem (Lijphart 1971).

Variation on the Degree of Reform. The quantitative analysis suggests that the degree of pension privatization has a curvilinear effect on reversals; countries with moderate pension privatization are the most likely to abandon pension privatization. I selected three cases with moderate pension privatization to demonstrate this process, but also select three cases which vary. Of these three cases, Russia had the least extensive pension privatization, Poland had the most extensive pension privatization, and Hungary was to be found in the middle. Russia is somewhat of an exception on the low end of moderate pension privatization, but is just nearly within a standard deviation of the mean for all countries that privatized pensions. Thus, the cases demonstrate both why moderate pension privatization produces reversals and why there was variation in the type and degree of reversals depending on domestic conditions.

Variation on Partisanship. The partisanship of the government alone is an insufficient explanation for reversals. To date, right-wing governments have been overwhelmingly responsible for reversals. Reversals were by right-wing governments in eight of the eleven countries that did so. There is more variation, however, in the partisanship of which governments introduced reforms. In the Polish case, the left-wing government under Solidarity Electoral Action introduced the reforms in 1999 and a right-wing government under Civic Platform reversed. Likewise, in Hungary, the left-wing MSzP government introduced pension privatization in 1998 and the right-wing Fidesz government dramatically abandoned the reform in 2010. By contrast, in Russia, the same center-right political party (Unity which became United Russia) both introduced and reversed reforms.

By comparing the Polish and Hungarian reversals to Russia, we can better understand the role played by partisan politics. The justification for reversals – avoiding higher taxes and deficits – was more in fitting with right-wing governments. And this justification was used even when a right-wing government had introduced reforms as in the Russian case. Thus, a right-wing government might be best viewed as a necessary but not sufficient condition for reversal. The extent to which pension privatization had been pursued was a critical causal factor even when the reversal appeared politically motivated for other reasons. Furthermore, the Hungarian case reveals that Fidesz had revised pension privatization during previous administration without recommending its reversal and that Fidesz made some attempt to avoid doing so in 2010 before cutting contributions to the second tier.

Variation on EU membership. Two of the cases – Hungary and Poland – were EU members, while Russia, of course, is not. This allows me to consider the role of the European Union in the Hungarian cases compared to the Russian case where its influence was absent. Policy diffusion in Russia mattered in a different way. In Poland and Hungary, the degree of pension privatization combined with pressure from the EU to stay within particular deficit guidelines meant that reversal was a particularly appealing option.

I begin with a consideration of the Russian case in Chapters 5 and 6, which demonstrates how and why a reversal of pension privatization is likely to occur. In Chapter 7, I then go on to examine the Hungarian and Polish reversals with an emphasis on similarities with the Russian case and variation in how reversals were pursued.

5

Russia's Staggered Reversal of Pension Reform

> Naturally, there are many who would like to get their hands on that money.
> Duma deputy Valentina Pivnenko speaking about Russian retirement savings
> in October 2001[1]

Russia has long faced difficulties in sustaining its expensive PAYG pension system. The substantial resources involved and the political and social implications of retirement policy have driven battles over pensions. There are many groups – bureaucrats, politicians, private pension funds, and investment companies – who would like to control those resources. Having implemented a significant overhaul of the pension system in 2002, the Russian government subsequently nearly entirely abandoned a significant component of the pension system, only to announce a possible retention of pension privatization in the Spring of 2015. In the ongoing battle over the retirement savings of Russian citizens, this reversal – and the subsequent policy volatility – shifts money from private investors back into state management and then possibly back to the private sector again.

The Russian case provides theoretical leverage in understanding the reversal and manipulation of pension privatization, particularly when juxtaposed with the experiences of Hungary and Poland. The reversal of Russian pension privatization is, in some ways, a least likely case of reversal. The same party of power that introduced pension privatization – United Russia (and its predecessor party, Unity) – also backed its reversal. Additionally, a decade had passed between adoption and reversal, enough time for the policy to have been extensively implemented and to see substantial growth in private pension funds, but not enough time to see any significant change in the fiscal, socioeconomic, or

---

[1] Quoted in Chandler (2004, p. 149).

demographic factors used to justify the introduction of pension privatization. Thus, we have an interesting theoretical and empirical puzzle regarding the failure of Russia's policy of pension privatization.

Russia is also an important case of pension reform in terms of understanding the broader economic and social reasons involved. The Russian economy is one of the largest to undergo a transition to a market economy, but its pursuit of market-oriented reforms has been inconsistent. Åslund (1995) argues that the Russian reforms failed to go far enough and were limited by the lack of political support for them. Frye (2010) explains how political polarization limited the development of consistent reforms; despite Yeltsin's exhortation to make reforms irreversible, he appeared focused on their short-term political benefits, even according to the account in his own memoir. The Putin years brought a mix of market-based policies alongside political moves that decreased the level of political competition. But not all of Putin's market-oriented reforms have survived either. To delve further into why reforms have been inconsistent and why particular reforms have failed, it is useful to consider a specific instance of reversal such as pension privatization.

Pension policy is a central part of how well the Russian economy will continue to function. Investment rankings are based partially on the sustainability of pension systems and government deficits, which are directly affected by pension costs (Vittas 2000). The financial investment community has further identified aging populations as a critical area of economic policy. A 2010 report by Standard & Poor's expressed concern about how governments' failure to address the cost of an aging population on public finances would hurt sovereign ratings.[2] There was little optimism that governments would handle aging populations well. Standard & Poor's concluded that

Against the backdrop of large deficits in some countries, we expect undertaking budgetary consolidation and pension or health-care system reforms simultaneously will prove politically challenging, and could lead to delays in policy implementation. In our view, the maneuvering room has shrunk and delays in policy implementations may generate additional political, economic, and budgetary costs. (p. 2)

Not only were pension policies considered critical to economic and market performance, but recent trends were raising serious questions about the long-term prospects for countries like Russia.

Russian pension reforms also carry large social implications. Russia has one of the world's largest and fastest-growing pensioner populations, making it an important instance in which to understand how the government handles the challenge of supporting a costly, aging population. In 2012, Russia had over 18 million citizens over the age of 65.[3] In a 2008 report, *From Red to Gray*, the

---

[2] Standard & Poor's, "Global Aging 2010: An Irreversible Truth," October 7, 2010.
[3] Word Development Indicators (2014).

World Bank documented the declining and aging populations prevalent among the post-communist countries of Europe, Central Asia, and the Caucuses. By 2025, the World Bank estimates that 25 percent of the population in most of these countries will be over the age of 65. Russia, in common with many other post-communist countries, also has a shrinking population; it fell from 149 to 143 million between 1990 and 2005 and is expected to fall as low as 111 million by 2050. The shrinking size of the population, particularly among younger cohorts, makes it even more difficult for the government to support retirees.

The findings presented here are based on extensive field research in Russia on pension and social reform. I conducted 48 interviews from 2006–2013 with government bureaucrats, politicians, representatives of private pension funds and investment companies, professional associations, and other experts.[4] The lengthy nature of this research provides insight into the adoption of pension privatization, its consequences, and the politics of its ultimate demise. The extended nature of the research has also allowed me to conduct follow-up interviews with several experts on Russian pension politics, thereby offering an understanding of continuity and change in pension politics over time. In addition to interviews, I use data on Russia's fiscal situation, the development of private pension funds, and indicators about the evolution of Russia's pension system. Finally, I draw on existing survey data and original survey data collected in the Fall of 2014 to better understand the public reaction to the reversal.

The Russian case bolsters the findings based on cross-national trends by demonstrating why a moderate degree of pension privatization reform makes reversing pension privatization most likely. The Russian case further assesses my expectations about how reversals will occur and how they will vary in type. Staggering the Russian reversals allowed policymakers to test for possible negative reactions from the public and investors. The decision to allow voluntary contributions to the second tier shows a more limited degree of reversal than some countries (like Hungary) but much more extensive backtracking than others (like Poland). The reasons for Russia's particular version of reversal can be traced to the reasons it was adopted, the nature of the reform, policy diffusion, and domestic politics.

I begin by laying out the options available to the Russian government in choosing whether to revise or to reverse the 2002 pension privatization reforms. I then consider why pension privatization was adopted initially, what changed after its adoption, and how the reform's design and fiscal and political

---

4 Field research was conducted over the course of six trips to Russia: Summer 2006, Spring 2007, Fall 2007, Summer 2008, Summer 2011, and Summer 2013. I do not identify interviewees by name to protect their confidentiality and anonymity, but throughout the text I identify the affiliation of the person with whom I spoke and the date and location of the interview. With one exception, all interviews were conducted in Moscow, Russia.

conditions served as the foundation for reversal. Next, I explore how the degree of pension privatization, the lack of politically influential domestic stakeholders, and policy diffusion explain why the Russian government chose reversal over alternative options.

Reversing and Revising the Russian Pension System in 2012 and 2013

Reversing pension privatization was neither an obvious nor an inevitable choice for the Russian government. There were several options for the Russian government in relation to the 2002 reform:

1) *Revisions to bolster the PAYG component.* The government could have kept pension privatization, but cut benefits or raised the retirement age. The 2012 and 2013 reforms did include parametric reform measures, notably the switch to calculating benefits based on a point system. Neither reducing benefits nor raising the retirement age was ever seriously considered at the time.

2) *Revision to bolster the pension privatization component.* One option was to make Latin American-style revisions intended to bolster the operation of the private pension. This would include measures to improve the regulation and transparency of funds and to increase competition among funds in order to decrease administrative costs and improve performance. The Russian government did take some steps to improve the regulation and oversight of private pension funds.

3) *Reversal of pension privatization.* Eliminate the second tier altogether so that no portion of retirement contributions, either voluntary or mandatory, would be invested privately. The 2012 and 2013 pension reforms nearly eliminated the second tier.

Ultimately, the Russian government chose a combination of revising the first tier, strengthening the regulation of risk management in pension savings, and nearly entirely eliminating contributions to the second tier.[5]

First, regarding the first tier (referred to as the insurance portion of pensions in Russia), a point system was introduced, according to which pension benefits would be determined (Federal Law No. 400-FZ and No. 424-FDZ, passed December 28, 2013). The point system was intended to strengthen the connection between contributions and benefits. A longer period of employment is

---

5 *Laboratoriia Pensionnoi Reformy*, "Gosduma prinyala pyat' federal'nykh pensionnykh zakonov i utverdila pensionnuiu reformu," December 23, 2013. A summary of the legislative changes to pensions in 2012 and 2013 can be found in Alina V. Evtikhova and Vitalii V. Seregin, "Izmeneniia pensionnom zakonadatel'stve v Rossii," *Pensionnoe Obozrenie*, No. 3 (19), July–September, 2014.

now required – fifteen years instead of five – in order to receive the minimum pension payment.

Second, private pension funds were required to stop collecting contributions until they re-registered as joint stock companies (Federal Law No. 410-FZ, passed December 28, 2012). Russia's Central Bank (the Bank of Russia) now oversees private pension funds and is responsible for handling the re-registration process. Private pension funds that do not collect mandatory pension contributions have until 2019 to register. All private pension funds must re-register before they will be allowed to accept any new contributions. The Russian Central Bank's new role reflects one way in which the state reasserted its influence over the pension system. Re-registration had the effect of eliminating many smaller private pension funds and thereby reducing competition for the larger funds.

Third, in December 2012 the Russian legislature voted to temporarily reduce contributions to the second tier from 6 percent to 2 percent, a change which would become permanent unless citizens opted to keep the 6 percent contribution before December 31, 2013. The short-term losses to private pension funds were estimated to be as high as $16 billion.[6]

A year later, in December 2013, the government went further and almost entirely cut contributions to the second tier. Unless an individual chooses to have 6 percent of her wages invested in the funded component with a private pension fund or investment company before the end of 2014, she will cease contributing any portion of her wages to the funded component. The deadline for choosing where one's contributions go (which applies to those currently in the privatized system) was extended to December 31, 2015 (Federal Law No. 351-FZ).

In several ways, the 2012 and 2013 measures showed a marked effort to bring pension resources back under the state's control. The state reasserted its influence in part by decreasing contributions to the second, privatized tier of the pension system. The re-registration process further asserts the state's influence over private pension funds. In February 2014, draft legislation from the Ministry of Labor further recommended that the state Pension Fund be brought under the executive branch.[7] If adopted, bringing the Pension Fund into the executive branch, within what is called the "power vertical" in the Russian system, signifies an enormous and unprecedented shift. As a result the government would also have responsibility for directly overseeing the operations of the state Pension Fund, which has not previously been the case. As part of its oversight,

---

[6] Evgenia Pismennaya and Vladimir Kuznetsov, "Russia Pension Funds May Cede $16 billion to VEB in 2014–2015," *Bloomberg*, September 23, 2013.

[7] Petr Netreba, "Penssionnyi fond proshaet'sia s molodost'iu," Kommersant, February 18, 2014; *ITAR-TASS*, "Mintrud predlagaet utochnit' pravovoi status Pensionnogo Fonda Rossii," February 18, 2014.

the government would be responsible for approving the Pension Fund's budget and, perhaps most significantly, would determine what should be done with any available funds. The stated justification for this move is in part to help the government ensure that the state Pension Fund is financially solvent; the Pension Fund currently receives significant subsidies from the federal budget. The rationale is that the executive would take over the national pension system to ensure better operations and management.[8]

In April 2014, Prime Minister Dmitry Medvedev publicly insisted that the measures being taken in Russia were neither a permanent nor a wholesale reversal of the privatized system.[9] It is true that the reversal and revisions do leave some openings for the private pension funds. The second tier will continue to exist, and legislation could conceivably expand the role of private pension funds in the future. Further, the government has promised that the current suspension on contributions to private pension funds is only temporary. Nonetheless, the measures adopted in 2013 make it unlikely that private pension funds will play a significant role in the national system. After December 31, 2015, the second tier will only be open to voluntary contributions. The pension privatization measures adopted in December 2001 will only apply to those who opted in before 2016 and will subsequently be phased out.

Pension policy continued to be debated in 2015 with an uncertain future for the accumulative portion of the pension system. In Spring 2015, Medvedev announced that the accumulative portion of pensions would not be eliminated. This announcement was reiterated by Putin in October 2015 when he also promised that the accumulative portion would continue to exist despite the short-term freeze on contributions.[10] Although these announcements are not formal legislation, they are an important signal of the executive's position and the likelihood of the accumulative portion continuing to exist in some form. In August 2015, the Central Bank and the Ministry of Finance announced that they supported extending the decision period in which citizens could choose whether to stay in the accumulative system through 2017 or even 2018.[11] More recently, in November 2015, the Ministry of Finance announced a proposal to extend the decision period through 2020 citing in part citizens' confusion about the changing rules.[12]

Government officials continue to debate the right course for pension policy. In September 2015, it was announced that the moratorium on contributions

---

8 Ibid.
9 "Sushchestvennyi korrektirovok v deistvuiushchuiu pensionnuiu sistemu ne potrebuetsia," *Interfax*, April 22, 2014.
10 "Prezident poobeshal ne otmeniat' yfrjgbntk'nuiu sistemu pensii," *Interfax*, October 13, 2015.
11 Ekaterina Metelitsa, "B pravitel'stve v TsB reshili sokhranit' sberezheniia 'molchunov' do 2018 goda," RBK, August 18, 2015.
12 "Minfin predlozhil na 5 let prodlit' vybor varianta pensionnogo obespecheniia," Interfax, November 3, 2015.

to the accumulative portion of pensions would be continued into 2016. This was now the third time the government had announced a moratorium on contributions to the accumulative portion of pensions.[13] Legislation extending the freeze on contributions was passed in mid-October.[14]

The announcement about an extension of the moratorium provoked a backlash from private pension funds and the head of the Central Bank, Elvira Nabiullina, who referred to the move as a "not very good decision," explaining that "It will mean that we gladly solve a short-term problem, but plugging holes sacrifices the long-term perspective because the accumulative part of pensions is built on long-term foundations of the whole pension system."[15] As evidenced by Nabiullina's statement, the continuation of the moratorium was considered by some to be a transparent move by the government to address short-term fiscal challenges. Indeed, the government has justified the freeze in contributions by citing the need to deal with short-term deficit problems.[16] Lower oil prices and sanctions are contributing to Russia's current recession and generating pressure to find short-term sources of revenue. There continues to be speculation about how long the government will continue to extend the moratorium on contributions to the accumulative portion of pensions beyond the most recent announcement.

If the accumulative portion of pensions continues to exist, one possibility is for the government to encourage or require private pension funds monies to be invested in domestic infrastructure projects.[17] The Ministry of Economic Development has emphasized the utility of using pension savings for domestic infrastructure projects. Keeping some amount of contributions to the accumulative portion of pensions while funneling the money to domestic projects would be a clever way for the government to avoid officially abandoning the reform while benefiting from the use of the savings.

Recent developments are consistent with my theoretical expectations: where pension privatization was pursued to a moderate degree, governments are most likely to backtrack when there is a fiscal incentive to do so. The key is that in the case of moderate pension privatization, neither public opinion nor lobbying pressure are constraining factors. Rather, where pension privatization was moderate, pension policy is much more the purview of elites.

---

13 Olga Kuvshinova, Margarita Papchenkova, and Phillip Sterkin, "Pravitel'stvo v tretii raz zamorozilo nakopitel'nye pensionnye vznosy: Moratorii na nakopleniia snova vremenno prodlen–na 2016 god," *Vedomosti*, September 30, 2015.

14 *Laboratoriia Pensionnoi Reformy*, "Gosduma v vesenniuiu sessiu rassmotrit vopros o paspredelenii 'zamorozhen nykh' pensionnykh nakoplenii," October 19, 2015.

15 Ibid.

16 "Prezident poobeshal ne otmeniat' nakopitel'nuiu sistemu pensii," Interfax, October 13, 2015.

17 Vedomosti, "Minek: NPF ezhegodno budut popolniat'sia na 400–500 mlrd rub, polovina mozhet byt' investirovana v infrastrukturnye proekty," August 15, 2015; Ekaterina Metelitsa, "Den'gi budushikh pensionerov napravili v zhil'e i dorogi," RBK, August 19, 2015.

Explaining Russia's Reversal: Overview of the Argument

The 2002 pension reforms were adopted partially as a component of Putin's state-building strategy and to limit the influence of powerful bureaucracies – like the state Pension Fund – that operated independently of the presidency. During Putin's second term, however, his consolidation of power meant that he no longer needed to use pension privatization as a means of curtailing the state Pension Fund's power. Furthermore, pension privatization proved to be costly and incompatible with other policy promises, including a refusal to raise the retirement age.

The Russian reversal can be explained by pressure resulting from the financing gap generated by pension privatization in combination with a financial crisis, the lack of domestic opposition to backtracking, and the global context in which reversals occurred. This chapter addresses the fiscal pressures created by pension privatization and how financial crisis spurred reform. Chapter 6 addresses the lack of domestic stakeholders sufficiently invested in pension privatization to fight seriously for its survival.

The process by which the adoption and reversal of pension privatization occurred reflected a typical policymaking process for Russia, particularly for the Putin era: one bureaucracy took the lead in crafting a proposal which was circulated among other actors and received feedback from policy experts and "quasi-state" civic entities which represented social interests (Remington 2014b). At the adoption stage in 2002 and the reversal stage in 2012 and beyond, however, different bureaucracies and interests took the lead in drafting proposals. Politicians' incentives to back pension privatization in 2002 changed so that by 2012 and 2013 politicians had strong political incentives to favor its reversal.

First, an annually recurring financing gap made reversal fiscally and politically desirable in the short term, particularly in the context of the financial crisis that began in 2008. Russia's reversal does not provide a long-term solution to the fiscal challenges of Russia's pension system, nor does it allow for long-term increases in spending. The amount of revenue estimated to be gained by the state is put at some \$7–11 billion annually (the total holdings of private pension funds were about \$50 billion); the state Pension Fund's total deficit in 2013 was \$58 billion.[18] Abandoning the second-tier contributions only provides a source of short-term revenue. Nonetheless, the short-term pressure to access resources tied up by transitioning the entire population into the privatized system proved to be a prime motivation to backtrack.

Russia's domestic political battles occurred amidst the backdrop of reversals in other countries and a shift in the position of the World Bank in promoting particular pension reforms. That other countries were able to reverse pension privatization and face little backlash from citizens and international

---

[18] "An Unaffordable System: Russia's prime minister signs a disastrous pension reform," *The Economist*, October 6, 2012.

organizations, and that they avoided investor flight, cemented the reversal of pension privatization as a viable policy option. The change in the World Bank's position marked an important permissive condition for reversal, although its sway appears to have been weaker in Russia than in other countries.

Second, reversal was politically feasible because of the lack of politically influential domestic stakeholders. In the welfare state literature, domestic stakeholders are given a central role in promoting the survival of a policy. Pierson (2000), for instance, writes that

Institutions as policies may encourage individuals and organizations to invest in specialized skills, depend on relationships with other individuals and organizations, and develop particular political and social identities. These activities increase the attractiveness of existing institutional arrangements relative to hypothetical alternatives. As social actors make commitments based on existing institutions and policies, their cost of exit from established arrangements generally rises dramatically. (p. 259)

This notion of interest groups, however, suggests that all policies will spark interest groups entrenched in the policy's survival which makes change unlikely. Indeed, the idea of path dependency emphasizes that policies in modern societies are lasting and difficult to change.

The role of potential domestic stakeholders is critical. In the case of debates surrounding pension privatization in Russia, there were two potential stakeholders – the private pension sector and citizens. The private pension funds had a clear, strong preference for pension privatization to continue, given that they profited directly; however, they did not have enough influence to prevent a reversal. Larger political developments also meant that the private pension funds did not have the opportunity to become influential in the legislative process. In addition, the partial nature of pension privatization in Russia limited the structural role that the private pension funds (and investment companies investing in pensions) played in the Russian financial system. Among Russian citizens, survey evidence reveals very little support for pension privatization. Public opinion matters greatly to Putin and Medvedev, but the public was not strongly invested in the survival of this policy, even though pension privatization had, at least partially, changed the rules of the retirement game.

Past is Prologue: The Adoption of Russian Pension Privatization

The Russian government adopted an overhaul of its pension system in December 2001, with an implementation of the reform beginning in 2002 and continuing over the next few years (Maleva and Sinyavskaya 2005). Russian pension privatization measures adopted in December 2001 cannot be fully explained by demographic and fiscal pressures (as several alternative reforms existed), Putin's support in the Duma (as he had not consolidated his power and faced several sources of opposition), or international pressure (in part because the World Bank was officially excluded from policy deliberations). The benefits of pension privatization were also long-term, costly, and uncertain. Yeltsin – who had handpicked Putin as his successor – had not backed pension privatization in any of his official proposals for market-oriented pension reform.

In the early 2000s, alternative pension reform options included different structural and parametric measures. Structural reforms refer to changes in the nature of the system itself. In addition to pension privatization, structural reforms could include NDC measures in which individual contributions would be credited with a notional rate of return to determine future benefits. NDC systems have the advantage of encouraging individuals to consider the link between contributions and benefits, while avoiding the risk of private investment (Holzmann and Palmer 2006). Parametric measures include steps like cutting benefits, raising the retirement age, and eliminating special categories of retirees (Cangiano et al. 1998). Some experts advocated for parametric measures as a reasonable, and possibly even better, option than structural overhauls. Barr and Diamond (2008) considered parametric cuts to be a less risky, more stable alternative to addressing the challenges faced by PAYG systems.

A common explanation is that Putin was able to get liberal welfare state reforms passed because the Duma was supportive of his agenda (Chandler 2004; Cook 2007). Putin did have one legislative advantage over Yeltsin; the win by the Unity Party in the fall of 1999 gave the Duma a center-right leaning that was more in keeping with Putin's agenda. Unity, however, failed to secure a majority, winning only 16 percent of the seats. Unity's limited success necessitated strategic compromises with others, including the Communist Party and the nationalist Liberal Democratic Party of Russia. Putin's party of power, United Russia, was not formally created until December 2001 and did not win an outright majority until the 2007 parliamentary elections. Although Putin would later significantly consolidate power within the executive, he had not done so in 2000 and 2001.

Even if Putin had simply preferred – for whatever reason – to pursue market-oriented pension reform, a plausible alternative would have been one based on Yeltsin's 1998 pension reform proposal. This entailed an NDC system in which the state Pension Fund played a central role and private investors were restricted to the realm of voluntary retirement savings. Because Putin was Yeltsin's handpicked successor, an adoption of the 1998 reform concept would have been an expected and politically viable step. Bureaucratic opposition to any market-oriented reform meant that the more radical option of privatization was a much more challenging path. The trajectory of reform in January 2000 suggested that a likely direction for pension reform under Putin would be an NDC system mixed with parametric reforms. With a more cooperative Duma, Putin's chances of successfully backing an NDC reform were greater.

Finally, international pressure does not offer a sufficient explanation for why Russia adopted pension privatization. Although the World Bank often successfully promoted pension privatization, in Russia the World Bank was officially excluded from policy deliberations. The Russian government also declined additional loans from the World Bank for pension reform in the 2000s. The last World Bank loan to Russia, which included support for the pension system, was disbursed in 1997 as part of a Social Protection Adjustment Loan (SPAL) of $800 million, the largest World Bank loan ever made to a country in Europe and Central Asia.[19] The loan was to be used for a variety of social initiatives. Regarding pensions, the loan was to be used to help improve the administration and collection practices of the state Pension Fund and also to support structural pension reform, including some degree of privatization. Notably, however, a proposal to privatize pensions never became part of the Yeltsin administration's official pension reform proposals.

Rather than the usual suspects that might explain pension reform, Putin favored market-oriented reforms like pension privatization in part to promote a certain kind of state-building. This is consistent with previous work that has emphasized that state-building was a top priority for the early Putin administration. Tompson (2002) writes

> Putin has moved to strengthen the power of an already strong presidency and to recover for the federal centre much of the authority devolved…This is a political project to which Putin would doubtless be committed even if he had no interest in structural reform, but it dovetails well with the structural reform agenda: tax reform and monopolies reform, in particular, will strengthen the centre and curtail regional authorities' power, while Putin's success in changing federal relationships will make it easier to press ahead with these reforms despite regional opposition. (p. 948)

In this explanation, structural economic reforms would, conveniently, help strengthen the power of the federal government. A major reorganization of federal relations began in 2000 almost immediately after Putin's election in March. Putin's early centralization of power included notable moves like the introduction of several Federal Districts (Goode 2004; Sharafutdinova 2010). The Federal Districts constituted a new level of government bureaucracy intended to help oversee the implementation and functioning of federal policies. In keeping with the centralizing changes and a decrease in regional power, Russia's upper legislative house, the Federation Council, was reorganized and took away seats from regional governors and speakers and instead had governors and speakers appoint representatives (Remington 2003). Putin's early economic structural reforms did not simply coincide with these attempts to strengthen the federal government's power; rather, they were tools to help undercut the parts of the state apparatus that would undermine the president's larger agenda.

Building on his initial political advantages, an important next step for Putin was the passage of policies that strategically undermined sources of opposition

---

[19] World Bank Press Release No. 97/1408 ECA, "World Bank Loan Supports Russia's Social Reforms," June 26, 1997.

within the state. Doing so allowed Putin to concentrate policymaking power in the executive permanently, rather than just remaining a popular president with a supportive legislature. Structural reforms, as a state-building tool, are an important addition to existing explanations: Putin's early economic policies were an integral part of his political tactics rather than the product of them. These early moves were later eclipsed by the more obvious power grabs that happened in Putin's second term, possibly explaining the relative lack of scholarly attention to Putin's state-building efforts early in his first term.

Pension reform was an important component of Putin's larger liberalizing economic reforms. Putin's economic agenda – including pension reform – was directed by liberal economic advisors who promoted a wide range of market-oriented policies in the areas of taxation, land privatization, labor laws, and business regulations. Indeed, we can see that Putin's larger state-building strategy informed not just areas like pensions but also very different policy areas like judicial reforms (Wilson Sokhey 2015). German Gref, a former head of the Ministry of Economic Development and Trade, was instrumental in developing and implementing this agenda. Aleksei Kudrin, the Minister of Finance, was also influential in promoting Putin's market-oriented policies. Gref and Kudrin, along with others, developed a wide range of pro-market policy proposals including pension privatization.

In addition to being part of the larger package of reforms, pension privatization had the added benefits of diminishing the influence of the state Pension Fund. Pension privatization was certainly the product of Putin's larger economic agenda and not entirely – or even primarily – an attempt to reduce the power of the state Pension Fund, but it was certainly politically beneficial to diminish the role played by this large and frequently corrupt body. In the early 2000s the state Pension Fund posed a potential obstacle to Putin's presidential administration in several ways. First, the Pension Fund could propose and comment on legislation and lobby Duma deputies accordingly, particularly those on the left like the Communist Party. The lack of strong political parties in Russia meant that major ministries were often responsible for mediating the demands of interest groups and passing these demands on to the government (Jensen 2001). To the extent that bureaucrats in the Pension Fund disagreed with the executive about policy goals, this posed a serious problem in building bureaucratic and public support for reforms. Cook (2007) describes social fund administrators, like those who manage the Pension Fund, as a "second set of veto actors against liberalization" who worked with representatives in the Duma to produce legislation that would preclude reform (p. 131). The public and governmental role of the Pension Fund, therefore, presented a serious challenge in passing any legislation with which it disagreed.

Second, the sheer amount of money controlled by the Pension Fund and its monopoly over the distribution of pensions gave it power. From 1993 to 1997 the Pension Fund commanded an annual average of $15 billion in resources, with expenditures and revenue that each averaged about 6 percent of GDP annually.[20] Larger deficits began to emerge in 1998, which necessitated larger transfers from the federal budget (Orlov-Karba 2005, p. 71). Nonetheless, in 1999, shortly before pension reform debates began under Putin in 2000, the Pension Fund had a $10 billion budget.[21]

The operations of the Pension Fund in managing and paying out benefits were important for the presidential administration to maintain support among pensioners who relied on the regular payment of pensions. Pensioners are an electorally important group, with those over the age of 65 making up 10 to 13 percent of the population since 1990.[22] Furthermore, Yeltsin had promoted the idea that the executive was personally accountable for pension arrears, as he took responsibility for ordering back payments to be covered in highly publicized moves (Javeline 2003). When the then relatively unknown Vladimir Putin was appointed prime minister in August 1999, one of his first orders of business was to meet with the head of the Pension Fund to demand the payment of pension arrears.[23] If the Pension Fund functioned poorly, or its budget was mismanaged, it would reflect badly on the president.

Scandals throughout the 1990s revealed the misuse of the Pension Fund's substantial resources, suggesting that it had a great deal of unofficial power. The Pension Fund's resources were "off-budget," meaning it collected payments directly, and its funds were not counted as part of general government revenue. The Pension Fund also collected contributions in cash so that some characterized it as a large slush fund, the resources of which could be diverted to banks or regional governors. An audit revealed that between 1995 and 1998 there was $1 billion for which the Pension Fund could not account. Some even speculated that Pension Fund monies may have been used to help finance Yeltsin's re-election in 1996, although these claims were never substantiated.[24] Another audit of the Pension Fund was commissioned by two outside companies in December of 1999 – just before Putin took office as president – in large part because the World Bank was with holding the final disbursement of a structural adjustment loan until an audit was conducted.[25]

Furthermore, top Pension Fund officials had documented links to the private financial sector, which was the most viable source of political opposition to Putin at the time. For instance, Mikhail Zurabov – appointed the head of the Pension Fund in June 1999 – had a brother who was also the head of one

---

[20] Data are from the Russian Ministry of Finance as reported in Denisova et al. (1999, p. 12).

[21] The Pension Fund's annual budget is available online at www.pfrf.ru.

[22] Demographic data are taken from the World Development Indicators.

[23] ITAR-TASS News Agency, "Russian Premier Instructs State Pension Fund to Speed Up Arrears Payments," September 3, 1999.

[24] For a summary of the accusations against the state Pension Fund in the 1990s, see: Melissa Akin, "Scandal-Ridden Pension Fund Gets New Chief," *The Moscow Times*, June 2, 1999.

[25] Interfax News Agency, "Pension Fund Auditors Picked," December 10, 1999.

of Russia's largest domestic banks, *Russkii Standart*.[26] In short, the Pension Fund posed an independent source of power due to its budget, its policymaking capacity, and its ability to finance political candidates and parties opposed to Putin. Putin had a strong incentive to find structural means to limit the power of the Pension Fund in relation to the executive.

Bureaucrats at the Pension Fund vehemently opposed any privatization measures that would have diminished their role as the lone manager of Russia's retirement funds (Chandler 2004; Cook 2007). Zurabov, then the new head of the Pension Fund, proposed instead that the solution was to break the link between wages and pensions, instead determining benefits on the basis of the minimum subsistence level.[27] One option might have been to replace the head of the Pension Fund with someone who favored Putin's position. Simply replacing the head of the Pension Fund would have been politically costly to Putin, however, and potentially made it even harder for him to implement policy. Any new head of the Pension Fund would only seek to enhance her own bureaucratic power too.

The private pension funds had the largest direct stake in seeing the establishment of a system in which mandatory retirement contributions could be privately invested. Private pension funds had existed in Russia since 1992, operating in the sphere of voluntary retirement savings (Karasyov and Lublin 2001). Although there were initially only a few, a change in legislation in 1995 made it easier to register private pension funds; the number of funds jumped to 255 and stayed relatively constant through the 1990s and 2000s.[28] As of 2002, several of the private pension fund founders (4 percent) were industrial businesses, including gas and oil companies. Credit organizations, insurers, and investment companies constituted about 20 percent of the founders of private pension funds. Even government bureaucracies established some private pension funds, although they accounted for only about 5 percent of all founders. Social and religious organizations were responsible for about 7 percent of the private pension funds (Mudrakov et al. 2002, p. 23, 52–55). About 50 percent of the funds were located in Moscow and St. Petersburg.

Many of the largest private pension funds had been founded by businesses associated with the largest businesses in Russia's natural resources industries. Of the twelve largest companies in Russia in the natural resources industries, ten had established private pension funds.[29] This included natural resource

---

[26] Melissa Akin, "Scandal-Ridden Pension Fund Gets New Chief," *The Moscow Times*, June 2, 1999.

[27] "State Pension System Faces Collapse," *Segodnya* (Moscow), October 6, 2000.

[28] Data on the number of private pension funds are provided by the Ministry of Labor of the Russian Federation, Inspectorate of Private Pension Funds, and are available upon request.

[29] For a list of the oligarchs and the companies associated with them, see: Peter Rutland, "Introduction: Business and State in Russia," in *Business and the State in Contemporary Russia*, 2001, ed. Peter Rutland, pp. 20–21. A list of the private pension funds, including data on their size, is available From Russia's National Association of Private Pension Funds (in Russian) at: http://napf.ru/main_activities/napf_funds.

companies like Gazprom, LUKoil, Sibneft, Yukos, and Norilsk Nickel. Most of the major banks had also established private pension funds, including Alfa Bank, Bank Moskva, Inkombank, Oneksimbank, Most-Bank, and Rossiiskii Kredit. As of 2004, the three largest private pension funds (by net worth) – GAZFOND, LUKOIL-Garant, and Suruneftegaz (Mudrakov et al. 2002, pp. 52–55) – controlled 65 percent of pension reserves and 95 percent of investments, and they also managed the funds of 68 percent of individuals privately investing their retirement savings (Orlov-Karba 2005, p. 155).

Businesses and organizations in the private pension sector had the resources, expertise, and connections to advise the government. Perhaps more importantly, the Kremlin wanted their help. The Putin administration actively sought the advice of business associations as a source of alternative proposals that could put pressure on major state bureaucracies; this even included empowering small businesses that would not otherwise have had much influence (Markus 2007). Balzer (2003) describes this as a shift to "managed pluralism" in which more groups had access to the Kremlin, but in which they did so under the supervision and control of the president. Attempts at managed pluralism are not always successful, which Balzer notes, but Putin was able to use his popularity and legislative advantage to successfully push for the establishment of this new system of interest articulation.

Rather than relying as extensively on personal connections, Putin favored a model in which the government collectively bargained with formal business organizations, some of which were created with the express backing of the government (Yakovlev 2006; Fish 2005). For instance, to represent the interests of small and medium-sized firms, Putin encouraged the creation of *OPORA* in the Spring of 2000.[30] Large businesses continued to be represented by the *Rossiskii Soyuz Promishlennikov i Predprinmatelei* (RSPP), although the RSPP served a different role under Putin than Yeltsin.[31] The RSPP was founded in 1990, and while initially opposed to major economic restructuring – as its founding members were mostly managers of state-owned enterprises – it later came to champion market-oriented reforms as the mangers of formerly-owned state enterprises began to profit from the new capitalist system (Kubicek 1996). Hanson and Teague (2005) characterize the RSPP as a "frequently-shaken kaleidoscope," rather than a typical economic interest group, in large part because of its transition from an organization of state enterprises to a political tool of pro-market businesses (p. 664). With the rise of managed pluralism under Putin, the RSPP has played a role that would be more typical in a corporatist system in which the government works through businesses via formal organizations. The RSPP's own mission statement reveals that one of its current primary goals is drafting and commenting on legislation.[32] It maintains specific committees

---

[30] Simon Ostrovsky, "Kremlin Befriends Small Business," *The Moscow Times*, December 7, 2001.
[31] In English, the RSPP is the Russian Union of Industrialists and Entrepreneurs (RUIE).
[32] Available at: http://eng.rspp.ru/about.

to comment on legislation in a wide range of policy areas, including taxation, trade, the environment, and labor policies, including pensions.

The Putin administration was eager to work with firms in the private pension sector, as evidenced by regular consultations between the Gref team (assembled by the Putin administration to direct pension reforms) and private pension funds. In turn, firms in the private pension sector were happy to oblige. Those involved in policy negotiations confirmed that the RSPP and the private pension funds worked closely with the government concerning technical issues surrounding pension reform.[33] The RSPP regularly collaborated with other business associations – including the *Natsionalnaya Assotsiatsiya Negosudarstvenni Pensioni Fondov* (NAPF) – in advising the government on pension reform.[34] There was a great deal of overlap across many of these groups. For instance, the then head of NAPF's board of directors was also the head of the RSPP's committee on pension reform, as well as the director of a private pension fund.[35]

NAPF was created by the League of Private Pension Funds in December 1999 to represent the interests of the sector to the government. Regular publications from NAPF offered specific policy recommendations. NAPF also held conferences and organized working groups that brought together high-level bureaucrats, Duma representatives, and those working in the private pension sector. NAPF's inaugural meeting was in February 2000, only a month after Putin had become the acting president. By June 2001, a working group of the NAPF Board of Directors and the Ministry of Labor formed an expert council on private pension fund provision in order to provide policy advice.[36] This collaboration between the Ministry of Labor and the newly founded NAPF represents a significant shift in relations between the private pension funds and the government during the Putin era. Due to the Kremlin's interest in its proposals, NAPF was enjoying an inclusion in the policy process that its predecessor, the League of Private Pension Funds, had not.

There were also regular collaborations between key bureaucrats and the private pension funds, providing formal venues in which the Putin administration considered proposals coming from the private sector.[37] This was a marked change from the Yeltsin administration. Under Yeltsin, policy decisions were made by a small group of the president's advisors and personal connections (Jensen 2001). There was a clear shift in how (and which) private businesses were able to shape the policy process in the 2000s. In 2001, the Putin administration actively sought the assistance of these private firms in backing its preferred proposals.

---

[33] Interview with private pension fund representative, June 23, 2008, Moscow, Russia.
[34] In English, NAPF is the National Association of Non-State Pension Funds.
[35] Interview with private pension fund representative, June 23, 2008, Moscow, Russia.
[36] Interview with private pension fund representative, December 3, 2007, Moscow, Russia.
[37] Interview with private pension fund representative, June 23, 2008, Moscow, Russia.

In May 2001, the RSPP published an official proposal for pension reform and one that was in opposition to the stance taken by the Pension Fund. The RSPP stated

All of these questions [in relation to pension reform] can be decided today. And they cannot and should not be decided in accordance with the position of the Pension Fund. It is obvious that the Pension Fund is not interested in the competitive institutions which are the basis for an effective comparison of state and private pension systems according to their administrative resources (in part related to their absolute size and in part to dynamic changes), and according to the effective management of financial resources. (RSPP 2001)

The RSPP's official objection to the Pension Fund's position on pension reform criticized an adherence to an outdated model of collective responsibility, rather than individual contributions. They also emphasized the macroeconomic consequences of reform, pointing to how the Pension Fund's position would promote high state debt and allow pensions to be managed by a largely unchecked, inefficient state power. As such, the RSPP was a clear and forceful advocate against a source of bureaucratic opposition to Putin.

Bureaucrats in the Ministry of Economic Development and Trade began promoting strikingly similar pension proposals to those advanced by business associations. An economist who served for many years as an independent consultant before joining the Ministry of Economic Development and Trade noted that private pension funds were especially influential during this period.[38] Pro-market reform bureaucrats in MEDT linked an economic recovery with financial sector reforms, including pension privatization. Influential bureaucrats like Mikhail Dmitriev, a deputy minister in the Ministry of Economic Development and Trade, linked market-oriented pension reforms to an improvement in pension benefits and recovery from financial crisis (Dmitriev 2000). A report initially prepared in 1999 concluded that "the program of pension reform in the Russian Federation, adopted by the Government of Russia in May of 1998, currently needs to be corrected in connection with the worsening of financial conditions of the pension system as a result of the economic crisis" (Dmitriev et al. 2002).

The initial version of the pension reforms passed its first reading in the Duma in mid-July 2001. Even just one month before the passage of the final reform package in December of 2001, however, it was unclear whether the state Pension Fund would win its battle to maintain a monopoly over the country's retirement savings.[39] That the bill passed in the first reading reflected that the government was mostly concerned with the expansion of the state savings

---

[38] Interview with representative of the Ministry of Economic Development and Trade, October 16, 2007, Moscow, Russia.

[39] "Will Pension-Reform Package Change How Russians Retire?," *The St. Petersburg Times*, 13 November, 2001.

that were accumulated in the Pension Fund, rather than allowing private investment.[40]

One of the major issues still left to be resolved was that, if private investment was allowed, what proportion of mandatory contributions a citizen could choose to have invested privately. Although the debate over the percentage of private investment was not the most public aspect of the reform – public debates instead focused on providing benefits for current retirees and rhetoric about creating a sustainable system – this was a crucial aspect of the system's design and a key point of contention for those debating pension reform. The Pension Fund maintained that if any private investment was allowed, it should be capped at 2 percent of contributions, rather than the 6 percent being proposed by pension funds. The difference between these two figures was substantial; it meant an estimated difference of up to $2.4 billion in 2004 alone (mandatory contributions were projected to continue rising so that the amount of capital at stake would continue to grow annually).[41]

The private pension funds and the RSPP continued to argue that allowing the existing system to continue was detrimental to current and future pensioners, the development of the larger financial market, and the national economy. In this way, the new form of interest group politics that had emerged under Putin allowed the private funds to counter proposals coming from the state Pension Fund by effectively linking pension privatization with broader macroeconomic consequences in the minds of policymakers. They made their case by arguing that

Russian stock market capitalization today is around $50 billion. In the account of the Pension Fund in 2001 alone (without the introduction of a savings element) there is about 2.5 billion dollars. With the introduction of a savings element, in 5–6 years there would already be financial resources in the Pension Fund worth nearly half of the capital market. Putting these resources in the financial market would of course improve the conditions of the entire economy … Adopting the model of pension reform proposed by the Pension Fund would not only hurt the quality of pension provision for current and future pensioners, it would also hurt the growth of savings in the system … and have negative consequences for the national economy. (RSPP 2001, p. 3)[42]

The claims from private funds that the state Pension Fund's proposal would hurt the national economy were very useful for Putin by providing a strong economic rationale for the structural shift. These arguments also highlighted

---

[40] Interview with representative of Ministry of Economic Development and Trade, October 18, 2007, Moscow, Russia.

[41] Interview with representative of the Ministry of Economic Development and Trade, October 18, 2007, Moscow, Russia.

[42] The actual amount of money in the entire Pension Fund in 2001 was over $10 billion. The RSPP was likely referring to the annual revenue collected by the Pension Fund in 2001, which is closer to the number cited. Translation by author.

the magnitude of what was at stake. Pension privatization meant that the state Pension Fund would lose access to substantial resources.

Ultimately, President Putin backed – and the Duma passed – a version of the bill that allowed up to 6 percent of wages to be privately invested. Last-minute changes in legislation to allow a greater degree of mandatory contributions to be privately invested are particularly telling as evidence that the Putin administration was seeking to limit the role played by the state Pension Fund. A senior bureaucrat in the Ministry of Economic Development and Trade explained that "Especially in the second reading there were very big changes, in particular, private investment companies were influential in the second reading. And this is the version of the system that was ultimately adopted."[43] By making changes just before the last version of the bill was adopted, the Putin administration cleverly avoided further mobilization by the state Pension Fund in opposition to the reform. Contrary to a trajectory in January 2000 suggesting that an NDC system might be adopted, the Russian government adopted a mixed system combining elements of NDC and pension privatization. Given the political and bureaucratic strength of the Pension Fund, this outcome is especially dramatic and surprising. The Pension Fund, while still powerful, was no longer the sole proprietor of the nation's pension system.

The influence of the state Pension Fund decreased substantially after the adoption of the 2002 pension reforms in several notable ways. To understand the size of this shift away from the state Pension Fund, consider the growth of the private pension funds before and after the 2002 reforms (from 1999 to 2009) as presented in Figure 5.1. During this time, there was a more than fourteenfold increase in the size of the private pension sector, and the number of citizens with private pension savings more than tripled. As of 2010, about 5 percent of those eligible to transfer their savings had done so, and there were about $450 million of mandatory contributions that were being privately invested (in addition to voluntary savings invested with these funds) (Degtyarev 1999).

Ultimately, in 2010 – even with only 5 percent of those eligible having transferred their savings into private management – there was a quadrupling in the net worth of the private pension funds, which increased by about $5 billion (in constant 2000 USD).[44] This was money that would otherwise be in the state Pension Fund.

The Ministry of Labor noted that the passage of the 2001 pension reforms did in fact give a substantial boost to the potential development of the private pension funds. In 2002, they predicted that in three years there would be a tripling in the amount of pensioner reserves and a 68 percent increase in the

---

[43] Interview with representative of the Ministry of Economic Development and Trade, October 18, 2007, Moscow, Russia.

[44] Figures on the growth of the private pension sector are calculated based on data on the total holdings of the private pension funds. Data are from the Inspectorate of Private Pension Funds, which is part of the Ministry of Labor of the Russian Federation.

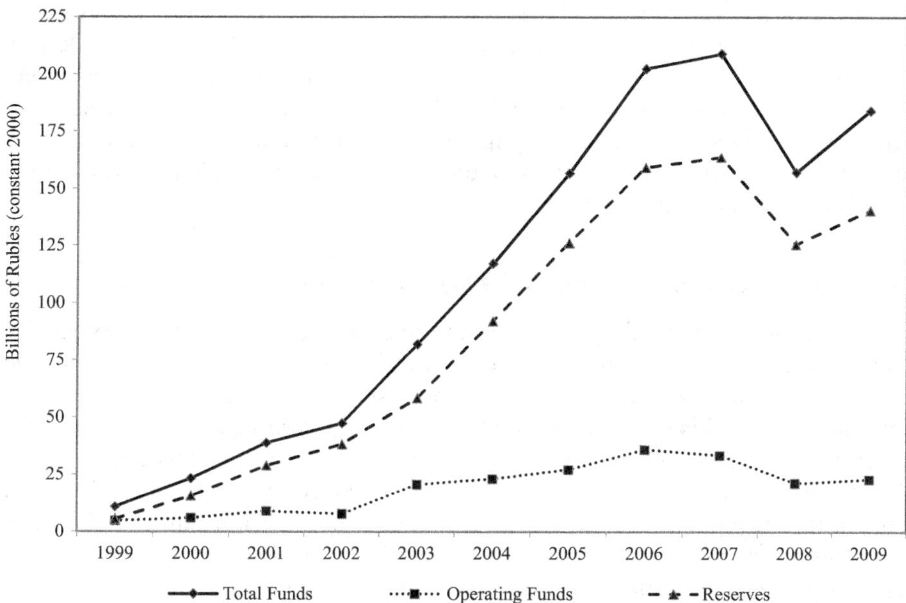

FIGURE 5.1 Russian Private Pension Fund Indicators, 1999–2009

number of participants. While the gains by 2005 were not quite as much as projected, it was clear that the industry saw this as a very big gain for its potential growth. Data from January 7, 2002 show an increase in private pension fund reserves and participants less than a month after the passage of reforms and a further increase in the number of private pension funds by July 2002 (Mudrakov et al. 2002). In early 2002, the private pension funds had not actually been allowed to manage mandatory contributions – the legislation was not implemented nearly so quickly – but the passage of the reform itself seems to have given the sector a positive boost.

The state Pension Fund was not even allowed to regulate the new privatized portion of pensions. The Ministry of Finance and the Central Bank – rather than the state Pension Fund – were responsible for implementing the pension reform. Specifically, this was a power struggle over who would license and regulate private pension funds and investment companies that wished to participate in the new system. The resolution of this bureaucratic conflict was reported as "one of the main intrigues of pension reform."[45]

The state Pension Fund was only able to hamper implementation of pension privatization temporarily. The Pension Fund initially refused to transfer individuals' contributions to any private companies, claiming that it was waiting

---

[45] Liza Golikova "MinFin Zastavili Podelit'sia s FKTsB Kontrolem Nad Pensionnoi Reformoi," *Kommersant,* February 17, 2003.

for a list of federally-insured banks, and that without such a list, it refused to transfer even a single kopek to what it considered unreliable sources.[46] Despite bureaucratic resistance, as early as 2002 additional legislation to help implement the reform was being adopted, and experts were hailing the reform as a major step forward in creating competition between state and private pension provision (Yakushev and Kolobaev 2002). By 2002, Russia's pension system had been considerably overhauled.

Recurring Financing Gap Created by Pension Privatization in Russia

The fiscal pressure faced by the Russian government came from the expensive nature of its PAYG system, its degree of privatization, and the fiscal situation it faced after the 2007 financial crisis. The first of these – the cost of the PAYG system – was and is quite costly for the Russian government. Before the introduction of pension privatization, Russia's federal government was responsible for covering between 4 and 13 percent of the Pension Fund's annual budget shortfall (Orlov-Karba 2005, p. 71). The size of the Pension Fund's deficit and subsequent federal transfers to the Pension Fund peaked in 1997, at 13 percent of the Pension Fund's annual budget, just before Russia's financial crisis in 1998.

The Pension Fund's annual shortfalls have substantial implications for Russia's federal budget. Figure 5.2 shows the Pension Fund's annual deficit from 2009 to 2014.[47] In the aftermath of the financial crisis beginning in 2007 and 2008, the size of the Pension Fund's deficit grew as there was a decline in contributions from wages. The Pension Fund's annual deficit more than doubled in only a few years, going from \$6.1 billion in 2009 to more than \$12.7 billion in 2012. As a result, the government was facing an increasingly significant challenge in covering retirement benefits.

The second major determinant of fiscal pressure on the Russian government is the extent to which the government privatized the pension system. The Russian government chose a pension scheme that was more limited than that adopted in the extensive pension privatization schemes introduced in countries like Chile and Kazakhstan, but nonetheless meant that significant resources would be diverted away from the PAYG system. The pension privatization laws adopted in December 2001 allowed a citizen born after 1967 to choose to have a portion of his or her wages invested with a private pension fund or investment company that had been approved by the government.[48] The default option was

---

[46] Liza Golikova, "Mikhail Zurabov Pokazal Bankam Fikus: Pensionnyi Fond s Chuzhimi Den'gami Prosto Tak Ne Rasstaetsia," *Kommersant*, February 5, 2004.

[47] Russia's Ministry of Finance publishes data on the Pension Fund's budget, which is available at http://info.minfin.ru/pf.php (accessed July 2014, available data from 2009–2013) and available upon request.

[48] According to the initial legislation, for men born in 1952 or earlier and women born in 1956 or earlier, none of the contributions to the second tier would be allocated to the second tier. For men

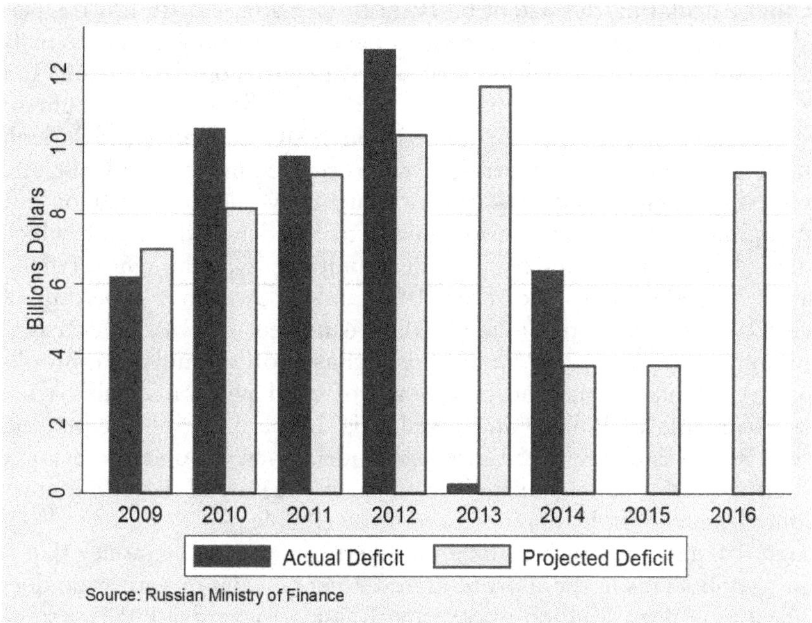

FIGURE 5.2 Russian Pension Deficits, 2009–2016

that 6 percent of wages would go into an individual account that was managed by the state-owned commercial bank, Vneshekonombank, and 8 percent would be credited to an NDC account. By 2012, 14 percent of citizens who were eligible to do so had chosen to have their money privately invested.[49] Even those in the default option had 6 percent of their wages diverted to individual accounts, rather than having their contributions cover the government's current obligations. As a result, a total of 14 percent of wages was diverted away from covering the government's current pension obligations.[50]

Ultimately, these contributions to individual accounts would constitute some portion of a citizen's future benefits. One pension fund manager noted,

born between 1953 and 1966 and women born between 1957 and 1966, the percentage was initially set at 2% of contributions to the second tier. However, subsequent legislation passed in 2004, excluded all of those born before 1967 from participating in the accumulative portion of pensions. See: Federal Law No. 204-FZ, "On internal changes in the second part of the Tax Code of the Russian Federation" (passed on 29 December, 2004). This specific design of the reform is also discussed in Orlov-Karba (2005, p. 108).

[49] "Otmena nakopitel'noi pensii: sotsial'nye riski i vozmozhnosti," *Fond Obshchestvennoe Mnenie*, 2011–2012; full report available in Russian upon request.

[50] A detailed description of the system adopted in 2001 can be found in the official government commentary on the law: *Kommentarii k pensionnomu zakonodatel'stvu Rossiiskoi Federatsii*, Ministry of Healthcare and Social Development of the Russian Federation and the Pension Fund of the Russian Federation, Moscow: 2007.

however, that calculating the size of one's future pension – much less the percentage that would be based on the defined benefits portion – was extremely complicated; he himself, as the head of a private pension fund, could not calculate the size of his future pension.[51] Although the precise amount of future benefits to be based on the funded and NDC portion were difficult to determine precisely, Russia contrasted with other countries like Chile and Kazakhstan, in which all citizens' future benefits would be based on the funded component. Russia was more similar to Sweden and Poland, which also combined NDC and mandatory funded components, although in Poland 9 percent of wages went to the second tier, and in Sweden 2.5 percent of wages went to the second tier (compared to 6 percent of wages in Russia) (Immergut and Andersen 2007; Müller 2003). Based on a simulation, Brooks (2009, p. 43) calculates that the percentage of total pension coming from the private accounts in Poland and Sweden is 49 percent and 17 percent, respectively. Russia is closer to the Swedish model, given its lower percentage of contributions and because private investment in the second tier is voluntary and has only been chosen by a minority of those eligible.

Although Russian pension privatization diverts an amount of money that is significant to politicians in the short term, reversing pension privatization does not provide a long-term solution to covering Russia's expensive PAYG system, which still incurs annual deficits. As Figure 5.2 shows, the reversal of pension privatization in 2013 did subsequently result in a large temporary decline in the Pension Fund's deficit. The shortfall in 2013 was a relatively measly $284 million. The 2014 Pension Fund deficit, however, is projected to exceed $3 billion and continue increasing in subsequent years. Even the reversal of Russia's partial pension privatization cannot shore up its PAYG system for long. In Fall 2012, *The Economist* criticized the reversal proposal, noting that the entirety of private pension fund holdings of $58 billion could only cover the Pension Fund's current full debt of $50 billion in the short term.[52] As the Pension Fund continues to accrue large annual deficits, eliminating pension privatization provides little relief, and a return to 2012 levels of Pension Fund deficit poses a serious long-term fiscal challenge.[53]

Finally, the Russian government's larger fiscal situation affects the recurring financing gap generated by pension privatization. Figure 5.3 shows the Russian government's surpluses and deficits from 2002 to 2011.[54] The Russian government enjoyed a surplus in the 2000s, until the financial crisis resulted in deficits in 2009 and 2010, with a recovery beginning in 2011.

---

[51] Interview with the head of a private pension fund, September 25, 2007, Moscow, Russia.

[52] "An Unaffordable System: Russia's prime minister signs a disastrous pension reform," *The Economist*, October 6. 2012.

[53] Russia's Ministry of Finance publishes data on the Pension Fund's budget that is available at http://info.minfin.ru/pf.php (accessed July 2014, available data from the period 2009–2013) and available upon request.

[54] Data are from the 2013 World Development Indicators.

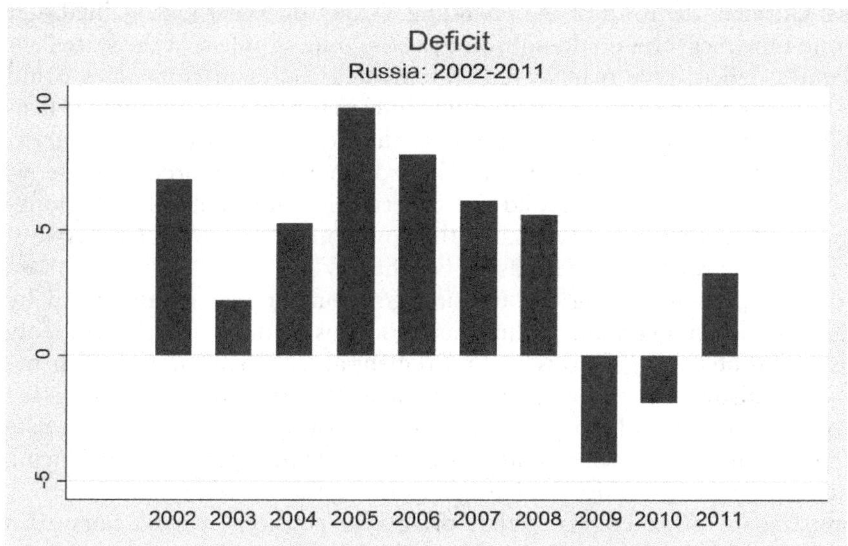

FIGURE 5.3 Government Deficit in Russia, 2001–2011

The financial crisis also resulted in the Russian government drawing down the fiscal reserves built up from oil and natural gas revenue. A Stabilization Fund was created in 2004 that was financed by revenue from oil and natural gas. In 2008, the Stabilization Fund was split into a Reserve Fund to help maintain a balanced federal budget and a National Wealth Fund tasked with providing financial support for social welfare programs, including Russia's pension system. The Reserve Fund has been significantly depleted; it began with $125 billion in 2008, only to decline to a low of about $25 billion in 2011, before beginning to recover in 2013. At $87 billion in early 2014, the Reserve Fund still represents a small portion of its starting value. The Wealth Fund began with $32 billion in 2008 and has increased in value to $87 billion by January 2014 (going from a value worth about 2 percent of GDP in 2008 to 4 percent of GDP in 2014).[55] The Wealth Fund's resources could go a long way toward addressing the Pension Fund's annual deficit, although this also is not a long-term solution. If there is a return to the 2012 level of annual Pension Fund deficit (of more than $12 billion), the Wealth Fund's holdings would be able to cover the shortfall for less than a decade. The head of the European Pension Fund, Evgenii Yakushev, announced that the Welfare Fund had played a bad joke on the pension system by not fully assessing the cost of pension rights.[56]

[55] Data on the Reserve Fund and Wealth Fund are available from the Russian Ministry of Finance at http://www.minfin.ru/en/reservefund/statistics/amount/index.php?id_4=5817 (accessed July 2014)

[56] Evgeniya Pismennaya, "Luchshe ne kopit'," *Vedomosti*, July 16, 2012.

Evsei Gurvich, the head of the Economic Group of Experts, explained that other one-time measures could not solve the ongoing problem of the state Pension Fund's deficit. One plan to sell state-owned shares in companies could generate about $12 billion, an amount woefully inadequate to address the Pension Fund's continual annual shortfalls.[57] Another economist, Sergei Guriev, then the head of the Center for Economic and Financial Research in Moscow, also noted that suspending second-tier contributions did not solve the long-term problems with pension financing; the government had to choose between either increasing revenue or decreasing benefits.[58]

The fiscal pressure facing the Russian government was compounded by promises made to maintain or increase social spending. Putin repeatedly promised that he would not raise the retirement age. Decreasing current benefits or even raising the retirement age for those near retirement was therefore ruled out as a serious policy option. Instead, the government continues to vote for increases in current benefits, as evidenced by Duma deputies introducing legislation proposing to raise the base pension for those over 75.[59]

Compared to other countries that privatized pensions, Russia pursued a moderate degree of pension privatization. The Russian case demonstrates why a moderate degree of pension privatization – in which politicians are more tempted to change course and doing so is still politically feasible – make reversal most likely. Russia's recurring financing gap, combined with the fiscal crisis, meant that reversing pension privatization was a tempting source of short-term revenue for Russian politicians. At the same time, the extent of pension privatization had not also been extensive enough to generate powerful domestic stakeholders. Had more pension money flowed into the hands of private firms, or citizens linked their future benefits more closely with the performance of individual accounts, the Russian reversal of pension privatization would have been less likely. Had less pension money been diverted to individual accounts, Russian politicians would have been less tempted to backtrack to gain temporary funds.

Fiscal and Political Incentives to Reverse Pension Privatization

Bureaucratic consensus about pension privatization in Russia never existed, but this dissent did not undermine the reform until there was a change in political and fiscal conditions. Proposals to substantially revise or even reverse Russian pension privatization began as soon as the laws were adopted in 2001 and implemented in 2002. The state Pension Fund initially tried to block the

---

[57] "Pensionerov podeliat na 'molodykh' i 'starykh' i budut platit' im po-raznomu," RBK Daily, March 18, 2011.

[58] "Nakopitel'noi chasti pensii – byt'," *Praim*, July 10, 2012.

[59] "Deputaty predlagaet nachisliat' fiksirovannyu doplatu k pensii s 75 let," *Laboratoriia Pension-noi Reformy*, July 16, 2014. The justification was, in part, that few Russians live this long, so the cost to the government would not be significant.

implementation of reforms, but, as noted above, it had only limited success in doing so. In 2008, political battles over pension reform were actively being debated, with some maintaining – with remarkable foresight – that the most interesting developments were yet to come.[60] For nearly a decade, Russian pension privatization continued to be implemented despite ongoing opposition from the state Pension Fund.

Amidst the aftermath of the 2008 financial crisis, Russia's electoral and fiscal timelines created pressure to revisit the issue of pension policy. By 2011 the Russian government was recovering from deficits incurred during the recent financial crisis and facing increases in the state Pension Fund's annual deficit. Duma elections were scheduled for December 2011, with presidential elections following in March 2012. Additionally, in Fall 2012 a federal budget would be drafted in preparation for its adoption in Spring 2013. Thus, 2011 and 2012 became critical years for debating what to do about Russia's pension system.

As with the adoption of pension privatization, the debate about reversal included high-level policymakers and politicians with limited public input. The major bureaucracies were responsible for legislative proposals and thus became the center of pension policy debates. In 2011 the Ministry of Health-care and Social Protection (MHSP) initiated the discussion about pension reform with a report that set the foundation for backtracking on the 2001 reform. The report, entitled *Results of Pension Reform and a Long-term Perspective on the Development of the Russian Federation's Pension System with an Account of the Influence of the Global Financial Crisis*, emphasized global experiences and the lack of justification for pension privatization and the reform's failures. The report emphasized the role of the World Bank in the adoption of pension privatization and the organization's subsequent shift in its position. The experiences of countries like Chile and other Latin American countries were highlighted as examples of the failure of pension privatization. The authors noted, for instance, that more than half of those covered by pension privatization in Chile also had to receive government support.

Furthermore, the Health Ministry's report backed Putin's position that raising the retirement age should not be considered, arguing that neither raising the pension age nor raising contributions to individual accounts would solve the problems in Russia's pension system. The report concluded that

The solution to this problem, as shown by international experience and especially the consequences of the financial crisis, lies not with increasing the share of the mandatory accumulative pension program [i.e., pension privatization] nor increasing the pension

[60] Interview with representative of the National Association of Private Pension Funds (NAPF), June 23, 2008.

age, but in the modernization of the institutional social insurance relationship in the pension system.[61]

Thus, the report laid the foundation for, at the very minimum, avoiding an increase in contributions to individual accounts (the "mandatory accumulative pension program" in Russian bureaucratic language). It further emphasized that the focus must be on the first tier, the social insurance portion of pensions. The Health Ministry report, however, was not an official legislative proposal, but rather a starting point for discussion about the reforms.

The Ministry of Labor, building on the Health Ministry's report, provided the basis for an official legislative proposal. In Fall 2012 the Ministry of Labor, under new leadership as of Spring 2012, published a report entitled "A Strategy for the Development of the Russian pension system through 2030." The Ministry of Labor notes the importance of maintaining sustainable pension benefits and the importance of fiscal stability in the pension system. Three major areas of reform are noted: (1) reform of pension contributions for the "self-employed" (which included the many citizens receiving unofficial income and who did not have an official employer making contributions on their behalf); (2) reform of short-term (disability) pensions; and (3) a reform of the savings portion of pensions (which constitute the second tier, i.e., the privatized portion of pensions). These areas echoed long-standing issues of concern regarding Russian pensions. For instance, experts have long identified the problem of unofficial, undocumented wages as undermining any pension reform Russia pursues.[62]

Regarding the second tier, the Ministry of Labor concluded that contributions to the individual accounts in the savings portion should be entirely voluntary and highlighted a number of concerns about the privatized portion of pensions. Problems with the privatized portion included the following: a lack of effective guarantees for returns, resulting in citizens and employers being uninterested in participating; a failure to develop voluntary savings; a lack of control and regulation of investment risk, ineffective oversight, high administrative costs (such as commissions); and problems with the legal infrastructure of funds.

The Labor report also cites the Pension Fund's deficit as a major concern. In addition to pointing out the problems with maintaining a privatized portion of pensions, the report lists several measures for improving the long-term financing of the pension system, including raising taxes on wages and increasing contributions from the "self-employed." It is telling just how unpopular

---

[61] Ministry of Healthcare and Social Protection of the Russian Federation, "Itogi pensionnoi reformy i dolgosrochnye perspektivy razvitiia pensinnoi sistemy Rossiskoi Federatsii s uchetom vliianie mirovogo finansovogo krizisa," Moscow, Russia, 2011.

[62] Interview with economic advisor at Federation Council, September 6, 2006, Moscow, Russia; Interview with academic expert, September 5, 2006, Moscow, Russia.

the issue of raising the retirement age is among Russian citizens that the report could recommend raising taxes but not the retirement age. Other experts also emphasized the "double burden" of the reformed system, in which current contributions would be diverted to individual accounts instead of covering current benefits.[63]

Although promoting a reversal of pension privatization, the Labor report justified its position by claiming to support market-oriented pension reform. For instance, the report supported keeping a three-tier system (although the second and third tiers would be based on voluntary contributions). The report further argued it was critical to consider the pressures of having a global economy and international experiences, although it was vague about the particulars of doing so. At a minimum, using this language reflected a concern with the reaction of investors to the reform.

As part of this effort, supporters of reversal attempted to paint the money saved in the second tier as being wasted contributions that were simply lining the pockets of private companies. Maxim Topilin at the Ministry of Labor argued that although the idea has been that pension savings in the financial market would contribute to long-term investments, the money was just being pocketed.[64] At the time, the government sided with supporters of reversal and the main conclusions of the Health Ministry's report. In July 2012, Russian news sources reported that,

According to government officials, the Ministry of Labor has a strong economic argument: currently savings are simply wasted in the accounts of Vneshekonombank, a huge sum taken away from financing the current social system and payment obligations.[65]

The state-owned bank, Vneshekonombank (VEB), currently manages the savings of individuals in the default option; these individuals had not chosen to transfer their mandatory retirement contributions from VEB into private pension funds and constitute about 86 percent of those eligible to do so. In short, the report pointed out the obvious fact that this money could instead be used to cover the sizable deficit in the Pension Fund.

Those opposed to reversing pension privatization included the Ministry of Finance, the Ministry of Economic Development and Trade, independent experts, and private pension funds and investment companies. This followed the pattern established during debates about the adoption of pension privatization, with the economic and finance ministries favoring pension privatization and the welfare ministries opposing it. In previous debates about the adoption of pension privatization, the Ministry of Finance and the Ministry of Economic Development and Trade were considered two of the most influential

---

[63] Alexandra N. Gvozdenko and Olga N. Chernyshova, "Nalogovaia nagruzka mozhet zadushit' biznes," *Pensionnoe Obozrenie*, 1(1), January–March, 2010.
[64] Ibid.   [65] Evgeniya Pismennaya, "Luchshe ne kopit'," *Vedomosti*, July 16, 2012.

bureaucracies.[66] In contrast to previous debates, however, the welfare ministries were drafting the legislative proposals and defining the terms of the policy debate. The economic and welfare ministries were on the defensive.

Several bureaucratic shakeups in 2011 and 2012 signaled Putin's desire to exert the Kremlin's control over key parts of the bureaucracy responsible for pension and budgetary reform, as well as internal power struggles. In September 2011, Aleksei Kudrin, the Minister of Finance since 2000 during Putin's first term in office, was asked to resign his post after publicly criticizing the government's budget proposals and announcing that he could never work in a government headed by Medvedev as prime minister.[67] Kudrin's successor, Anton Siluanov, has worked at the Ministry of Finance since 1992, is a member of United Russia, and specializes in budgetary politics.

A few months later, in the spring of 2012, the heads of the Ministry of Economic Development, the Ministry of Healthcare, and the Ministry of Labor were all replaced, suggesting that Putin wanted to make sure the Kremlin had control over these bureaucracies, whose work was critical for the pension reforms being considered. The change in leadership was accompanied simultaneously by a bureaucratic reorganization. The Ministry of Healthcare and Social Protection became just the Ministry of Healthcare and the Ministry of Labor became the Ministry of Labor and Social Protection, with a corresponding shift in responsibilities.[68]

At the Ministry of Healthcare, Veronica Skvortsova replaced Tatiana Golikova. While Golikova is an economist with a background in Russia's Ministry of Finance, Skvortsova is a medical doctor with an academic background. At the Ministry of Economic Development, Andrei Belousov replaced Elvira Nabiullina. Belousov has extensive experience working for the Putin administration on economic and financial matters. Nabiullina became head of the Central Bank. Only a year later, in the summer of 2013, however, the head of the Ministry of Economics would change again with Belousov being replaced by Aleksei Ulyukaev, who had previous experience at the Ministry of Finance and Russia's Central Bank. Maxim Topilin was promoted from within and took over as the head of the newly organized Ministry of Labor and Social Protection.

The new appointees were promoted from within and did not represent fundamentally different policy positions from those of their predecessors. For instance, the new Minister of Finance, Siluanov, publicly noted that abandoning the second tier was only a temporary fiscal solution and did not solve the

---

[66] Interview with academic expert, September 4, 2006, Moscow, Russia.

[67] "Kudrin Steps Down as Finance Minister," *The Moscow News*, September 26, 2011. Some speculated that Kudrin was reacting to his disappointment at not having been named the next prime minister himself.

[68] A previous reorganization in 2008 had already changed the Ministry of Economic Development and Trade to the Ministry of Economic Development, with trade issues subsequently being delegated to the Ministry of Industry and Trade.

long-term problem of balancing the pension system.[69] The Ministry of Finance noted further that a reversal was unnecessary since the private pension funds were profitable.[70] With the notable exception of Kudrin, who had publicly criticized Putin and Medvedev, most of the former ministers had backgrounds as presidential advisors.[71] The reshuffling of bureaucratic leadership, nonetheless, enabled Medvedev (serving as president in 2012) and Putin (the then PM) to signal a new direction in policy to the public, preceding the 2012 presidential elections without undermining support from high-level bureaucrats. A similar tactic had been used in 2007 when Golikova and Nabiullina were first appointed before the presidential elections in December 2008. In fact, there had been concern by some about a shift in policy when Golikova was appointed head of the Ministry of Healthcare because of her background at Russia's Ministry of Finance.[72]

Legislative debates were limited because United Russia had overwhelming control of the Duma. . While United Russia supported the proposal, the three other parties in the Duma – the Communists, the Liberal Democratic Party of Russia, and A Just Russia – opposed it. The Communists and the Liberal Democratic Party of Russia raised objections, but neither party focused on the proposals to reverse pension privatization. Ultimately, the Communist party voted against the reform while the Liberal Democratic Party and A Just Russia abstained from voting. Dissenting views focused mainly on changes to the first tier, with deputies complaining that the new point system formula was so complicated that even some experts had difficulty understanding it.[73]

Echoing the passage of the pension privatization reforms in the fall of 2001, measures to suspend contributions to individual accounts were passed very quickly by the Duma. The first version was adopted in September, the second in November, and the final bill in December 2012. The quick passage of the legislation reflects the two years of policy debates preceding their adoption in which bureaucrats and politicians worked out the policy details. Furthermore, the legislation was adopted almost simultaneously with the presidential elections in December 2012. If there was any backlash from the public or private sector, neither the Duma nor the president would face electoral challenges for several years, with the next rounds of elections due in 2016 and 2018, respectively. Because the legislation passed its first two readings in the Duma with little public comment, however, there was likely limited concern about a negative reaction.

---

[69] Evgeniya Pismennaya, "Luchshe ne kopit'," *Vedomosti*, July 16, 2012.

[70] "MinFin: pensionnye nakopleniia ne nado otmeniat', potomu chto oni prinosiat pribyl'," *Finmarket*, August 6, 2012.

[71] Alexei Nikolskii, Maria Zheleznova, and Natalya Kostenko, "Vliianie administratsii prezidenta na pravitel'stvo usilitsia," *Vedomosti*, May 23, 2012.

[72] Interview with an advisor to private pension funds, October 19, 2007.

[73] "Novaya pensionnaia formula neponiatna dazhe samim parlamentariiam," *Kommersant*, November 19, 2013.

The measures passed in December 2012 temporarily reduced contributions to the second tier from 6 percent to 2 percent and suspended contributions to private pension funds until they re-registered as open or joint stock companies. Citizens could opt to continue to pay 6 percent of their contributions to the second tier; if they did so, however, the money had to be placed with a private pension fund or investment company. Initially, citizens had until the end of 2013 to choose, but this deadline was later extended until the end of 2014.

Discussions in 2013 continued to highlight the cost of pension privatization and were part of the discussion about the new budget to be adopted the following spring. The 2012 legislation only reduced contributions to the second tier and allowed citizens to choose to keep 6 percent of their wages going to individual accounts with private pension funds or investment companies. The partial backtracking on second-tier contributions made it seem possible that private pension funds could either retain some role in the mandatory national retirement system, or possibly convince the government to change some of the rules to ones more favorable for the private sector. The government promised that the mandatory contributions being diverted temporarily to the state-owned bank, Vneshekonombank, would be returned once private pension funds re-registered. Instead, proposals emerged to further and permanently eliminate mandatory contributions to a second tier. The Ministry of Finance countered with a proposal to change the rules about early and short-term pensions. Even the Ministry of Finance, however, did not propose either a reduction in benefits or the raising of the retirement age.[74]

With minimal reaction from the public and the limited ability of the private pension sector to influence the political system, legislation passed in 2013 was also adopted quickly, with little debate in the Duma. In December 2013, the Duma passed legislation that virtually eliminated the main component of the reform passed twelve years earlier. A Russian citizen could opt to have all of his or her wages managed by a private pension fund, but the individual was required to make this decision by the end of 2014, after which he or she would not be allowed to switch back.[75] A second tier of the pension system would exist, but it would be based on voluntary contributions to an individual account.

Spreading out the reversal of pension privatization over two years gave politicians a trial run to gauge reaction in the public and private spheres, including among international investors. Delaying the final reversal until 2013 also allowed politicians to avoid making pension reform a major electoral issue in 2011 and 2012.

The second reversal was, however, passed after the budget was already adopted. Because the budget for 2014–2015 had already been passed with the

---

74 "Predlozheniia MinFina po pensionnoi reforme sokrashchaiut defitsit PFR," RIA Novosti, June 28, 2012.

75 Ekaterina Donskikh, "Luchshe 2% ili 6%? Kakie otchisleniia na nakopitel'nuiu pensiiu vygodnee," *Argumenty i Fakty*, No. 25, June 23, 2013.

more temporary and limited reversal, Putin and United Russia had some flexibility in deciding whether or not to keep a stronger component of pension privatization. The ability to continue accessing additional short-term revenue from mandatory contributions proved to be a compelling motivation to make the second tier entirely voluntary. Some went so far as to speculate that it was the pension reversal that financed Russia's intervention in Crimea.[76] Ultimately, the government chose to abandon what had become an important part of the pension system. Developments in the spring of 2015 suggest that this is still an unresolved issue and that there is a high degree of volatility in Russian pension policy.

Policy Diffusion

Fiscal pressures and the weak role of domestic stakeholders in the public and private sphere explain the motivation and ability to reverse in Russia, but pension policy is developed in an international context. The World Bank had advocated the adoption of pension privatization (Orenstein 2008). The adoption of pension privatization was especially subject to diffusion pressures because it was a costly reform (Brooks 2007), and it allowed policymakers to make what has been called an "inferential shortcut" in solving a complicated policy problem (Weyland 2006). Consensus about pension privatization within the World Bank began to decline in 1999 and became highlighted even further in 2005 and 2006, when reports were published criticizing the premature implementation of pension privatization in some countries (Orenstein 2011). This shift in the World Bank's position on pension privatization, and subsequent reversals and revisions in countries around the world, informed the Russian government's consideration and deliberation over reversing pension privatization.

In an increasingly globalized world, both in terms of the economy and the flow of information, policy diffusion often plays an important role in the spread of policies (Meseguer and Gilardi 2009), particularly where market-oriented policies are concerned (Meseguer 2005). Although the Russian government often makes an effort to make policy decisions appear independent of international organizations such as the World Bank, there is evidence that the government both learned from and justified the reversal of pension privatization on the basis of experiences in countries in Latin America and Europe. Furthermore, Russia's reversal came after a wave of backtracking that was especially concentrated among other post-communist countries in the region. The change in the World Bank's position and the experiences of other countries can be seen as permissive conditions that made pension privatization possible. It is hard to imagine, however, that the Russian government would have reversed – or at least that it would have done so to such an extent – had

---

[76] Leonid Bershidsky, "Russian Pensions Paid for Putin's Crimea Grab," *Bloomberg Review*, June 23, 2014.

the position of international organizations like the World Bank not altered and had other countries not done so successfully.

The Russian government explicitly considered international opinion and experience when formulating policy, including the positions of international organizations and experts. The adoption of pension privatization had drawn extensively on international experiences, including those of Latin American reformers like Chile (Piñera 2000). At a minimum, the experiences of other countries were used to justify the Russian government's decision to backtrack. Although it is difficult to distinguish between policymakers' use of global trends as a justification versus actual learning, it appears that Russian policymakers were actually looking to glean important lessons from the experiences of other countries, not just reference them as excuses for reversal. The 2011 Health Ministry report that initiated policy discussions about pension privatization extensively references international opinion and the experiences of other countries. Overall, the report portrays internatiional opinion about pension privatization as being overwhelmingly negative. The authors write that

In the past 10 years there has been published a series of fundamental research, critically rethinking the experiences of the functioning of state pension systems that adopted in whole or part the accumulative [mandatory funded] principles. Notable among this research is a report by the Nobel Laureate in economics, Joseph Stiglitz, who held the post of vice-president of the World Bank from 1997–2000 and a report by a professor at the London School of Economics, Nicholas Barr.[77]

In fact, international opinion has been much more mixed than the report suggests, and experiences with pension privatization around the world have revealed shortcomings of privatized pension systems as well as benefits (Orenstein 2008; see especially pp. 179–193).

The Health Ministry report further emphasized that Russia adopted pension privatization "under the existing recommendations of the World Bank in the Russian Federation." This, in fact, may be an exaggeration. Experts on Russian pension reform indicated that the World Bank and the experiences of other countries were not central factors in the decision to reverse pension privatization.[78] The 2001 report accurately notes a shift in the World Bank's advocacy of pension privatization. This shift, however, did not extend to the World Bank endorsing reversals. Indeed, the World Bank representative to Russia publicly opposed reversing the 2001 pension privatization reform measures.[79] Amidst debates about maintaining Russia's privatized system in the Fall of 2012, the director of the World Bank in Russia, Mikhail Rutkovsky,

---

[77] Ministry of Healthcare and Social Protection of the Russian Federation, "Itogi pensionnoi reformy i dolgosrochnye perspektivy razvitiia pensinnoi sistemy Rossiskoi Federatsii s uchetom vliianie mirovogo finansovogo krizisa," Moscow, Russia, 2011.

[78] Interview at the Ministry of Economic Development and Trade, June 27, 2013, Moscow, Russia; Interview at Center for Strategic Development, June 25, 2013, Moscow, Russia.

[79] *RIA Novosti*, October 9, 2012.

announced that, "The Russian pension system introduced in 2002 is very robust and the savings element [i.e., the privatized portion] is considered to be a very important part of the system and we advise politicians reforming the system not to risk compromising this structure."[80]

The experiences of countries like Chile were cited as examples of the failure of pension privatization. The Health Ministry notes that more than half of those included in Chile's privatized system had to receive additional state support because their benefits from the privatized system were insufficient. The Health Ministry does not acknowledge, however, that, aside from Argentina, not all of the South and Latin American countries that privatized pensions subsequently abandoned the policy. Instead, the Latin American countries adopted measures intended to bolster the survival of the system and improve its performance (Kritzer et al. 2011; Kritzer 2008). Writing about the Chilean reforms, Kritzer (2008) explains that "The International Monetary Fund supports these changes because they strive to retain the basic features of the individual account system and, at the same time, address its major shortcomings" (p. 81). By the IMF's account, the Latin American countries that privatized pensions did not indicate policy failures that needed to reverse course – as the Russian Health Ministry report suggests – but rather areas of improvement for what were generally sound policies.

The incomplete review of the experiences of the Latin American countries indicates that, although the Russian government did explicitly consider the experiences of other countries, policymakers at the Ministry of Health used the experiences of other countries in part to justify their moves and not only as a learning tool. This is consistent with research that democratic regimes are more likely to engage in policy learning (Meseguer and Escribà-Folch 2011). The Russian government is less competitive and less democratic than its postcommunist counterparts who reversed pension privatization. Although there is evidence that Russian policymakers were learning from others' experiences, they may have been doing less so than policymakers in other countries.

International experiences continued to be cited in policy discussions in 2012 and 2013. The 2012 Russian Labor Ministry report also noted that it considered global trends and norms in pension privatization, although it did not reference specific examples from other countries. The report cited a need for international collaboration on pension policy, although it failed to mention any specific initiatives to do so or any international organizations with which the Russian government was working. As policy discussions continued in 2013, international experts were consulted. A roundtable in November 2013 included representatives of the International Labor Organization and the OECD.[81]

---

[80] *RIA Novosti*, October 9, 2012.
[81] "Pensionnoi reforme neobkhodimy nezavisimaia ekspertiza i maksimal'no otkrytoe obsuzhdenie – eksperty," *Laboratoriia Pensionnoi Reformy*, November 15, 2013.

Finally, the experiences of other countries were useful in assessing how investors would respond to a reversal in pension privatization. The Russian government had been enjoying surpluses, before the 2008 financial crisis resulted in deficits in 2009 and 2010. In 2014, the costly Russian intervention in Ukraine and subsequent sanctions raised further concerns about investing in Russia. Russia's pension reforms were certainly closely related to other considerations about the financial sector.

The financial ramifications made it especially necessary for decisions about pension reform to take into consideration the expected reaction of investors and the experiences of other countries. International investors and ratings organizations had mentioned the importance of pension reform, suggesting that reversals might send a negative signal. Russian experts suggested that backtracking on market-oriented reforms like pension privatization would send a uniquely bad signal. One economist noted that although not adopting pension privatization might not have sent a bad signal, reversing pension privatization sent a uniquely bad signal that the government was not committed to market-oriented reforms.[82]

Reversals in other European countries also preceded the reversal measures in Russia, often by several years. These reversals included Estonia (2009, 2010), Hungary (2010), Latvia (2001), Lithuania (2009, 2010), Poland (2011), Romania (2009), and Slovakia (2006, 2007). None of these reversals prompted large-scale investor flight. Even the complete abandonment of the privatized pension system in Hungary did not prompt significant concerns from investors, in contrast to the worries about the market consequences of the Argentinian reversal. The stock market dropped 11 points on the day the nationalization of private pension funds was announced and an additional 27 percent over the next month.[83] Nonetheless, the Argentinian renationalization of ten private pension funds in 2008 prompted only a temporary decline in national stock market performance.

In five of the eight countries that reversed before Russia – Argentina, Lithuania, Poland, Romania, and Slovakia – stock market capitalization increased after the reversal of pension privatization (World Development Indicators 2014). In those countries in which market capitalization declined after the reversal of pension privatization – Estonia, Hungary, and Latvia – reversals were made in 2009 and 2010, meaning the decline could very plausibly be attributed to the global financial crisis. Certainly, the performance of these countries' stock markets cannot be attributed solely – or even primarily – to the reversal of pension privatization. Nonetheless, because other countries did not appear to suffer any massive long-term investor flight resulting from the

---

[82] Interview with an economist at Higher School of Economics, July 11, 2011.

[83] Alexei Barrionuevo, "Argentina Nationalizes $30 billion in Private Pensions," *New York Times*, October 21, 2008; "Harvesting Pensions: A pre-election boost for Cristina," *The Economist*, November 27, 2008.

reversal of pension privatization, the Russian government could worry less about the effect of backtracking on stock market performance.

Finally, the staggered nature of Russia's reversal of pension privatization allows the government to see if its initial backtracking provoked any major backlash. Following the first round of reversal in December 2012, there was no major reaction from international investors. Similarly, the subsequent reversal in December 2013 also did not provoke any major reaction. In 2014, investors in Russia were more concerned with the government's actions in Ukraine. Nonetheless, the reversal of pension privatization does not appear to have instigated any major reaction from investors in the Russian economy.

The diffusion mechanism here is distinct from what influenced the spread of pension privatization. In this case, Russian policymakers could observe whether reversals provoked a negative reaction from investors and international organizations. The Russian case confirms that learning is an important mechanism of policy diffusion, although it also suggests that governments use others' experiences to justify policy moves they may have pursued anyway. Here, learning functioned as a shortcut, as has been documented in other cases of diffusion (Berry and Baybeck 2005). Russian policymakers were able to find solutions that have been successfully pursued in other places as a justification for reversing pension privatization in Russia.

6

Russian Domestic Stakeholders and Backtracking on Pension Reform

> And so, the 2002 reform is done … forget about it.
>
> Ivan Zargaryan, "Requiem for the 2002 Pension Reform," June 2014[1]

Despite forecasts that Russia's reversal of pension privatization was permanent, in spring 2015 Putin met with representatives of the private sector and subsequently announced that the mandatory accumulative portion of pensions would remain in place.[2] The lesson of the Russian pension reform repeatedly appears to be that pension reform is the domain of elite negotiations with top-down policymaking; the fluctuations in policy appear to follow the interests of ruling politicians, rather than public opinion or interest group lobbying.

The previous chapter explains the rationale by which Russian policymakers made their decision to reverse pension privatization. In this chapter, I examine both the role of domestic interest groups, including the lobbying efforts of private pension funds to preserve a social security system from which they profited, and also the role of public opinion. These groups were potential stakeholders in pension privatization. I explain how lobbying and public pressure neither spurred nor prevented backtracking on pension privatization. This finding complements existing work which finds that public opinion has an independent effect on welfare state formation (Brooks and Manza 2006). Although I would by no means deny that public opinion often plays a central and critical role in social policies, in the case of pension privatization in Russia, public opinion was not driving change. Nonetheless, as Brooks and Manza (2006) note, public opinion research concerning the

---

[1] Ivan Zagaryan, "Rekviem po pensionnoi reforme 2002 goda," *Pensionnoe Obozrenie*, June 3, 2014.

[2] Petr Netreba and Yana Milukova, "Medvedev reshit sud'bu nakopitel'noi pensii v sleduiushchuiu sredu," *RBK*, April 14, 2015.

"

welfare state is important because for a long time it was not incorporated into our studies of where social policies come from.

Lack of Politically Influential Domestic Stakeholders in the Private Sector

Debates about pension reform in 2011 did not initially spark a strong reaction from the private sector. Fears that mandatory contributions would be entirely eliminated were not yet at the forefront of their concerns. At the time, the head of one private pension fund estimated that there was only a 50–50 chance that the proposal by the Healthcare Ministry in 2011 would come to fruition.[3] Another expert thought the proposal was unlikely to ever pass, noting that he thought policymakers had already dismissed the idea to liquidate the second tier.[4]

Furthermore, many private pension funds and investment companies themselves acknowledged the problems in their sector and supported the efforts to improve regulation and transparency. Private pension funds had faced accusations about fraud and mismanagement for several years. In 2011, the state Pension Fund refused to honor nearly one million requests from citizens to transfer mandatory contributions to private pension funds. Although the state Pension Fund was largely secretive about its reasons for refusing to do so, there were suggestions that the applications may have been fraudulent.[5] Private pension funds were also accused of switching investments between funds without their clients' knowledge.[6] Acknowledging these problems, Konstantin Ugrumov, the head of the National Association of Pension Funds (NAPF), publicly stated that "[c]urrently the sale transactions of private pension funds are on an illegal, opaque level."[7] Vitaly Plotnikov, the head of a private pension fund known for consolidating smaller funds, further noted that one specific challenge was that consolidating pension funds usually occurs through changes in the structure of the board, which risks future legal challenges and might result in losing the funds' holdings.[8]

Despite support from private pension funds for better regulation, the funds complained that their businesses were being sabotaged and that the Ministry of Healthcare and Social Protection had failed to back the introduction of laws that would make it possible to pay out pensions to those who were currently retiring and had money invested in the second tier. Although the Ministry of Economic Development and Trade had proposed additional

---

[3] Interview with head of a Russian private pension fund, June 30, 2011, Moscow, Russia.

[4] Interview with economist at Higher School of Economics, July 11, 2011.

[5] Alexander Mazunin, "Pensionnye nakopleniia ne perevodiatsia/PFR ne priznal dogovory grazhdan s chastnymi pensionnymi fondami," *Kommersant*, March 28, 2011.

[6] Ekaterina Karlenko, "Pensii kochuiut mezhdu fondami bez vedoma grazhdan,"*BFM.RU*, June 29, 2012.

[7] Natalya Biyanova, "Sobirateli pensii," *Vedomosti*, April 12, 2011.   [8] Ibid.

legislation, the Healthcare Ministry maintained that no additional measures were necessary. At stake were the indexation rules that private pension funds were allowed to use and how much they would be allowed to pay out to their customers.[9]

Firms in the private pension sector appeared to be trying to make the best of things amidst what was potentially a very bad policy shift for the sector. Those in the private pension sector actively published commentaries on the proposals and participated in seminars. Although those in the private pension sector had no official input into the 2011 MHSP report or the 2012 Ministry of Labor report, they did participate in conferences, at least one of which was sponsored by the Research Institute of Labor at the Ministry of Healthcare and Social Protection.[10]

The private sector responded swiftly to the 2012 report from the Ministry of Labor. Notably, the editorial board of the Russian journal *Pension Observer* addressed an open letter to Prime Minister Medvedev, asking him to suspend the implementation of the Ministry of Labor's report (which served as a template for the legislation adopted in December 2012).[11] NAPF publicly highlighted the shortcomings of the reversal, pointing out that the number of private pension funds had consolidated since 2008 and that the total holdings in the sector had more than doubled. Those favoring the survival of the individual accounts emphasized that the importance of maintaining a central role for the private pension funds was necessary not only in planning for future pensions, but also in promoting financial literacy and the development of an investment culture.[12] Mikhail Dmitriev, credited as one of the main designers of Russian pension privatization and the president of the state-financed Center for Strategic Development, criticized the government for avoiding modernization of the risk management system and instead focusing on turning funds into joint stock companies.[13]

Despite arguments about the benefits of pension privatization for the financial sector, even in the private pension sector there were skeptics about how much pension privatization had actually strengthened Russia's financial sector. The head of one private pension fund stated that the private pension funds had little influence on Russia's financial sector either before or after the financial crisis. He acknowledged that long-term capital and investment are certainly important for the financial sector, but there was simply not enough

---

[9] Anton Trifonov, "Pensionnoe bezzakonie," *Vedomosti*, April 28, 2011.

[10] "8–9 Noiabria 2011 god v NII truda sostoitsia seminar 'Pensionnaia sistema Rossii: vyzovy XXI veka i puti modernizatsii'", *Laboratoriia Pensionnoi Reformy*.

[11] "Otkrytoe pis'mo Predsedateliu Pravitel'stva RF D.A. Medvedevu," *Pensionnoe Obozrenie*, No. 4 (12) October–December, 2012.

[12] Viacheslav V. Ismailov, "Razvitie sistemy NPF. Chastnoe Mnenie," *Pensionnoe Obozrenie*, No. 4 (12) October–December, 2012.

[13] *Laboratoriia Pensionnoi Reformy*, "Pensionnoi reforme neobkhodimy nezavisimaia ekspertiza i maksimal'no otkrytoe obsuzhdenie – eksperty," November 15, 2013.

capital in the private pension sector to have had much influence on the financial sector.[14] In short, because pension privatization had not been more extensive, the private pension sector did not have the positive influence which its proponents had hoped.

Private pension funds were not part of the formal discussions with the Ministry of Healthcare and Social Protection or the Ministry of Labor in formulating policy. Nor did the private pension funds have any extensive collaboration with the Ministry of Economic Development or the Ministry of Finance, both of which opposed reversals. Indeed, by 2012 the Ministry of Economic Development was no longer very involved in commenting on pension reform, according to high-level officials employed there.[15] In the early 2000s, private pension funds were regularly consulted, and they provided policy reports that bureaucrats and politicians referenced (Wilson Sokhey 2015). In the early 2000s, however, the Kremlin favored the position backed by the private sector and could draw on policy analysis from private pension funds for support. The Kremlin, now publicly backing reversal proposals, no longer needed to make an effort to include the private sector.

In the summer of 2013, when additional reversal measures were being debated, the head of a private pension fund expressed guarded optimism about the trajectory of reform.[16] He praised the government's measures for increasing awareness about the funded portion of pensions, but argued that the government's plan was not a long-term solution and that it was opposed by many experts. Another expert also expressed some optimism that the private pension funds would be able to recoup losses incurred by the then-temporary reversal legislated in December 2012. Although the heads of private pension funds were not influential on the government, experts emphasized that their expertise was useful to policymakers.[17]

Despite the hope that private pension funds might still come out all right, in December 2013 additional legislation permanently eliminated most of the contributions to a second tier, which could be invested by private pension funds and investment companies. Private pension funds in Russia will be almost entirely confined to managing voluntary contributions and are at risk of losing the contributions that were originally to be redirected temporarily to the state-owned commercial bank, Vneshekonombank.

Heads of private pension funds were clearly opposed to the reversal of pension privatization, but lacked influence over the legislative process.

---

[14] Interview with head of private pension fund, June 30, 2011, Moscow, Russia.

[15] Interview with representative of Ministry of Economic Development, June 27, 2013. This particular representative has been employed at the Ministry of Economic Development since 2007 making their perspective on the Ministry's changing role in pension reform particularly insightful.

[16] Interview with head of private pension fund, June 24, 2013, Moscow, Russia.

[17] Interview at Center for Strategic Development, June 25, 2013, Moscow, Russia; Interview at Ministry of Economic Development, June 27, 2013.

Furthermore, the private pension funds were typically part of larger financial institutions, whose larger fortunes did not depend solely, or even primarily, on Russia's partially privatized pension system. For example, the head of a private pension fund indicated that his firm made little money from pension investments. They continued to participate in managing mandatory contributions to the second tier simply to show that they offered a full package of financial services.[18] Thus, private pension firms had a limited incentive to engage in any more pressure on the government than they already were. The larger financial institutions, of which private pension funds were a part, were likely better off focusing on their ability to profit in other areas.

Furthermore, Russia's partial pension privatization and limited role for private pension funds suggests that the private pension portion of the financial sector was not very structurally important to the larger economy or structurally critical to the financial sector. When firms are structurally important, the mere threat of their exit from the market may be sufficient to compel politicians to act in their favor (e.g., the exit, voice, and loyalty game described by Hirschman 1970; see also Lindblom 1977). Przeworski (2008) emphasizes this point, concluding that

A science of politics that ignores economic constraints on popular sovereignty misses what all democracies have in common, namely, that they exist in societies where the future of all depends on the decisions of some, those who control productive resources. Popular sovereignty is constrained by private ownership of collective resources. (p. 16)

In the case of Russia's private pension funds and investment companies working in the private pension sector, the firms did not exercise any structural leverage. Their sector's size and wealth, although much greater after the 2002 reforms, lent private pension funds limited influence on the Russian government.

From the beginning, Russian pension funds have also been heavily invested in short-term government treasury bonds, on which there were no investment restrictions. Orlov-Karba (2005) details restrictions on Russian pension fund investments, including the percentage of investments that were allowed to come from various sources including:

- Stocks and bonds from foreign governments (20 percent)
- Currencies (20 percent)
- Securities from a single issuer (5 percent)
- Stocks and bonds from a single company (10 percent)
- Securities from regional government (40 percent)
- Municipal bonds (40 percent)
- Agricultural collective (50 percent rising to 80 percent)
- Joint stock companies (20 percent rising to 65 percent)
- Single type of bond (35 percent)

---

[18] Interview with the head of a private pension fund, September 25, 2007, Moscow, Russia.

In 2005, private pension funds had an average of 70 percent of their investments in short-term government treasury bonds (Orlov-Karba 2005: 151).[19] Currently, Vneshekonombank – the state-owned bank that is managing all contributions to the second tier until these contributions are phased out – invests solely in government securities, mortgage papers backed by the state, and rubles and foreign currency funds. Vneshekonombank states that it is currently working to diversify its investment options to include all government bonds, including bonds from companies owned by the state.[20]

Given the large proportion of pension savings in government bonds, the Russian government could have chosen something similar to the Kazakh route for backtracking on pension privatization. In 2013, the Kazakh government chose to continue mandatory contributions which are individually credited and tracked, but has brought the management of second-tier contributions entirely under state control under one consolidated fund.[21] Instituting state management, however, would not have freed up the annual recurring financing gap incurred by diverting contributions to a second tier of individual accounts. That the Russian government did not choose to simply assert state control over the mandatory second-tier contributions provides further evidence that fiscal pressures were a primary motivation in reversing pension privatization.

The restrictions on private pension investments – which are a large part of why they invested heavily in government bonds – also reveal the constrained role that private pension funds were allowed to play in the financial sector. Ultimately, the interests in the private sector supporting the survival of pension privatization were not politically influential enough to overcome politicians' motivations to access second-tier contributions.

Lack of Public Support for Pension Privatization

Those opposed to the reversal tried to argue that reversal would instigate public outrage. Dmitriev, credited as one of the key designers of Russia's reformed pension system, claimed that reversing pension privatization would provoke a social reaction comparable to when the government monetized benefits.[22] Monetizing benefits – which entailed switching from benefits-in-kind to cash payments – resulted in large-scale protests by pensioners across the country.

---

[19] Orlov-Karba (2005) reports that 121 pension funds had 50% of their reserves in short-term government treasury bonds (called GKOs), 85 funds had more than 75% in GKOs, and 66 funds had all of their money in GKOs.

[20] See Vneshekonombank's statement regarding pension investments at http://www.veb.ru/en/agent/pension/ (accessed August 15, 2014).

[21] Raushan Nurshayeva and Mariya Gordeyeva, "Kazakhstan mobilises pension fund assets to spur growth," *Reuters*, January 23, 2013: IMF Country Report No. 14/258, "The Republic of Kazakhstan: Financial System Stability Assessment," Washington DC, July 8, 2014.

[22] Dina Ushkova, *Izvestiya*, "Otkaz ot nakopitel'noi sistemн budet vospriniat obshchestvom kak monetizatsiia l'got," August 22, 2012.

Because the Russian government pursued only a partial pension privatization and let the default option be for citizens *not* to have money invested with private pension funds, there was ultimately a lack of public support for the reform. Inequality in Russia has risen sharply since the fall of communism, although there is significant variation in the extent of inequality by region (Remington 2011). As a result, the public has paid more attention to issues like the level of existing benefits and less attention to issues like pension privatization (which arguably increased inequality). Because pension privatization was not more extensive, reversing was not as unpopular as some had speculated. Theories of path dependency suggest that policies create feedback loops in which actors are invested in the current system (Pierson 2000; Rose 1990). The case of Russian pension privatization demonstrates a case in which feedback loops were not created. Citizens were not supportive of pension privatization, in part because it was only a relatively limited part of their retirement benefits.

Survey evidence reveals that while most of the Russian public was aware that the second tier of pensions existed, few strongly supported its continuation; most were indifferent or opposed to keeping the second tier, particularly if the money was deposited into private pension fund accounts. The Public Opinion Fund conducted a survey based on a representative sample of 3,000 people in 46 regions of Russia (out of 81 total regions) in July 2012.[23] Eighty-eight percent responded that they knew about the second tier or had heard something about it. Only 10 percent of respondents said that they were hearing about it for the first time during the survey. Sixty-three percent of respondents further knew whether their contributions to the second tier were being managed by the Russian state (in the Pension Fund) or by private pension funds. The high level of awareness about the second tier reflects that most citizens knew it existed and where their own savings were being held. Far fewer – only 23 percent – were certain about the exact amount in their pension funds.

Only 25 percent of those covered by the second tier (those under 45) thought they were better off with the mandatory second-tier contributions. Thirty-one percent said they were better off *without* mandatory second-tier contributions, and 32 percent said it made no difference. Even though a quarter of those covered said they were better off with second-tier contributions, 37 percent (of those under 45) viewed the Labor Ministry's proposal to reverse pension privatization favorably. A mere 18 percent viewed the reversal proposal negatively. The polling data, then, indicated that the public would not object to a reversal of the system.

The reasons given for supporting or opposing reversal in the survey were different from the arguments being made by public experts for reversal (mostly by those associated with the administration, the Ministry of Labor, and the Ministry of Healthcare and Social Protection). The most oft-cited reason for

---

[23] "Otmena nakopitel'noi pensii: sotsial'nye riski i vozmozhnosti," *Fond Obshestvennoe Mnenie,* 2011–2012; full report available in Russian upon request.

supporting the reversal (for 11 percent of respondents) was that individuals were opposed to mandatory contributions because they felt that people should be allowed to choose. None of the criticisms about a lack of confidence in private pension funds, excessive administrative fees, or a lack of guarantees about returns (all of which were criticisms of the private pension market in the Labor report) were mentioned.

In response to an open-ended question, the most cited reason for opposing reversal (for 7 percent of respondents) was that people would not save independently for their own retirement. The Public Opinion Fund presented additional survey evidence that Russian citizens were, in fact, either unwilling or unable to save for their own retirement. In response to a different question, only 13 percent reported that they were willing and able to save for their own retirement. Some took this evidence of an unwillingness to save as support for keeping mandatory contributions to the second tier. Even if it is true that Russians would not save a sufficient amount for their own retirement (a problem not limited to Russia), the more important survey results for the government were that the public would not object to a major overhaul of the second tier. Perhaps because individuals did not prioritize retirement savings, eliminating mandatory retirement contributions did not seem particularly troubling to them.

The Russian public did not show any significant reaction to the discussions about pension reform from 2011 to 2013 and did not balk at initial measures to restrict contributions to the second tier. Even those who are well educated and comparatively well informed about their options have demonstrated little concern about the changes. In summer 2013, one such individual indicated that they were currently contributing to a private pension fund, but were uncertain which one they had chosen and had not yet decided whether to go with the 2 percent or 6 percent option being offered at the time.[24] Such a reaction may be entirely rational; given a general lack of distrust or expectation of policy changes, worrying about a relatively small portion of one's retirement contributions may make little sense.

Some have noted that the recent pension reform debates in Russia have been primarily a discussion amongst elites and note the importance of increasing social awareness and inclusion in pension reform discussion. When asked which social groups were most influential in terms of the course of pension reform in Russia, one expert considered for several moments before admitting he could not think of a single specific interest group that was active with regard to pension policy.[25] Policy debates about reversals have raised concerns again about the lack of social involvement. Writing about pension reform, the economist Sergei Guriev comments that,

---

[24] Interview at the Ministry of Economic Development, June 27, 2013
[25] Interview at the Ministry of Economic Development and Trade, October 15, 2007, Moscow, Russia.

But I think in 2014 society will begin to understand that it does not understand one of the main economic mechanisms on which almost everyone's future directly depends. This awareness will create a murmur, a desire to understand. When society understands a bit more, they will begin to grumble more. And that's good because building opposition will inevitably be suppressed, but when there are economic protests, they will be somewhat heard and, importantly, protesters will have a chance to find allies within the elites.[26]

Guriev optimistically suggests that public awareness will grow and further suggests that this could translate into influence on elites if those opposed to the recent pension reform find allies among the elite. Yet no such protests have emerged, and social opposition has not sought out allies in the elites. Furthermore, although there are bureaucratic elites who oppose the reversal of pension privatization, citizens would find few (and relatively weak) political parties or politicians willing to back their opposition. As of 2014, the recent reversal of pension privatization had not provoked any major public backlash or demonstrations.

The Russian Public Opinion Research Center (WCIOM) also conducted surveys inquiring about public opinion and pension reform from 2013 to 2015. In a nationally representative survey conducted on October 31, 2013, WCIOM asked a series of questions about the accumulative portion of pensions.[27] Only 24 percent of respondents claimed to know the amount of funds in their accumulative portion of their pensions (we do not know whether individuals actually knew the correct amount). Forty-seven percent responded that they did not know and 25 percent responded that they did not have an accumulative account (which would apply to those born before 1967).

A 2013 WCIOM survey also indicated that 57 percent of Russians did not know about the moratorium on the accumulative portion of Russian pensions that had been put in place.[28] At the time, 27 percent were opposed to the moratorium and only 19 percent were in support of the moratorium. Sixty percent of respondents reported being interested in the changes in the pension system.

Original Survey Evidence from 2014 and 2015

I drafted original survey questions which lend additional insight into the role of public opinion by directly inquiring into knowledge about the ongoing pension reforms and support for these measures. The surveys consist of a nationally representative survey of 1,600 Russian citizens polled by Levada in November 2014 and in October 2015.

---

26   Sergei Guriev, "Peresmotr pensionnoi reformy," *FinMarket*, 2014.

27   Russian Public Opinion Research Center (WCIOM), Press Release No. 2443, "Kopit' na pensiiu: zachem i skol'ko?"

28   Olga Grosheva, "Ludei, konechno, napriagaet reshenie vlastei zabrat' ikh den'gi," *Kommersant*, October 22, 2013.

The results of my original survey questions in Fall 2014 and Fall 2015 differ somewhat from previously conducted surveys – including the WCIOM surveys discussed above – particularly with regard to the level of support for reversals, although the results are consistent. For instance, in October 2015 I find that 19 percent somewhat or completely agreed with the moratorium on contributions to the second tier – the same percentage supporting the moratorium in the WCIOM survey in 2013. My survey results, however, show only 18 percent either somewhat or completely disagreed with the moratorium compared to 27 percent opposed in the WCIOM survey.

The different times at which the surveys were conducted is likely part of the reason that there are different responses. The Public Opinion Fund survey was conducted in Summer 2013 and the WCIOM polls were in Fall 2013 and Spring 2015. There could be something unique about Fall 2014 and Fall 2015 when the reversal was underway, but still had at least a somewhat indeterminate status. The questions are also not identical. Differences in question wording and response categories are likely producing different responses.

Nonetheless, the survey results are consistent in showing low levels of awareness and limited opposition to the government's reversal. Also telling is that standard socioeconomic indicators are not consistent predictors of preferences for pension policy even though these policies influenced wealthier, white-collar people more than others. This is consistent with my expectation that public support for reversal played virtually no role in instigating backtracking; rather it was the lack of strong public sentiment in favor of reversing that helps explain the turnaround.

Table 6.1 presents the responses to the question about supporting the reversal of pension privatization. Several knowledge questions tap into whether an individual is aware of current reforms. More than a third of respondents – and often nearly half – said that it was "Hard to say." Indeed, even the broadest question in 2014 about whether any changes were being made to the pension system had 45 percent answer with "Hard to say." Less than half of the respondents gave the correct answer in response to any of the knowledge questions. General awareness about the reversals was quite low.

To an outside audience the first two knowledge questions may seem overly detailed or specific. The Russian media, however, reports regularly on the changes being proposed and legislated with regard to the pension system although this is not typically front-page news. The largest and most publicized change to the insurance portion of the pension system was the switch to a point system. Furthermore, headlines frequently included the percentage of contributions that would be devoted to the accumulative portion of pensions. For instance, an article in *Argumenty i Fakty* on June 30, 2013 ran a story with the headline "Better 2% or 6%? Which variant of the accumulative pension is more profitable"; the article itself was a Q&A answering questions that readers had sent in about the recent changes to the pension system. In principle, then, the Russian public had the opportunity to get news about the changes to the

TABLE 6.1 *Knowledge about Recent Pension Reforms in Russia, 2014 and 2015*
Correct answers are highlighted

	Oct. 2014 Insurance Portion Points	Oct. 2014 6% wages to accumulative	Oct. 2014 Accumulative changes	Nov. 2015 Keeping accumulative	Nov. 2015 Insurance Portion Points
True	45%	39%	26%	36%	41%
Not True	22%	23%	29%	17%	14%
Hard to Say	33%	38%	45%	47%	45%

Surveys conducted by the Levada survey company; nationally representative survey of 1,600 Russians in October 2014 and nationally representative survey of 1,602 Russians in November 2015.
True/False Statements:

1. October 2014: The insurance portion of pensions will be based on an individual coefficient (points) based on the level of wages, the level of seniority, and age at the time of retirement.
2. October 2014: Through the end of 2012, employers sent a sum equal to 6 percent of wages to the accumulative portion of pensions for all employees born in or after 1967.
3. October 2014: The Russian government is currently *not* in the process of decreasing or changing the accumulative portion of the pension system for those born in or after 1967.
4. November 2015: In the spring of 2015, Prime Minister Medvedev announced a decision to preserve accumulative pensions.
5. November 2015: The insurance portion of pensions will be based on an individual pension coefficient (points) derived from the level of wages, work experiences, and age at retirement.

pension system, but it appears that a relatively small segment of the population was paying attention to these changes.

Questions from the fall of 2014 and 2015 inquire about support for the Russian government's changes to the pension privatization system. Table 6.2 presents a summary of the responses to these questions.

In 2014, nearly a quarter of respondents (23 percent) said it was "Hard to say" and 18 percent said they would "Neither agree nor disagree" in response to the question about support for reversing pension privatization. This means that 41 percent of respondents expressed no opinion either way about the reversal of pension privatization. Of those expressing a preference, 35 percent disagreed with reversing pension privatization and 23 percent agreed with reversing pension privatization.

In 2015, 36 percent agreed with maintaining the accumulative portion of pensions (a figure nearly identical to the percentage that opposed reversals just a year earlier). Now, however, only 13 percent disagreed with preserving the accumulative portion (compared to the 23 percent who agreed with reversing a year earlier). Differences in question wording may explain, at least in part, why opposition to reversal shifted – as well as the government's stance on the issue. In 2014, the Russian government was backing reversal and in 2015 it was backing keeping some form of the accumulative portion of pensions. Support

TABLE 6.2 *Support for Reversing Pension Privatization in Russia, 2014 and 2015*

	November 2014: Support Reversal of Accumulative Part	October 2015: Support Preserving Accumulative Part	October 2015: Support Moratorium	October 2015: Clear & consistent pension policy
Completely Disagree	14%	5%	9%	13%
Somewhat Disagree	21%	8%	9%	14%
Neither Agree nor Disagree	18%	18%	19%	19%
Somewhat Agree	16%	18%	11%	11%
Completely Agree	7%	18%	8%	6%
Don't Know		10%	13%	11%
Hard to Say	23%	24%	32%	26%

Surveys conducted by the Levada survey company; nationally representative survey of 1,600 Russians in October 2014 and nationally representative survey of 1,602 Russians in November 2015.
Statements:

1. November 2014: I support the reversal of the accumulative portion of the pension system.
2. October 2015: I support preserving the accumulative portion of the pension system.
3. October 2015: I support the idea of extending the moratorium on contributions to the accumulative portion in 2016.
4. October 2015: The Russian government has been clear and consistent in making pension policy.

for extending the moratorium was split almost evenly between those who agreed (18 percent) and disagreed (19 percent) with nearly half (45 percent) responding that they either did not know or it was hard to say.

To get a more general assessment of how Russian citizens were responding to these changes I asked whether respondents thought the Russian government has been clear and consistent in its pension policymaking. Only 17 percent of respondents in 2015 agreed that the government had been clear and consistent in making pension policy. Thirty-seven percent responded that they either did not know or it was hard to say if policy had been clear and consistent. Although the public may not have thought that the Russian government was being clear and consistent, this did not appear to make them opposed to reversals of pension policy.

Explaining Awareness and Preferences about Pension Privatization Reforms

Although knowledge and preferences are not the primary questions of interest, it is useful to consider whether the standard socioeconomic factors predict knowledge and preferences about pension privatization. Many policymakers assumed that pension privatization would change the social contract because of how it altered citizens' awareness of their retirement benefits and their preferences for particular savings' strategies and policies.

Analysis shows that education, income, and having a white-collar job are statistically significant predictors of knowledge about the recent pension reforms.[29] Being more educated, having a larger income, and having a white-collar job made one less likely to respond "hard to say" in response to all of the knowledge questions. Education and income also had a positive effect on giving a correct answer to the knowledge questions.

There is some evidence that having a white-collar job makes one less likely to respond "hard to say", but having a white-collar job only made one more likely to give a correct answer to the points knowledge question. The marginal effects show that a person with a white collar job was about 10 percent less likely to respond "Hard to say" to the "Any changes" or points questions (although the confidence intervals slightly overlap). Those with white-collar jobs were around 5 percent more likely to give a correct answer to the "any change" question; there was no substantive effect for either the points question or the 6 percent question. This is consistent with my expectations that professional jobs should make citizens more likely to be aware of changes to Russia's pension privatization system although the effect is relatively small.

Notably, the age groups affected by the implementation and reversal of pension privatization – those born after 1967 – were not less likely to respond "Hard to say" and were not more likely to give a correct answer to these knowledge questions. This speaks to the generally low levels of public knowledge about changes to the Russian pension system, even for those most impacted. Being under the age of 45 also did not influence one's support for reversing pension privatization even though these age groups were the most directly influenced.

Although certain groups were more likely to express a preference, socioeconomic status did not strongly predict – if at all – what that preference would be. Education and income were not consistently predictors of preferences for keeping the accumulative portion of pensions or extending the moratorium on contributions. Even being under the age of 45 did not influence one's support for reversing pension privatization, even though this was the age range most directly affected. That standard socioeconomic indicators fail to consistently predict preferences about pension reform provides additional evidence that this was not an issue about which even those who were most likely to care paid much attention.

The results of these original survey questions show that the Russian public was largely uninformed and apathetic about the funded component of the pension system. People with more education, higher incomes, and white-collar jobs were more likely to express a preference, but their socioeconomic status did not predict whether they would support the reversal of pension

---

[29] The full results of the statistical analysis are given in the data appendix to this chapter.

privatization or not. Indeed, the best-specified model appears to be the one predicting that one will "Neither agree nor disagree" with the reversal. For politicians who wanted to reverse pension privatization, the state of public opinion about pension reform was good news: citizens were likely to either be uninformed or lack strong preferences about what were potentially path-departing changes.

Implications of the Russian Case

The reversal of Russian pension privatization was driven neither by partisan bickering nor by a public backlash against a market-oriented transformation of the country's pension system. The design of Russia's partially privatized pension system, along with a financial crisis, prompted politicians to see reversal as a useful way to gain short-term revenue. The lack of politically influential domestic stakeholders in the private sector and the lack of public support for the privatized system made it politically feasible to backtrack.

One might think that the public's apathy and their low level of awareness are endogenous to the authoritarian nature of Russia's regime. While this is a reasonable conjecture, in this particular case it is unlikely that the public would have been more aware if a freer media had existed in Russia. As the Hungarian and Polish cases in the next chapter will establish, even in more competitive democratic regimes public concern about reversal appeared to be low. In the cases of moderate pension privatization, it appears that many citizens may have reasonably estimated that information about the privatized portion was not relevant to them.

Fiscal pressure played a central role in politicians' decision to backtrack on Russia's pension privatization measures, as revealed by two critical facets of reversal politics: the timing of the reversal and the nature of the policy debates surrounding reversals. The timing of reversal, in 2012 and 2013, reveals the important role played by these fiscal pressures. Electoral considerations, combined with the possible reaction from the private domestic sector and international investors, explain why the reversal was spread out over two years. Policy diffusion played a role too. The Russian government paid attention to policy moves in neighboring countries and how investors responded to these moves. That other post-communist countries, even very market-oriented ones, abandoned pension privatization without any significant public backlash or loss of investment, confirmed for the Russian government that the short-term benefits would outweigh the costs. In the long term, reversals mean that the fiscal stability of Russia's PAYG pension system remains in question, if the government refuses to consider raising the retirement age or reducing benefits. In the short term, however, backtracking reduces the Pension Fund's deficit and gives the government greater control over the pension system.

The Russian case provides three important insights. First, the Russian case lends insight into the central role played by the initial design of pension privatization. The extent to which Russia privatized pensions influenced its recurring financing gap and fiscal pressures, along with the extent to which domestic stakeholders existed in the public and private sphere, as well as the extent to which these interests were influential. Countries that pursued a similar degree of pension privatization included other post-communist countries whose experiences influenced the decision of Russian policymakers. The influence of the extent of pension privatization on the financing gap and the lack of domestic stakeholders also played a central role in the Hungarian and Polish cases, although, as we will see, in different ways than in Russia.

Second, the Russian case helps illuminate why partisanship is only part of the story of reversals. Eight of the eleven countries that have reversed pension privatization have done so under right-wing governments. In the Russian case, however, it was the same right-wing party and president who both introduced and backtracked on reforms. This helps establish that fiscal pressures and the lack of domestic stakeholders – rather than partisanship – were the decisive factor. Partisanship is probably better viewed as a contributing but insufficient condition for reversal. The public political justifications for backtracking on pension privatization were consistent with traditional right-wing, pro-market rhetoric about avoiding an increase in taxes or deficits. In the Russian case, this was combined with President Putin's commitment to avoid raising the retirement age. Ultimately, the extent of pension privatization implemented in Russia in 2002 undermined its survival.

Finally, the Russian case reveals how the learning process by which policy diffusion can occur is applicable across countries. In particular, because pension privatization was a market-oriented reform with significant implications for a country's financial sector, policymakers had reasons to be concerned with how investors would react to backtracking on such a major reform. Ratings agencies like Standard & Poor's included pension reform in their rankings of countries and implored governments to consider the fiscal sustainability of their national retirement systems. Russian policymakers, however, observed reversals in other countries and found that investors were not deterred. Policy diffusion played an important role in pension reform debates in Poland and Hungary too, but in a different way, as their reversals came earlier in the recent wave of changes to privatized pension systems.

The dramatic shifts in pension policy in Russia in the 2000s reveal that battles over national retirement policies are deeply political. These political battles entail a complex interplay of politicians' goals, bureaucratic agendas, public opinion, reactions from the private sector, and international experiences. At stake is a great deal of money and the well-being of millions of pensioners. Short-term costs and electoral timelines, though, make it difficult for governments to commit to long-term solutions that might bolster financial stability. Pension privatization is not the only way in which the Russian government, or any government, can establish a more financially stable retirement system. Any solutions, however, that require short-term costs for long-term benefit are more likely to be undermined, unless groups in the public and private spheres can become domestic stakeholders in their survival in the present.

Data Appendix to Chapter 6

The models below are based on original survey questions included on a nationally representative survey by the Levada Center in October 2014 and November 2015. All data and the original survey question wording are available upon request.

Standard demographic indicators are included in the analysis to account for the possible predictors of pension policy preferences described above. These include gender, marital status, education, income group, age, white-collar employment, and (un)employment. Gender and marital status are binary variables. Education includes eight categories: primary education or less; some middle school; trade school and some middle school; complete middle school; complete middle school and trade school; secondary school; some high school; and a high school degree. The income question is based on monthly income in thousands of rubles. For age, I include a variable capturing whether an individual is under the age of 45, the cutoff age in 2012 for those who would be included in the new privatized pension system (those born in or after 1967). For employment, I use two binary variables in the analysis: white-collar, which captures whether a person has a professional job (12 percent of respondents); and unemployed, which captures the small minority of respondents (3 percent) which reported having no job.

Predicting Knowledge about Pension Reforms in 2014

	Model 1 Points *Hard to Say*	Model 2 Points *Correct Answer*	Model 3 6% *Hard to Say*	Model 4 6% *Correct Answer*	Model 5 Change *Hard to Say*	Model 6 Change *Correct Answer*
Male	−0.01	−0.06	0.03	−0.13*	0.04	−0.01
	(0.07)	(0.07)	(0.07)	(0.07)	(0.07)	(0.07)
Under Age 47 (in 2014)	0.10	−0.06	0.04	−0.04	0.10	−0.08
	(0.08)	(0.07)	(0.08)	(0.07)	(0.07)	(0.08)
Married	−0.12	0.00	−0.16**	0.03	−0.21***	0.12
	(0.08)	(0.07)	(0.08)	(0.08)	(0.07)	(0.08)
Education	−0.09***	0.05***	−0.07***	0.0001	−0.06***	0.07***
	(0.02)	(0.02)	(0.02)	(0.02)	(0.02)	(0.02)
Income	−.000004***	.000006***	−.000005***	.000007***	−000005***	000002
	(.000001)	(.000001)	(.000001)	(.000001)	(.000001)	(.000001)
White Collar	−0.28**	0.20*	−0.06	−0.03	−0.26**	0.31***
	(0.11)	(0.10)	(0.11)	(0.10)	(0.11)	(0.11)
Work Situation Worse	−0.12	−0.04	−0.00	−0.15**	−0.04	0.04
	(0.08)	(0.08)	(0.08)	(0.08)	(0.08)	(0.08)
Region Size	−0.01	0.03	0.03	−0.03	−0.01	−0.02
	(0.03)	(0.03)	(0.03)	(0.03)	(0.03)	(0.03)
Voted for President	0.08	0.02	0.23*	−0.16	0.21*	−0.17
	(0.12)	(0.12)	(0.12)	(0.12)	(0.12)	(0.12)
Voted for Putin	−0.11	0.16	0.01	−0.05	0.06	−0.27***
	(0.11)	(0.10)	(0.11)	(0.10)	(0.10)	(0.11)
Constant	0.17	−0.74***	−0.15	0.0008	0.17	−0.69**
	(0.28)	(0.27)	(0.28)	(0.27)	(0.27)	(0.28)
Observations	1,373	1,373	1,373	1,373	1,373	1,373
Probability $> \chi^2$	.0000	.0000	.0000	.0000	.0000	.0000
Pseudo-R^2	.03	.02	.03	.02	.03	.02

Standard errors in parentheses, * $p < 0.10$, ** $p < 0.05$, *** $p < 0.01$

Predicting Preferences about Reforms in 2014 (Baseline is neither agree nor disagree) N = 1.063, Prob. > χ2 = .005

	Somewhat Disagree	Somewhat Agree
Married	0.09	0.15
	(0.14)	(0.14)
Under Age 47 (in 2014)	0.07	−0.04
	(0.13)	(0.14)
Male	0.13	0.11
	(0.13)	(0.14)
Education	0.01	−0.08**
	(0.04)	(0.04)
Income	0.000003	.000005**
	(0.000002)	(0.000002)
White Collar	0.07	0.16
	(0.18)	(0.19)
Work Situation Worse	0.13	0.09
	(0.14)	(0.15)
"Hard to say" response	−0.11	0.17
	(0.13)	(0.14)
Voted for President	−0.08	0.14
	(0.21)	(0.23)
Voted for Putin	0.18	0.45**
	(0.19)	(0.20)
Constant	−0.15 (.46)	−0.43 (.49)

	Completely Disagree	Completely Agree
Married	0.02	0.37**
	(0.14)	(0.17)
Under Age 45	0.02	0.10
	(0.14)	(0.16)
Male	−0.13	−0.01
	(0.14)	(0.16)
Education	−0.07*	−0.08*
	(0.04)	(0.04)
Income	0.000005**	−.0000001
	(0.000002)	(0.000003)
White Collar	−0.17	−0.24
	(0.20)	(0.24)
Work Situation Worse	0.28*	0.50***
	(0.15)	(0.16)
"Hard to say" response	0.08	0.33**
	(0.14)	(0.16)
Voted for President	−0.14	−0.08
	(0.22)	(0.24)
Voted for Putin	−0.08	−0.14
	(0.20)	(0.22)
Constant	0.28 (.47)	−0.49 (.52)

Predicting Preferences about Reforms in 2014

	Agree with Reversal	Disagree with Reversal	Neither Agree/Disagree
Married	0.17**	−0.03	−0.07
	(0.08)	(0.08)	(0.08)
Under Age 45	0.00	0.07	−0.11
	(0.08)	(0.07)	(0.09)
Male	0.09	0.01	−0.09
	(0.08)	(0.07)	(0.08)
Education	−0.03	0.04**	−0.07***
	(0.02)	(0.02)	(0.02)
Income	.0000008	.000002	−.000001
	(0.000001)	(0.000001)	(0.000002)
White Collar	0.13	0.06	−0.33**
	(0.11)	(0.11)	(0.13)
Work Situation Worse	0.15*	0.12	−0.22**
	(0.08)	(0.08)	(0.09)
"Hard to Say" response	−0.05	−0.41***	0.81***
	(0.08)	(0.07)	(0.08)
Voted for President	0.08	−0.12	0.06
	(0.13)	(0.12)	(0.14)
Voted for Putin	0.14	−0.06	0.05
	(0.11)	(0.10)	(0.12)
Constant	−0.98***	−0.35	−0.63**
	(0.27)	(0.25)	(0.28)
Observations	1,373	1,373	1,373
Probability $> \chi^2$	.12	.0000	.0000
Pseudo-R^2	.01	.03	.10

Standard errors in parentheses

* $p < 0.10$, ** $p < 0.05$, *** $p < 0.01$

Predicting Knowledge about Pension Reforms in 2015

	Points Hard to Say	Points Correct Answer	Medvedev Hard to Say	Medvedev Correct Answer
Male	0.006	−0.003	−0.01	0.004
	(0.07)	(0.07)	(0.07)	(0.07)
Under Age 48	0.13*	−0.15**	0.13*	0.01
	(0.07)	(0.07)	(0.07)	(0.07)
Married	−0.03	0.008	−0.10	0.04
	(0.07)	(0.07)	(0.07)	(0.07)
Education	−0.09***	0.08***	−0.05**	0.004
	(0.02)	(0.02)	(0.02)	(0.02)
Income	−0.000005***	0.000003***	−0.000004***	0.000003**
	(0.000001)	(0.000001)	(0.000001)	(0.000001)
White Collar	−0.01	0.09	−0.05	0.20**
	(0.09)	(0.09)	(0.09)	(0.09)
Family Better/Worse	0.06	−0.09*	0.09	−0.15***
	(0.06)	(0.06)	(0.06)	(0.06)
Region Size	−0.03	0.007	−0.01	−0.04
	(0.03)	(0.03)	(0.03)	(0.03)
Voted for President	0.44***	−0.27**	0.47***	−0.36***
	(0.11)	(0.11)	(0.11)	(0.11)
Voted for Putin	0.11	0.05	0.23**	−0.07
	(0.09)	(0.10)	(0.10)	(0.10)
Constant	−0.20	−0.19	−0.56*	0.47
	(0.30)	(0.30)	(0.30)	(0.31)
Observations	1,533	1,533	1,533	1,533
Probability $> \chi^2$	.0000	.0000	.0000	.0000
Pseudo-R^2	.04	.03	.03	.03

Standard errors in parentheses Levada survey, October 2015

* $p < 0.10$, ** $p < 0.05$, *** $p < 0.01$

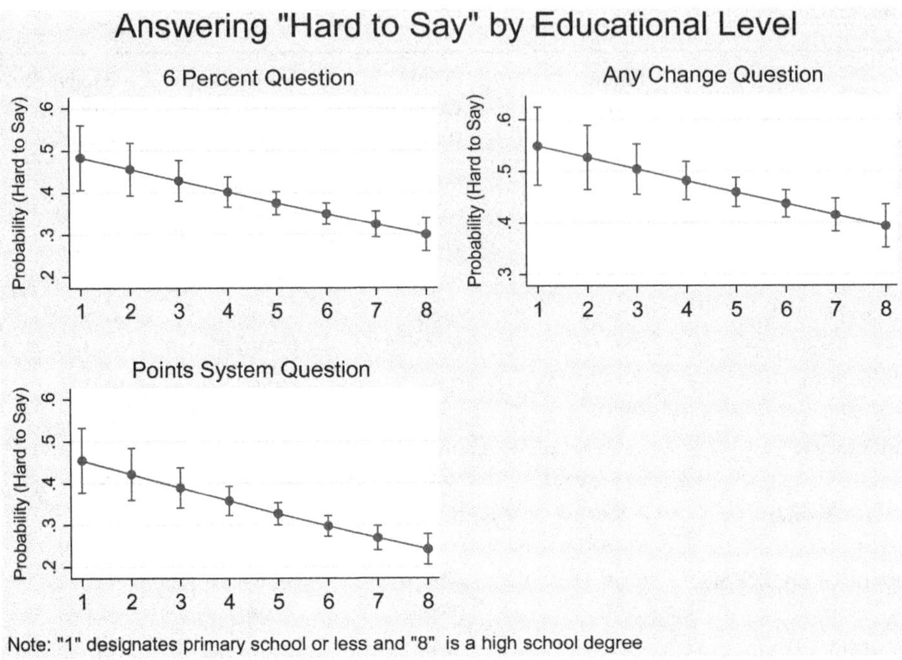

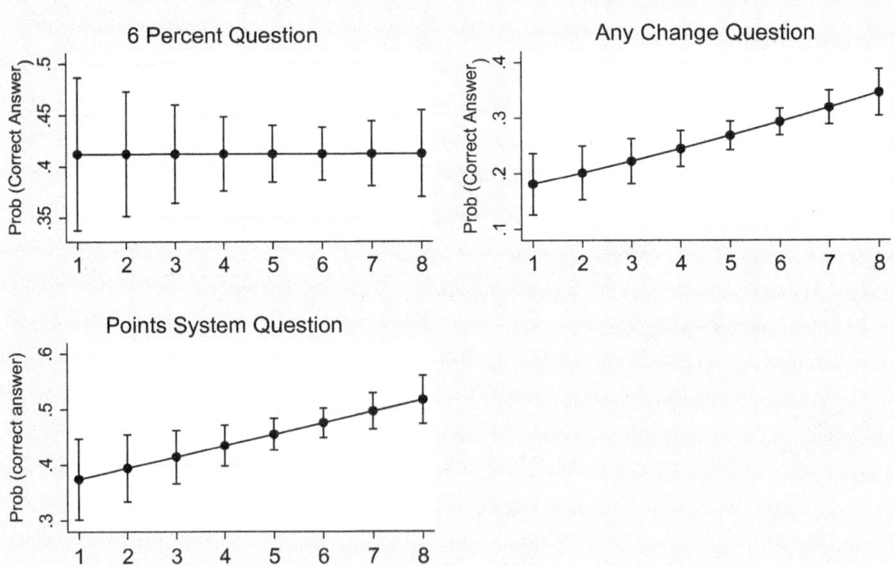

Marginal Effect of Education on Knowledge of Reform
Note: "1" designates primary school or less and "8" is a high school degree

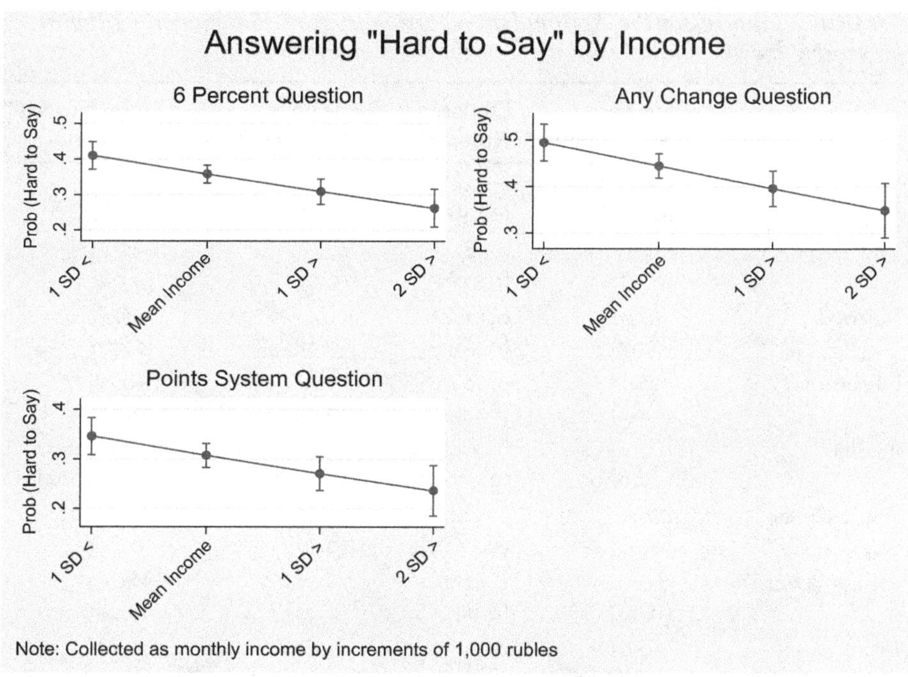

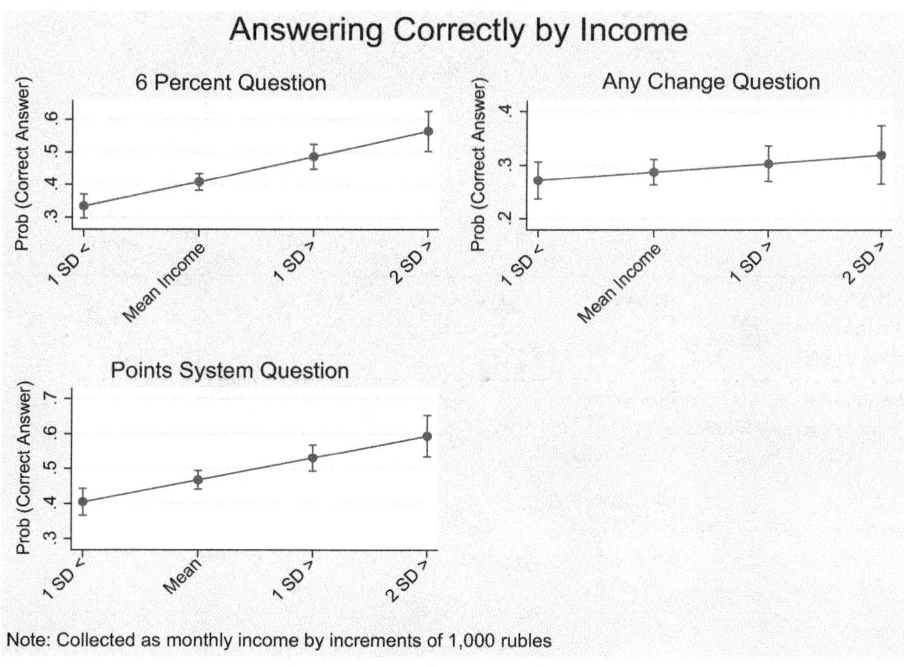

Marginal Effect of Income on Knowledge of Reform
Note: Collected as monthly income by increments of 1,000 rubles

Predicting Support for the Accumulative Portion in 2015 (Statement: I support preserving the accumulative portion of the pension system.)

	Support Accumulative	Oppose Accumulative	Neither Support/Oppose	"Hard to Say" Opinion
Male	0.02	−0.08	−0.002	0.009
	(0.07)	(0.09)	(0.08)	(0.08)
Under Age 48	0.07	0.02	0.07	−0.15[*]
	(0.07)	(0.10)	(0.08)	(0.08)
Married	−0.02	0.13	0.05	−0.05
	(0.07)	(0.10)	(0.08)	(0.08)
Education	0.04[**]	0.02	0.01	−0.08[***]
	(0.02)	(0.03)	(0.03)	(0.02)
Income	0.000006	0.000003[**]	−0.0000007	−0.000001
	(0.000001)	(0.000001)	(0.000001)	(0.000001)
White Collar	0.02	−0.28[**]	−0.01	0.05
	(0.09)	(0.13)	(0.11)	(0.11)
Family Better/Worse	0.07	0.22[***]	−0.16[**]	−0.13[**]
	(0.06)	(0.08)	(0.06)	(0.06)
Region Size	−0.05[*]	0.12[***]	−0.004	0.06[*]
	(0.03)	(0.04)	(0.03)	(0.03)
Voted for President	−0.01	−0.15	−0.14	0.16
	(0.11)	(0.14)	(0.13)	(0.13)
Voted for Putin	0.10	−0.33[***]	0.08	0.13
	(0.10)	(0.12)	(0.11)	(0.12)
Hard to Say (Knowledge)	−0.59[***]	−0.91[***]	−0.24[***]	1.04[***]
	(0.07)	(0.11)	(0.08)	(0.08)
Constant	−0.46	−1.66[***]	−0.43	−0.89[**]
	(0.31)	(0.41)	(0.36)	(0.35)
Observations	1,533	1,533	1,533	1,533
Probability $> \chi^2$	.0000	.00000	.008	.0000
Pseudo-R^2	.05	.11	.02	.15

Standard errors in parentheses
Levada survey, October 2015
[*] $p < 0.10$, [**] $p < 0.05$, [***] $p < 0.01$

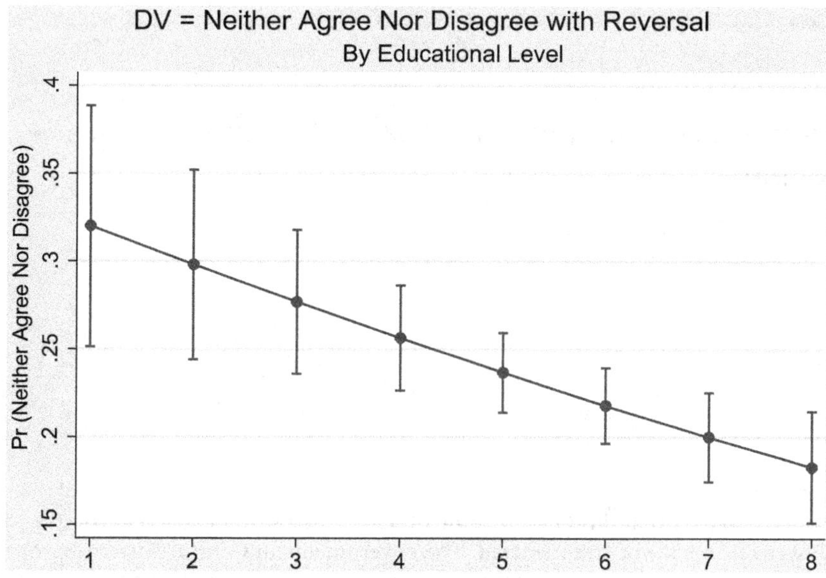

Marginal Effect of Educaiton on Reversal Opinion

7

Variation in Pension Policy Reversals: Hungary and Poland

There is a danger that this Orbánization of the pension system policies may spread all over Europe if not counteracted. The governments in Central Eastern Europe are under pressure to slow down fiscal consolidation or retreat to fiscal stimuli. The Hungary-Polish bad example risks giving more power and additional arguments to the populist voices in the region. This is why we have to stop the Polish government proposal now and defend the private pension savings of the people.
Marek Tatala and Fred Roeder, Editorial in *Forbes*, November 12, 2013

If a country like Poland cannot proceed with reforms, it makes you think whether it can be done at all.
Mamta Murthi, Country Director for Central Europe & the Baltics, World Bank, speaking about Poland's reversal of pension privatization in 2014

The reversal of pension privatization in Hungary and Poland reveals commonalities in why moderate reform makes backtracking more likely and why there is variation in the type and degree of reversal. The business community expressed concern that these reversals were a sign of a negative turn toward populist policies – in this case meaning measures contrary to the preferences of those in the finance industry – as evidenced in the *Forbes* quote above. These reversals, however, were not directly the product of popular demand and occurred even in a country like Poland, long characterized as a bastion of market-oriented reform. Rather, the Hungarian and Polish cases confirm that reversals were driven by the fiscal interests of politicians and the lack of resistance from domestic stakeholders. Although popular demand did not call for a reversal of pension privatization, in reversing pension privatization politicians were responding to popular pressure to spend in other areas and avoid tax increases.

The Hungarian and Polish experiences further reveal how and why there was variation in the type and degree of reversal due to unique domestic

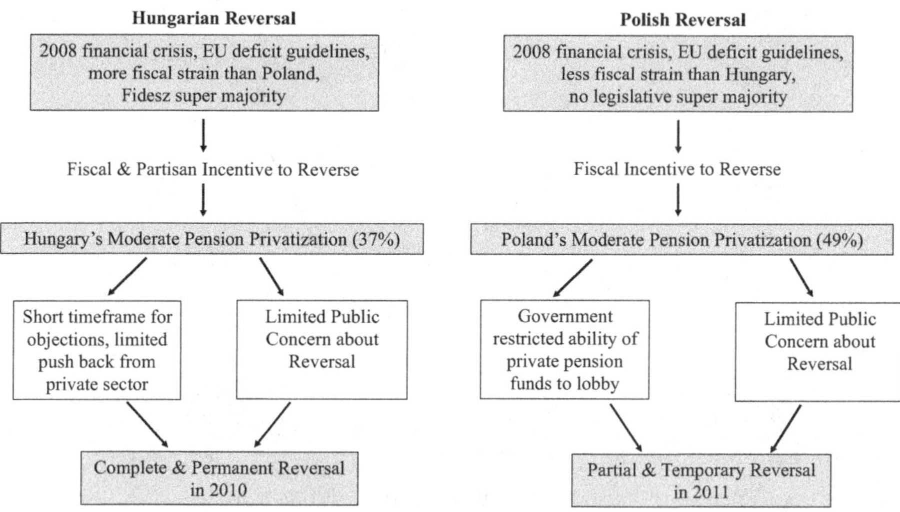

FIGURE 7.1 The Reversal of Pension Privatization in Hungary and Poland

circumstances. Figure 7.1 lays out the paths to different types of reversals in Hungary and Poland. The Hungarian government completely eliminated pension privatization with virtually no public or legislative debate in a single bill adopted in December 2010. The Polish government took a more cautious approach, pursuing a mix of temporary and permanent reductions in pension privatization.

Figures 7.2 and 7.3 depict the differences in the political climate and government deficits in Hungary and Poland from the time pension privatization

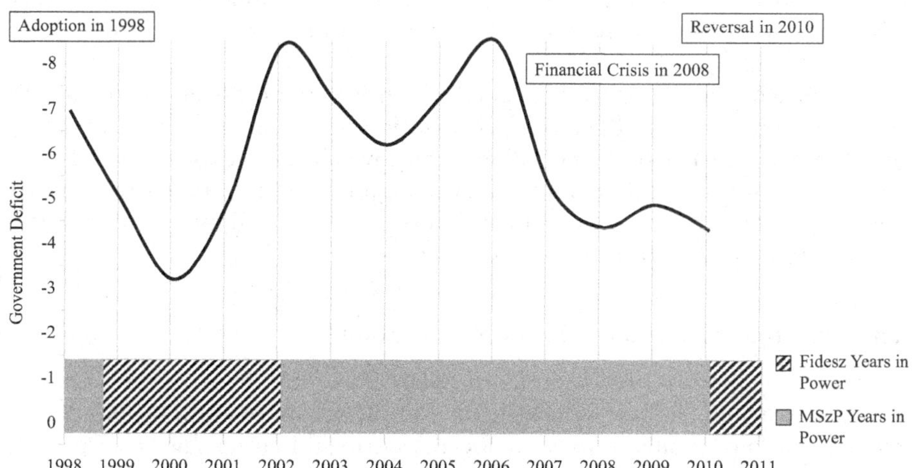

FIGURE 7.2 Timeline of Hungarian Pension Privatization and Its Reversal

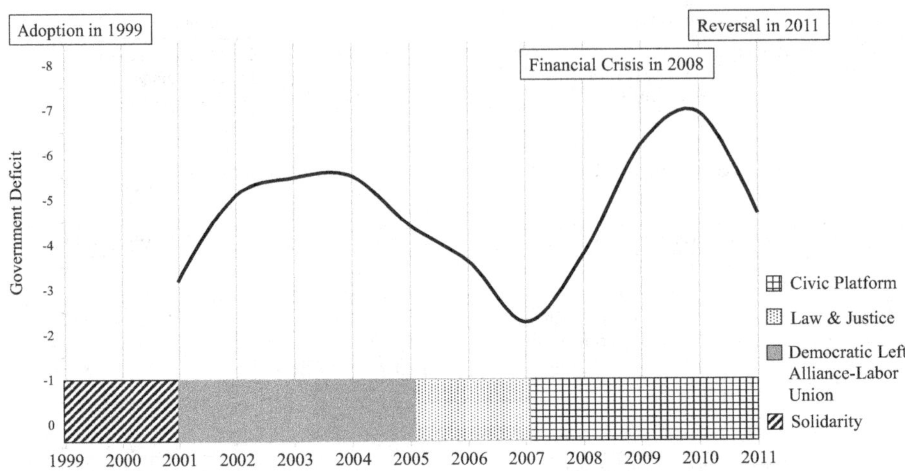

FIGURE 7.3 Timeline of Polish Pension Privatization and Its Reversal

was adopted until its reversal. The Hungarian approach reflected serious fiscal pressures to reverse and the super-majority obtained by the Fidesz party in 2010 whose campaign promises included lower taxes. The Polish approach reflected comparatively less fiscal pressure – Poland was the only EU country not to go into recession in the 2008 financial crisis – and a more competitive political arena in which the potential for a backlash from domestic stakeholders was greater. The Civic Platform won a legislative majority in 2007 and was re-elected with a legislative majority in 2011. The Polish reversal happened just after Civic Platform's re-election. The Polish case further bolsters the argument that reversals of pension privatization were not just about partisanship since Civic Platform did not consider backtracking during its first government from 2007 to 2011.

I begin with the Hungarian reversal which was the most dramatic and the only complete reversal of pension privatization in the region. I then juxtapose the Hungarian case with the Polish one which was staggered and partial. I compare both cases to the Russian experience highlighting the similarities regarding why moderate reforms were more likely to be reversed and the differences explaining why these three reversals varied.

The Hungarian Reversal of Pension Privatization

Hungary was the first post-communist country to adopt pension privatization, doing so in 1998, and it was also the first in the region to entirely abandon its radical, market-oriented reform of social security, initiating this latter process in 2010. Other reversals in the region have been temporary and partial. The Hungarian reversal followed on the heels of temporary and permanent backtracking on pension privatization in Estonia, Latvia, and Lithuania and the nationalization of ten private pension funds in Argentina in 2008. In contrast to the Baltic countries, however, the Hungarian government entirely scrapped its structural pension reforms adopted more than a decade earlier. Unlike Argentina, the Hungarian government initially marketed the reversal as voluntary – ostensibly giving citizens a choice – but permanently and completely backtracked in 2011 with additional legislation.

In some ways, Hungary was a less likely case for the reversal of pension privatization. Hungary was among the post-communist European countries that had effectively transformed itself from a communist-planned economy to a market-based one and had done so relatively quickly. Even in the late Communist era, the Hungarian government had pursued market-inspired reforms to promote the development of small businesses and open the economy that were atypical for the region at that time (Kornai 1991). The Hungarian government had been a leader in introducing other market-oriented reforms, including pension privatization. Hungary's early apparent success with transforming its pension system provided useful lessons for other countries in the region that subsequently adopted pension privatization measures. Unlike neighboring countries such as Russia, Hungary's financial sector in 1998 was also better prepared for the introduction of individual mandatory pension savings accounts.

In other ways, Hungary was a most likely case for reversal. Figure 7.2 depicts the alternations in power between the right-wing Fidesz Party and the left-wing MSzP (the Hungarian Socialist Party, which in Hungarian is the Magyar Socialist Party) which resulted in regular changes in economic and social policies. Hungary had also always had high deficits, which made it somewhat surprising that the government took on a policy like pension privatization that would result in higher deficits for decades after the new policy was implemented. As with *ex ante* expectations about the survival or failure of pension privatization in general (described in Chapter 2), there were reasons that we might have expected Hungarian pension privatization to succeed or fail, but none of these address why a country like Hungary abandoned pension privatization while others did not.

The Hungarian case demonstrates well why countries with a moderate degree of pension privatization were the most likely to reverse: a significant financing gap, combined with a lack of domestic stakeholders invested in the policies' survival, resulted in the failure of this radical, structural, pension overhaul to change the social contract in a meaningful, long-term way. Hungary also demonstrates why governments varied in how they pursued reversals. Because of domestic political and economic factors, the Fidesz government that came to power in 2010 did not need to be as concerned about a potential political backlash to reversal. The government did not need to gauge the public's reaction – in part because it had just won a landslide electoral victory – and did not worry about a reaction from private investors. As a result, Hungary was the first country in the region to wholly and abruptly eliminate its second tier with little public discussion and virtually no legislative debate.

Reversing and Revising the Hungarian Pension System in 2010

In September 2010, the Hungarian government announced its intention to allow citizens to switch back into the PAYG pension system. In December 2010, the reversal began, giving citizens only a few short weeks in which to make their decision by the end of January 2011 (Gál 2012). Citizens who kept making mandatory contributions to the private pension funds would forfeit any future benefits from the PAYG portion, even though they would have to continue contributing to the PAYG system. Ultimately, Hungarian courts ruled it unconstitutional to deny citizens their state pensions if they did not switch back, but the effect on getting citizens to switch back had already occurred.[1] This ensured that virtually all citizens (97 percent) switched back into the PAYG system.

In December 2011, the Hungarian government ensured that this reversal was complete by suspending all contributions to mandatory pension accounts. Initially the suspension was only for fourteen months, but it was then extended indefinitely.[2] If there was any doubt about the end of Hungarian pension privatization, the 2011 legislation confirmed that there was no going back. Over the course of just one short year, the Hungarian government had completely eliminated a radical, market-oriented, social policy that had substantially restructured the nature of the national pension system for the twelve years it was in effect.

This dramatic policy turnabout was effectively a one-step move by the government. The 2010 measures resulted in almost all of Hungary's citizens switching back. Only relatively minor follow-up legislation was required to put the final nail in the coffin of Hungarian pension privatization in 2011. This contrasts with Russia and Poland, where the governments have pursued multiple pieces of legislation curtailing the second tier. The Russian government passed two major pieces of legislation and began by partially backtracking before reconsidering saving the second tier in the spring of 2015. Likewise, the Polish government instituted temporary and partial cutbacks and subsequently considered more radical measures.

The Hungarian reversal is unique in that the government completely eliminated the second tier. The only other country to pursue a similarly dramatic reversal was Argentina in 2008. Most other reversals have been partial, and some remnant of the second tier has remained. The Hungarian government,

---

[1] Krystyna Kryzak, "Hungarian government vent to seize remaining private pension fund assets," *Investment & Pensions Europe*, November 27, 2014.

[2] Thomas Escritt, "Hungarian move essentially spells end of mandatory funded pension pillar," *Investment & Pensions Europe*, December 19, 2011.

however, was not interested in a phased-in reversal to gauge public or private reactions. In the Hungarian case, it is especially clear that the reversal was the product of politicians' motivation to gain access to short-term revenue.

The Hungarian government also did not make use of temporary measures before cutting pension privatization. The government could have chosen to suspend contributions to the mandatory funded portion of pensions, gauged the reaction, gained some short-term revenue, and then decided whether to pursue this path permanently. The Fidesz government elected in spring 2010 did not consider this path. The Hungarian government was following the lead of Argentina, whose dramatic reversal provoked relatively limited negative consequences, and the Baltic countries of Estonia, Latvia, and Lithuania, which pursued less radical means of backtracking in 2009 and 2010.

Why did the Hungarian government reverse pension privatization in 2010? And why did the Hungarian government choose to completely abandon pension privatization instead of reducing contributions to the second tier or temporarily suspending contributions to the second tier? The financial crisis beginning in 2008 further strained the Hungarian government's already challenging fiscal situation. Like many developed countries and the post-communist European countries in particular, Hungary has an aging population and an expensive PAYG pension system. The Hungarian government implemented a relatively moderate degree of pension privatization in 1998 as part of a political compromise, but this system meant that nearly a quarter of retirement contributions were being diverted away from covering payments in the PAYG system. The Fidesz government that came to power in the spring of 2010 saw an opportunity to backtrack as a means of gaining access to short-term revenue. Fidesz – the right-wing party that had alternated in power with the socialist MSzP party since the early 1990s – had run on a platform of promoting Hungary's national economic autonomy and addressing pressing issues like the government's rising debt and unemployment.

Pressure from neither the public nor the private sectors blocked Fidesz's move to eliminate the second privatized tier of the pension system. The privatized pension system initially enjoyed public support, but its reversal garnered very little attention and virtually no backlash. When pension privatization was initially introduced in Hungary, 50 percent of the workforce was required to sign up between 1998 and 2000. In later years, 25 percent of the workforce voluntarily joined the new privatized system. Firms working in the private pension sector had been influential allies of supporters of pension privatization when it was adopted (specifically firms backed members of the MSzP who were promoting pension privatization), but managers of private pensions funds had little role in discussions about reversals. Private pension funds only weakly mobilized to oppose the elimination of the second tier.

Because of the Hungarian government's growing deficit and the lack of domestic stakeholders in pension privatization, the Hungarian right-wing

Fidesz Party saw the opportunity to temporarily shore up finances in order to help meet its populist campaign promises and avoid raising taxes. The party had long opposed the partially privatized system introduced by the Socialist MSzP, but previously had confined itself to changes in the design of the system. Only in 2010 were there serious considerations about reversing the 1998 reforms.

The reason for the occurrence and nature of the Hungarian reversal is multifaceted: the ability to learn from the experiences of other countries, combined with the short-term fiscal benefits of doing so, and the European Union's unwillingness to be flexible on its deficit requirements, created a strong incentive to eliminate contributions to the second tier. The lack of strong domestic stakeholders in pension privatization meant there was no significant political obstacle to reversing pension privatization measures.

The Adoption of Hungarian Pension Privatization

Hungarian pension reforms were adopted by the left-wing former Socialist party as part of its package of market-oriented reforms. As in other countries, pension privatization was promoted as a means of bolstering retirement benefits in a financially sustainable way. Pension privatization was also supposed to give a boost to Hungary's financial sector and help attract investment, thereby boosting macroeconomic development.

The proponents of pension privatization included several different groups. A number of experts promoted the macroeconomic, fiscal, and social benefits of pension privatization and advocated for its adoption. Other experts believed that the necessary reforms of the PAYG portion were impossible unless citizens were distracted by the packaging of these parametric reforms alongside bigger structural changes (Müller 1999). As in other countries, the Ministry of Finance spearheaded the legislative proposal for pension privatization. Private pension funds were, of course, in favor of this structural overhaul from which they would profit.

Opponents of pension privatization included the bureaucratic apparatus in charge of the PAYG system, which would have less control under the privatized system. Several Hungarian economists were also vocal opponents of pension privatization. Some experts maintained that parametric reforms to the first tier would be sufficient to address problems of fiscal sustainability and adequate coverage and provided detailed analysis about the consequences of doing so (Augusztinovics and Martos 1996). The government never seriously considered confining the reforms to an overhaul of the PAYG system. Rocha and Vittas (2002) claim that the government did not consider more fundamental PAYG reforms because parametric reforms would be too easy to reverse, the government did not trust the state pension fund to operate well, PAYG reforms would not aid in the development of capital markets, and the private system was expected to gain higher returns.

There was very limited public debate about the pension reforms introduced in 1998. Unions and employers played some role in advising the government, but they did not significantly shape the legislation (Herman 2013). Although public discussions were limited, citizens had limited confidence in the existing PAYG system, making the introduction of an alternative more feasible (Müller 1999). This was consistent with the introduction of other market-oriented reforms in Hungary. The communist economic system was largely seen as having failed. Even in the late communist era, the Hungarian government instituted a number of reforms that were highly nontraditional for a communist country, including an income tax (Kornai 1992). Moreover, Hungary was a country in which the former Communist Party had been able to reinvent itself as a popular party with a legacy of instituting important reforms, even in the communist era (Grzymała-Busse 2002).

As in Russia, the private pension funds did play an important role in partnering with those in the government who favored the adoption of pension privatization. Private pension funds had invested voluntary retirement savings since 1993 and had the resources and organizational capacity to work well with policymakers and politicians. As in Russia, however, private pension funds were not the instigators of reform but rather the allies and partners of those in the government who wished to pursue pension privatization. Ultimately, Hungary's 1998 pension reform was a compromise that resulted in partial pension privatization alongside parametric reforms to the first, PAYG tier of pensions (Gál 2012). New entrants to the workforce were required to participate in the partially privatized system. Those already in the workforce were allowed to choose whether or not to enter the new, partially privatized system.

Hungary and Russia had very different political systems in the 1990s – and still do today – but we see similarities in the politics surrounding the structural overhauls of their pension systems. Politicians backed reforms with limited public input. The failures of the communist-era PAYG systems helped erode support for the status quo. Bureaucratic powers were the arena for debates over legislative proposals. Firms in the private pension sector served as important partners in promoting the reforms and pushing for their adoption. Significantly, Hungary and Russia both adopted relatively moderate degrees of pension privatization, which undermined the reform's long-term survival.

The Hungarian government paved the way for post-communist countries to adopt structural pension reforms in 1998. Kazakhstan – a country that is both politically and economically different from Hungary – also adopted pension privatization measures in 1998. The Polish government followed shortly thereafter, implementing pension privatization in 1999. Other countries looked to these early examples in making their own decisions about whether to pursue pension privatization. The early performance of the Hungarian and Polish reforms was especially influential on other countries, since these were two countries that had been leaders in market-oriented reforms.

Developments in Hungarian Politics between 1998 and 2010

Several important developments in Hungarian politics between the late 1990s and early 2000s played an important role in determining the fate of economic policies in general – and pension reform in particular. Three factors are of particular importance in this respect: Hungary's accession to the European Union; a shift in the political climate; and experiences with pension privatization.

European Union Membership

Hungary privatized pensions in 1998 and it attained EU membership six years later, in 2004. The European Union had neither required nor encouraged Hungary to adopt pension privatization as part of the accession process. Indeed, pension privatization goes much further as a radical, market-oriented social reform than policies adopted in almost any West European country (Appel and Orenstein 2013). In Western Europe, the only countries to adopt any kind of system in which mandatory retirement contributions are privately invested were Sweden and the United Kingdom. Influential EU member countries like Germany and France have never seriously considered pension privatization measures (Immergut et al. 2007). The lack of pension privatization in Western Europe also meant that individual countries in the region were not pushing for this particular policy.

The World Bank, not the European Union, provided logistical and technical support for instituting pension privatization as discussed above. Instead of backing structural pension reforms, the EU provided general guidelines, according to which governments were encouraged to adopt systems that were fiscally sustainable and provided adequate benefits. There were a variety of ways in which countries like Hungary could pursue these goals without adopting pension privatization. Parametric reforms to the PAYG portion of pensions could address these issues and were backed by some experts as a better alternative. Although the EU did not promote pension privatization, it also did not oppose it.

The biggest direct impact that EU guidelines had on pension privatization in Hungary was the organization's deficit requirement. The deficit requirements heightened the significance of the financing gap and the fiscal pressure created by pension privatization. The EU has held firm on the deficit guidelines, refusing to make adjustments for countries that privatized pensions more difficult for these countries to sustain.

Partisan and Constitutional Changes

There was a political shift to the far right in the 2000s. During the 1990s, Hungary had experienced regular alternations in power between the left-wing Socialist MSzP Party and the right-wing Fidesz Party. These alternations in power had been accompanied by regular shifts in pension policy. After the introduction of the partially privatized system by an MSzP government in 1998, the

Fidesz Party regularly altered the parameters of the second tier when it was in power.

Since the 2010 election, there has been a move to the right, which has included a consolidation of power by the Fidesz Party. Fidesz's partisan policy goals, in combination with the fiscal pressures faced by the government, resulted in a reversal of pension privatization. Here we can see that partisan policy goals played an important role in the effect of fiscal pressures. Since 2010, the party has consolidated its power in a number of ways, including controversial constitutional amendments that limit important democratic freedoms. Despite concern from the European Union and the international community, these constitutional measures passed and are still in effect. It is increasingly difficult for opposition parties, including the MSzP, to challenge the Fidesz Party.

Performance and Reactions to Hungarian Pension Privatization

Finally, an assessment of Hungary's pension reform emerged during this time period that served as a model for other countries and suggested that reversing pension privatization was not necessarily the logical next step. Only a year after implementation, a USAID report was published, entitled *Pension Reform in Hungary: Useful Experience for Ukraine* (USAID 1999). The report was based on a visit by 19 Ukrainian experts in May and June of 1999 with an eye toward pursuing a similar system in Ukraine. The Ukrainian delegation concluded that there were several important lessons to be gleaned from Hungary. Setting up a voluntary tier with private pension funds was advisable, as was instituting laws to ensure the legal protection of citizens' assets. The report also noted the importance of building a consensus of support for the reforms.

The Ukrainian government ultimately adopted pension reform in which the structural reforms were contingent on the completion of reforms to the PAYG portion which never happened. Pension privatization, as a result, never occurred in Ukraine. Nonetheless, the report's overall tone was positive and suggested that Hungary's system was expected to endure. The problems identified by the Ukrainian team were ones that were easily solved with additional adjustments to the system. The challenges Ukraine faced included developing a better record-keeping system with a centralized automated system, potentially high administrative fees, and regulations about transferring savings between funds. Critically, the report did mention the risk of a "great gap in the public finances" (p. 8) and noted that this could cause inflation and other problems. There was no concern noted, however, that the financing gap would undermine the reform's survival, nor was there a suggestion that countries should avoid pension privatization because of the financing gap.

Writing in the early 2000s, Rocha and Vittas (2002) concluded that the pension reform had largely been a success, despite challenges with its implementation. They write that

...[A]ny preliminary assessment of the Hungarian pension reform would be likely to conclude that the reform has been successful, especially considering the severe constraints imposed by initial conditions (e.g., large fiscal deficits, high contribution rates, high tax rates, very adverse demographic trends). The reform has reduced significantly the imbalances of the PAYG system and the implicit pension debt, while also introducing a mandatory, funded, and privately managed pillar that seems to be operating fairly well, despite the initial problems in the payment and registration system and some weaknesses in the regulatory framework. Moreover, the current shortcomings can be corrected during the next few years by the restoration of the original 8 percent contribution rate to the second pillar and the strengthening of the regulatory framework. (p.398)

This initial evaluation of the Hungarian system was positive and experts identified ways in which early problems could be corrected relatively easily. Specifically, recommendations included more transparency and better regulation, a standard prescription for countries that had privatized pensions. There was no mention of eliminating the second tier. Rather, Rocha and Vittas emphasize the system's popularity – evidenced by high rates of voluntary switching – and its initial successes. Backtracking on pension privatization was not an inevitable choice from the start and there were other obvious alternatives to bolster the system of which politicians and policymakers were well aware.

Recurring Financing Gap Created by Pension Privatization in Hungary

As in Russia and Poland, the degree of pension privatization played a central role in the political story about reversing pension privatization in Hungary. The timing of the reversal and its complete nature provide evidence that fiscal pressures were the primary motivation behind eliminating the second tier by creating a fiscal incentive for politicians to do so; the lack of domestic stakeholders and a legislative super-majority made a complete reversal politically feasible.

The fiscal pressures on the Hungarian government were determined by its increasingly costly PAYG system (which has remained only partially reformed), high government deficits, and a relatively moderate degree of pension privatization. Hungary's PAYG system was increasingly costly, particularly in light of its rapidly aging population. Hungary has one of the most rapidly aging populations in Europe, due to a combination of low birth rates and high emigration out of the country after the fall of communism.

In a 2008 World Bank report, Chawla et al. (2007) detail the region's demographic and social policy position. Hungary lost a significant portion of its population in the early 1990s and the country is projected to lose another 8 percent of its population between 2005 and 2025. Simultaneously, the percentage of the population over the age of 65 is projected to increase from 15 to 20 percent. The result is a shrinking portion of the working population whose contribution can cover the benefits of current retirees. Finally, spending on pensions is projected to increase from 10 to 15 percent from 2005 to 2025. Note that this projection was issued before the reversal in 2010; in other words, the Hungarian government was receiving a clear signal that the reforms adopted in 1998 were insufficient to address its still costly pension payments. The authors of the World Bank report did not suggest backtracking on the 1998 reforms, but rather instituting additional revisions of the PAYG system. Specifically, they recommended raising the retirement age and making the retirement age the same for men and women (which Hungary had already begun to do) and indexing pensions to consumer prices instead of wages to limit large increases in benefits.

Problems with Hungary's PAYG system – which were not restricted to its costs – led to suggestions that a critical component of pension reform involved parametric changes rather than structural ones (i.e., pension privatization). Other challenges with the PAYG system included providing a stronger and more transparent link between contributions and benefits and creating a more actuarially fair system in which men and women had the same (and higher) retirement ages.

Deficits are an important component of fiscal pressure. The Hungarian government ran high deficits throughout the period that pension privatization was in effect. At the time that the government chose to abandon the second tier of pensions (in 2010), the deficit had actually been improving for several years. Nonetheless, a 4 percent deficit was still quite high. Since 2009, Hungary's government debt has constituted more than 80 percent of GDP, despite recent moves to gain more revenue.[3] Hungarian deficits were not a new challenge. Kornai (1991) cites growing indebtedness as a challenge even in the late communist era. In the 1990s, Hungary retained its very high levels of debt while transitioning to the market.

In addition to deficits, an important component of the cost of switching from a PAYG system to one that is partially privatized is the extent of pension privatization. Hungary had adopted a relatively moderate degree of pension privatization, according to which 25 percent of contributions would go to mandatory individual accounts. According to Brooks' (2009) simulation, about 37 percent of one's future retirement benefits would be based on the individual contributions.

In promoting pension privatization, however, some claimed that the World Bank and other experts downplayed the transition costs of doing so by projecting unrealistically high investment returns (Simonovits 2009). As a result of this marketing, Hungarian workers were more aware of the benefits of pension privatization than the long-term fiscal consequences of doing so (Müller 1999). Fultz (2012) writes that

Thus, from the start, both new mixed pension systems [in Hungary and Poland] were dependent on future government actions – benefit cuts, increasing contributions or taxes, or borrowing – that were not widely understood by the populations. (p. 6)

---

[3] Deficit and debt data are from the World Development Indicators (2013).

The financing gap that would be generated by pension privatization was downplayed to help back the introduction of pension privatization, which, in turn, might become an entrenched policy as citizens planned their retirement based on their individual contributions, and private pension funds increasingly profited from the system.

Although concerns about the financing gap created by pension privatization were minimized by those advocating on behalf of pension privatization, politicians and policymakers were nonetheless very aware of the fiscal challenge of diverting current contributions away from covering current benefits. Despite the awareness of this fiscal challenge, the government did not incorporate the effect of pension privatization on deficits into government accounting until 2004 when Hungary joined the European Union (Simonovits 2011). Early estimates based on generational accounting showed that the 1998 reforms would improve the system's fiscal stability contingent on economic performance; specifically, productivity growth would indicate how much improvement was observed (Gál et al. 2001).

The annual shortfall in the public pension system for Hungary was estimated to be 1.4–2.2 percent of GDP for about forty-three years, which was the typical estimated cost of transitioning to pension privatization in the region (Fultz 2012; Orenstein 2013). Policymakers and experts were always keenly aware of the fiscal costs of switching from a PAYG to a partially privatized pension system. The Hungarian government did make some attempts to offset the financing gap caused by pension privatization by cutting future increases in cost-of-living adjustments, but a significant gap remained (Fultz 2012).

Reversing pension privatization was estimated to provide about $14.2 billion in revenue, which represents the value of private pension funds in Hungary's mandatory system.[4] Combined with other moves, including increased taxes on foreign companies, the government was actually generating more revenue than it needed in the short term, of which the private pension funds in the second tier were only a small portion. As a result, the Hungarian government's decision to backtrack appears especially short-sighted; reversal neither adds essential short-term revenue nor bolsters the country's long-term retirement system.

Political Incentives to Reverse Pension Privatization

The lack of attention to the financing gap would, however, ultimately undermine the long-term sustainability of the program. The financing gap did not result in a public backlash or discontent from the private sector which was generally profiting from pension privatization, albeit to a limited extent. Instead, the annually recurring financing gap created by pension privatization proved to be too tempting as a source of revenue for politicians to keep the policy in place, particularly in the context of financial crisis.

---

4 "Hungarian pensions: When solidarity is obligatory," *The Economist*, November 25, 2010.

Fidesz politicians had long opposed the partially privatized system introduced in 1998 and had sought to limit its scope and operations. Legislation introducing pension privatization was passed in late 1997 by a Socialist-led government. The Fidesz Party came to power after winning in parliamentary elections in the spring of 1998. The party had not campaigned on a platform of reversing the pension privatization measures, nor had pensions figured prominently in debates leading up to the election (Rocha and Vittas 2002). Nonetheless, upon taking power, party members began attacking the second tier. In particular, the new government suspended the increase in contributions to the second tier from 6 to 8 percent of wages.

Prior to the dramatic Hungarian reversal, however, Fidesz governments had never attempted to actually eliminate contributions to the second tier, even though the fiscal costs of doing so were identified early on as an important factor. The Fidesz Party replaced the MSzP-led government after elections in May 1998 and, along with its coalition partners, enjoyed an outright majority in the National Assembly. Rocha and Vittas (2002) note that in 1998, the Fidesz Party's desire to curb the recently adopted pension privatization may have been more related to the cost of reform rather than partisan bickering. The party did not campaign on reversing pension privatization, suggesting that this was not an electorally important issue. Because this fundamental structural pension reform had only just begun to be implemented a few months prior, the system was not at all entrenched in domestic stakeholders, and a reversal would have been relatively straightforward.

Instead of backtracking, however, the Fidesz Party chose to leave the 1997 legislation in place and modify the extent of reform. Contributions to the second tier were initially planned to increase from 6 to 8 percent, and the party pushed through legislation to keep the lower level of contributions. The new Fidesz government also changed the wage indexation formula, reducing the increase in nominal pensions from 18 to 14 percent. Although Fidesz politicians had publicly opposed pension privatization when it was introduced by the Socialists, their actions upon taking office suggest that there was not necessarily a fundamental ideological disagreement with the reform. The fiscal implications, not partisan ideology, drove the party's decision to limit the scope of structural and parametric reforms.

In 2002, a coalition of the MSzP and the Alliance of Free Democrats won 203 seats in the National Assembly, which gave them a majority, but only just slightly edged out the Fidesz–Hungarian Democratic Forum alliance, which had achieved 182 seats (out of 386 members total). This shift back to a Socialist-led government ensured that pension privatization would survive, at least for a time.

The 2006 elections once again brought a Socialist government into power. The 2006 campaign set the stage for the subsequent election in which the Socialists would suffer a major defeat. As was typical in the post-communist era, both the Fidesz and MSzP Parties campaigned with promises to increase spending on pensions.[5] The MSzP had a particularly credible claim in this regard; since 2002 government social spending had increased, and taxes had declined.

The Socialists won in 2006 but with a much narrower margin than in previous elections. A major scandal emerged after the election, which nearly overturned the recently elected government. The MSzP Prime Minister, Ferenc Gyurcsany, had reassured Hungarian voters that the government deficit was under control and improving at about 6 percent of GDP. Shortly after the election, however, the Central Bank released information that the actual deficit was closer to 10 percent of GDP.[6] The difference in estimates was partially because the Prime Minister was not taking into account pension privatization's effect on government financing. After revealing tapes were released, Gyurcsany was forced to admit that he had in fact lied to win the election. Massive protests ensued that constituted what some characterized as the worst anti-government violence since before the fall of communism.[7] The Hungarian PM, however, refused to resign. In part because the Socialists stayed in power, there was no threat to pension privatization at that time.

The Socialists' electoral success ended dramatically, but not unexpectedly, with the 2010 elections four years later. Parliamentary elections in 2010 brought the Fidesz Party back to power with a super majority. Hungarian citizens were particularly unhappy about the consequences of the 2008 financial crisis, which was continuing to drive high unemployment rates. The corruption scandal in the Socialist party – including the 2006 leaked video in which the MSzP prime minister admitted that his party had lied about the economy to win the election – further cemented Fidesz's victory.[8] The 2010 election was also notable for the electoral success of the far-right Jobbik Party, whose campaign platform included nationalist and anti-Jewish sentiments. The Jobbik Party won 17 percent of the vote, the largest success for a far-right party in Hungary in the post-communist period.[9]

The election of a Fidesz government with a super-majority allowed a number of controversial constitutional changes to be adopted (Rupnik 2012). Reversing pension privatization was not part of the 2010 Fidesz campaign platform indicating that this was not an issue which garnered a great deal of public political attention. Instead, the Fidesz Party campaigned on a wide array of populist promises including limiting payroll contributions. This echoed previous campaigns by Fidesz. In 1998, for instance, Fidesz ran promising to reduce pension

---

[5] Judy Dempsey, "Promises, promises, in Hungary Economists alarmed as parties woo voters," *International Herald Tribune*, April 19, 2006.

[6] Judy Dempsey, "Riots Fail to Force Hungarian Leader from Office," *International Herald Tribune*, September 20, 2006.

[7] Ibid.

[8] Judy Dempsey, "Hungary's Leader, Under Siege Over Lies, Refuses to Resign," *New York Times*, September 20, 2006.

[9] Dan Bilekfsy, "Hungarian Rightists, Both Center and Far Right, Advance," *New York Times*, April 12, 2010.

and health contributions despite previously promised increases in contributions (Simonovits 2000). Reversing pension privatization was not brought up until after elections in 2010. The timing of the reversal *after* Fidesz's election in spring 2010 suggests that politicians wanted to avoid a potential backlash to the fundamental changes being made to the pension system and to use these measures to fulfill other high-profile campaign promises. Just after the 2010 election, the government was also denied by the European Union for an adjustment in its budget guidelines. The EU Commissioner for Economic and Monetary Affairs, Olli Rehn, announced that the request for an adjustment to how the EU calculates deficits – and specifically a change that would take into consideration whether a country had privatized pensions – would be justified, but was simply not an option in the EU's current accounting system.[10] As a result, all of the EU member countries that had adopted pension privatization would have to meet the same deficit guidelines as those who had not.

The Hungarian government likely would have targeted pension privatization even without the burden of the EU's deficit guidelines, but this added pressure strengthened the impetus to do so. EU influence in this regard is discussed in greater depth below, but we should not overstate EU influence. For one thing, the Hungarian government had an incentive to emphasize (if not exaggerate) the burden of EU deficit guidelines in order to secure more favorable guidelines.

Because of Hungary's larger fiscal situation and the EU's refusal to change deficit calculations, the annually recurring financing gap being generated by keeping pension privatization in place starkly interfered with campaign promises made by the Fidesz Party. In particular, the party wanted to dramatically cut taxes in certain areas and promised to reduce unemployment as a response to the ongoing financial crisis. Although backtracking on pension privatization did not solve all of Hungary's fiscal problems in long term, it did provide temporary relief. It was estimated that the private pension accounts that were nationalized were worth \$14.2 billion (10 percent of GDP).[11] Combined with other measures, the funds from reversing pension privatization helped the Fidesz Party to fulfill its short-term campaign promises.

There are several reasons that a Fidesz-led government would choose to target pension privatization instead of using other means to fulfill its campaign promises. First, the amount of money being lost to general government revenue, or at least toward covering current pension payments, was easily identifiable and quantifiable. Cutting spending in other areas might be less obvious, and it may not be clear how much money the government would save by doing so. Second, reversing pension privatization was relatively easy from a logistical and administrative perspective. All that was required was diverting

---

[10] Zoltan Simon and Minka Rozlal, "EU Says Pension Accounting Change Sought by Poland, Hungary Not Possible," *Bloomberg News*, October 22, 2010.

[11] Margit Feher, "Hungary Forces Private Pension Fund Members Back to State Scheme," *Wall Street* Journal, November 24, 2010.

existing mandatory contributions away from individual accounts and back into the PAYG system. If citizens were generally apathetic or uninformed about the pension system, then reversal was even easier politically.

The Hungarian case helps explain why a right-wing party would want to abandon a policy traditionally labeled as a radical, market-oriented reform. Pension privatization was a reform whose costs would require higher deficits, higher taxes, or both. Although the Fidesz Party may not have truly been ideologically opposed to pension privatization, the cost meant that it was. That a right-wing party backed the elimination of a market-oriented reform is less surprising in the Hungarian context. The MSzP was a formerly communist party that reinvented itself by promoting market-oriented reforms and under which a number of market-oriented reforms had been introduced. The Fidesz Party also backed market-oriented reforms in different ways, but the alternations in power in the 1990s meant that policies were often modified.

Finally, one of the biggest reasons to target pension privatization over other ways to avoid an increase in taxes was that pension privatization was costly *and* there were no domestic stakeholders who would block its reversal. Unless Fidesz supporters (or potential supporters) or influential lobbyists would object to abandoning the second tier of pensions, there was little reason to maintain it.

In late November 2010, the Hungarian Minister of the Economy, Gyorgy Matolcsy, announced the reversal of pension privatization. The government framed the move as a choice citizens would have to make. Citizens could choose to stay in the privatized pension system or to go back to the PAYG system. If a citizen chose to stay in the privatized system, he or she would forfeit any future benefit from the PAYG portion of pensions. Citizens had only until the end of January 2011 to decide. The default option was to be switched back to the PAYG system. The choice was so heavily weighted in favor of switching back to the PAYG system that very few people remained in the privatized system.

In an interview in January 2011, Orbán defended the reversal of pension privatization as a means of fulfilling his party's campaign promise to protect pensions. Orbán explained the decision by saying

We made it clear in the election campaign and in the government programme that we would guarantee the value of pensions. This was the necessary step: this is the way we managed to save the pension system, which was on the brink of collapse. After an irresponsible experiment that has led to failure, Hungary is now returning to the family of West-European pension systems of state pension and voluntary pension funds. Under the pressure of the World Bank and the international money world, an unviable system had to be introduced and tested in Eastern Europe, which reached the so-called voluntary status through state coercion. This has now been ended…most people will gain. Those people who have lost their money owing to speculation with pensions in the stock exchange will now, when they switch back, receive the sum that someone had gambled away, because we look upon them as if they had not left the state system at all. Those who have been able to record a profit in recent years will, by returning, be able to take out their profit by 31 January without having to pay tax on it or will be able to credit it to their account.[12]

Orbán's statement is revealing in terms of both its tone and content. It is clear from his public announcement that the Fidesz Party had to defend its lack of mention of reversing pension privatization in the campaign. Indeed, there had not previously been any suggestion that the second tier should be eliminated, nor did the previous pension reform initiatives by the party suggest they would take this route. Orbán's statement further suggests that pension privatization was adopted under pressure from the international community, was never well suited in Hungary, and was inconsistent with West European systems that combined a PAYG portion with voluntary private savings. Finally, Orbán claims that most citizens would be better off with the reversal, suggesting that citizens had lost money because it was gambled away. In fact, other experts maintained that the poor returns were due in large part to high administrative fees combined with the recent financial crisis (Simonovits 2011). Orbán's explanation nonetheless reflects a politically savvy framing of a radical policy turnabout and was part of his larger economic strategy to promote what he referred to as Hungary's economic national autonomy.

Unsuccessful Opposition from the Private Pension Sector

Hungary's private pension sector enjoyed significant growth following the introduction of reforms in 1998. Hungary introduced a three-tier private pension system in 1998. By 2001, the assets of private pension funds in Hungary constituted 3.9 percent of GDP, reaching a high of 10.9 percent of GDP in 2007 (about $6.8 billion). Contributions to private pension funds in Hungary were 1.4 percent of GDP by 2008, which was about 0.9 billion dollars.[13] By 2010, the assets had increased substantially, to a worth of $14.2 billion.[14] These assets include voluntary retirement savings and represented a sector that was highly developed.

Private pension funds also represented a sector of firms that were potentially influential on the economy and the political system. The government had adopted pension privatization, at least in part, to promote domestic savings and had been successful in doing so. As a result, private pension funds were increasingly a group that mattered for the economy. The logic of firms' structural impact on the government suggests that even if the firms did not engage in explicit lobbying, the government would take heed of their preferences. A

---

[12] "Hungarian premier defends media law, pension changes, plans for new constitution," interview with Prime Minister Viktor Orbán by Peter Csermely, *Magyar Nemzet*, December 24, 2010.

[13] Data on the development of private pension funds is available from the OECD for Hungary, the Czech Republic, and Slovakia from 2001 to 2008. The figures in dollars given here are calculated using constant 2000 US dollars.

[14] Margit Feher, "Hungary Forces Private Pension Fund Members Back to State Scheme," *Wall Street Journal*, November 24, 2010.

classic version of this argument is the exit, voice, and loyalty game (Hirschman 1970) in which the mere threat of a firm's exit is sufficient to induce politicians to adopt favorable policies. Because of a fear of a decline in private pension savings or a loss of domestic capital, as the holdings of Hungarian private pension firms grew, politicians might be inclined to adopt policies beneficial to these firms that were becoming increasingly important for the Hungarian economy.

Firms working in the private pension sector did object to the reversal measures, but barely had a chance to mobilize before the measures were adopted by the Hungarian government. The first rumors about reversal emerged in Spring 2010 only months before the second tier was effectively eliminated at the end of the year. The reaction from firms in the private sector, both domestically and internationally, was negative but had no impact on the government's decision. Commentary from *The Economist* quipped, "Would you like to make a gift of your savings to the state in exchange for unspecified future benefits from a future government?"[15] An economist at ING in Budapest was quoted as saying, "This is effectively a nationalization of private pension funds. It's the nightmare scenario."[16]

Objections from the private pension sector had little influence on the government. The adoption of pension privatization in Hungary involved some consultation with employers and unions, but even this consultation was absent for the 2010 reversal. In part, the private pension sector in Hungary had relatively little time to organize, since the government's plans were announced in September 2010, and legislation was passed in December 2010.

The Hungarian Association of Pension Funds, *Stabilitás*, was founded in May of 2000.[17] *Stabilitás* attempted to fight the government's plan to reverse pension privatization in the fall of 2010. The organization did not rely on swaying public opinion in favor of keeping the privatized system in place. The association of private pension funds' decision not to focus on the public suggests that even those working in the industry did not think the privatized pension system had sufficient support among the public for its abandonment to provoke any significant backlash. *Stabilitás* relied primarily on making legal challenges to the law rather than courting public support. The association turned to the EU and requested an investigation of the planned reversal, arguing that it would violate citizens' constitutional rights.[18] *Stabilitás* also turned to the Hungarian Constitutional Court to challenge the laws. The president of *Stabilitás* resigned

---

[15] "Hungarian Pensions: When Solidarity is Obligatory," *The Economist*, November 25, 2010.

[16] Thomas Escritt, "Nightmare in Hungary as government nationalizes pension funds," *Investment & Pensions Europe*, November 26, 2010.

[17] *Stabilitás* provides a detailed history of its founding and main activities including its opposition to the reversal in 2010 at http://www.penztar-szovetseg.hu/#!penztarszovetseg/c23bq (accessed August 8, 2015). The organization was renamed the National Federation of Voluntary Pension Funds in 2015 after the mandatory privatized pension system had been eliminated and currently represents 93% of voluntary pension funds and 75% of national health insurance companies.

[18] Neil Buckley, "Hungary's Troubling Pension Reforms," *Financial Times*, November 26, 2010.

at the beginning of 2012 when it became clear that the private sector was not going to win any concessions from the government. A European pension fund lobbying group called Pension Europe condemned what it labeled the nationalization of pension funds, but has had little impact on actual legislation.[19]

Although the Hungarian government did not worry about learning about the private sector's reaction to reversal by initially using temporary or partial reversal measures, Fidesz politicians did seek to discredit the private pension funds after the fact. In early 2012, after the final death knell to pension privatization had sounded, the government accused the private pension funds of wrongdoing under the previous system and made allegations that the funds had gambled with the investment of retirement savings. An official investigation, led by a so-called "pension protection commissioner," Gabriella Selmeczi, announced that the funds did not earn an adequate profit in the mandatory system.[20]

In Russia, private pension fund managers engaged in a massive public campaign to encourage citizens to switch into the privatized system before the deadline to do so passed. We do not observe any similar campaign in Hungary. The design of the reversal in Hungary was so skewed toward pushing citizens to go with the default option of being transferred back to the PAYG system that such a campaign would have likely been very unsuccessful. The Hungarian pension funds also faced a much shorter deadline of only a couple of months, compared to a multi-year period in Russia.

Public Opinion about Reversing Pension Privatization in Hungary

Despite the strong reaction – on paper at least – from private pension fund managers and market advocates, there was little public reaction to the reversal. The lack of public reaction was surprising in part because of Hungary's success with market-oriented reforms. Hungary is a very market-oriented country, having undergone a significant economic transformation in the 1990s and as one of the countries to join the European Union in the first wave of expansion to the post-communist countries in 2003. Nonetheless, the Hungarian public appeared to be largely indifferent to the continuation of pension privatization.

Survey evidence conducted at the time showed contradictory results with some news outlets claiming that the majority of the public agreed with the reversal and others claiming the public was overwhelmingly opposed. One poll found that the overwhelming majority of citizens did in fact agree with the reversal, while another found that 55 percent did not agree and only 13 percent fully agreed; the same poll, however, also found that the level of

---

[19] Michael Glenister, "Pension funds not a source of short term capital, says lobby," *myInvestorCircle*, June 14, 2103.

[20] Thomas Escritt, "Hungarian government accuses pension funds of fraudulent practices," *Investment & Pension Europe*, January 9, 2012.

knowledge about the performance of private pension funds was quite low.[21] Another survey found that the majority of citizens did not trust the privatized portion. According to this survey, 38 percent said the private pension funds handled money poorly and only 24 percent said that they were satisfied with how private pension funds handled money; a whopping 38 percent, however, reported having no opinion about how much of their contribution was sent to the pension insurance system instead of the privatized portion.[22] Yet another survey found that 30 percent of respondents did not support returning to the state pension system and 24 percent were reluctant to go back with only a mere 7 percent saying they would definitely go back.[23]

The disagreement about Hungarian public opinion on pension privatization appears to have been both an issue of partisan framing and question wording suggesting that the public was, at the very least, not strongly opposed to the reversal of pension privatization. The MSzP attempted to get a national referendum on the issue shortly before the Parliament voted, but failed to get the 200,000 signatures necessary.[24] Whatever public opinion was, the Fidesz party did not seem especially concerned about a public backlash. No public protests or outcry followed the reversal in December 2010.

Seventy-five percent of Hungarian workers were in the privatized system at the beginning of 2010 before any reversal was made (Simonovits 2011). Fifty percent of workers had been required to participate in the second tier when the system was introduced in 1998, and another 25 percent later joined voluntarily. With such a high percentage of participation, a significant proportion of which was voluntary, we might think that citizens would be more supportive of the continuation of the system. There were, however, several notable problems with the implementation of pension privatization in Hungary. One major issue was the lack of returns to private pension funds. Taking into account administrative fees, Simonovits (2011) estimates that the average real interest rate was 0 percent from 1998 to 2004, meaning that citizens were not making any profit on their investments. Administrative fees were eventually restricted to 4.5 percent of contributions and 0.8 percent of assets under management, but not until 2008 (only three years prior to the reversal).

Because of problems with low returns and high administrative costs, Hungarian citizens had good reasons not to be too invested in the continuation of the privatized pension system. Some economists estimated that almost all citizens would be better off in the first tier, the PAYG portion of pensions.

Discussions about reversals in Hungary and other post-communist European countries coincided with decisions about how to design the system's payout phases. The first cohorts of those in the privatized system were just beginning to retire and claim benefits from the private tier. A number of challenges existed

---

[21] 168 Óra Online, "Nyugdíjkáosz: ha kiderül az igazság, majd lesz üvöltés," October 25, 2010.
[22] Ibid.   [23] Ibid.
[24] BELFÖLD, "Nyugdíj-ügyben a Fidesz szembemegy a közhangulattal," October 25, 2015.

with the payout phase, which had been inadequately designed in many countries. None of the countries, for example, had set out an integrated threshold replacement rate, which would guarantee a basic level of support for all pensioners upon retirement (Vittas et al. 2010). Other challenges included determining the default option and what alternatives citizens would have.

Vittas et al. (2010) detail the problems with the design of Hungary's payout system. In Hungary, citizens have the right to choose between a lump-sum payment and four types of annuities upon retirement. Annuity payments are based on a Swiss-style indexation formula that relies on an average of price and wage inflation. Critics, however, argued that this did not enable providers to insulate themselves from risk. The parliament passed a proposal in 2009 to redesign payout regulation. The President at the time, Laszlo Solyom, refused to sign the bill and referred the matter to the Constitutional Court, and to date, no legislation on this has been adopted. The proposal called for further restricting payout options, notably eliminating the ability to take a lump sum payment and offering only two annuity options. Public debate about payout options did not ensue, and given Hungary's elimination of its second tier shortly thereafter, the payout specifications are now a moot point. If the discussion about payouts had any effect, it was likely negative in portraying the system as overly complicated and restrictive.

Public protests did not emerge until 2011, when citizens objected to an increase in the retirement age for workers in special categories, including those in security services such as police, firefighters, and soldiers.[25] Protests in the summer of 2011 were referred to as the "Clown Revolution" because Prime Minister Orbán had promised to send a "clown affairs secretary" to negotiate with protesters who had started demonstrating in April 2011. Hungarian citizens showed little concern about the elimination of the second tier of pensions, but they were willing to protest changes in existing benefits in the PAYG tier. This bolsters the claim of some experts, cited earlier in this chapter, that the structural changes introduced in 1998 may have actually been easier to pursue than parametric changes to the PAYG portion of pensions.

The Hungarian Reversal in Regional Context

Elections in April 2010 brought Prime Minister Viktor Orbán to power and saw the rise of the far-right nationalist party, Jobbik, which secured 17 percent of seats, an unprecedented success for an extremist party that had existed since 2002 but had been operating on the fringes. Orbán ushered in a new direction for economic policy in part as a reaction to the financial crisis of recent years. Orbán backed several high-profile and controversial moves as part of what some have dubbed "financial nationalism." In particular, the Hungarian parliament signed measures that decreased Central Bank independence, increased taxes on financial institutions, promoted converting foreign currency loans, and

---

[25] "Hungarians stage 'clown' rally against benefit cuts," BBC, June 16, 2011.

postponed adopting the euro (Barnes and Johnson 2015). This was interpreted by outsiders as a move by Orbán away from Europe and a means of securing Hungary's autonomy.

Speculations about a Hungarian reversal of pension privatization began in the Spring of 2010, but no public discussion or political debates ensued, despite the upcoming elections in the summer of 2010. Discussions about reversal only began in the weeks after the election, when a Fidesz-led government came to power (Simonovits 2011). The first and primary legislation eliminating the second tier of Hungary's pension system was passed in December 2010. Initially, citizens had a choice to stay in the privatized system, although there were strong tax incentives to switch back to the PAYG system. Opting into the privatized system also required one to forfeit any benefits from the PAYG portion.

The Hungarian government subsequently passed legislation that required citizens to switch back into the PAYG system, although at that point the vast majority of citizens had already done so. The Hungarian reversal was primarily a one-time elimination of contributions to the second tier of pensions.

The dramatic shift in Hungary's economic policy initiated by Orbán in 2010 did not indicate that his government was not concerned with Hungary's place in the global economy. Rather, Orbán sought to protect Hungarian autonomy and to resist the influence of international organizations, but only up to a point, specifically up to the point that he could refuse international assistance. For instance, when negotiations with the IMF for a standby loan were unsuccessful in July 2010, the government initially announced that IMF support was unnecessary. Over the next year, however, there was a fall in the value of the Hungarian currency, the forint, and the rating of Hungarian bonds was lowered to so-called "junk" status. Ultimately, the government reinitiated talks with the IMF in November 2011 (Barnes and Johnson 2015). Orbán's strategy reveals that the Hungarian government did indeed care about the reaction of international organizations and, to a much lesser extent, foreign investors. This concern with securing aid from international organizations was unsurprising: Hungary had been the first EU country to accept an emergency bailout from the IMF in 2008 (Barnes and Johnson 2015). Despite nationalist rhetoric, the Hungarian government had to concern itself with approval from international organizations.

The Hungarian government was able draw on the experience of several other countries to learn about the consequences of reversing pension privatization. Hungary's reversal followed the dramatic renationalization of private pension funds in Argentina. Given that the Argentinean government recovered quickly, the Hungarian government could be reasonably assured that its market could withstand this dramatic shift in policy.

Hungary's reversal also followed temporary reversals that had been legislated in Estonia, Latvia, Lithuania, and Romania, which likely reassured the government that reversing pension privatization was a feasible policy option. Like Hungary, the Baltic countries are EU members and face the same deficit guidelines as Hungary. The Baltic reversals were especially informative in several respects.

Argentina's experience with reversing pension privatization had important lessons for Hungary, as the countries shared important similarities. Argentina and Hungary had both struggled with high levels of government debt. The Argentinean government had defaulted previously. Both countries also pursued a moderate degree of pension privatization. Argentina differed from other Latin American countries in that Argentina pursued a more limited degree of pension privatization. Chile, El Salvador, the Dominican Republic, Bolivia, Peru, and Colombia were among the countries with the most extensive levels of pension privatization.

Estonia, Latvia, and Lithuania had pursued temporary and partial reversals that were very different from the radical turnabout pursued in Hungary. In fact, the Hungarian government received negative signals from investors in reaction to its economic policies in 2010. The forint devalued against the euro, and sales of treasury bills declined.[26] It is difficult to determine whether investors were reacting to the entire slate of policies being accused of being anti-business or the reversal of pension privatization in particular. Nonetheless, Hungarian politicians had reasons to consider a more moderate version of reversing as a trial run, although they did not.

In the Hungarian case, unlike Russia, we see that the European Union's deficit guidelines played an important role as discussed above. The Hungarian government – along with Poland and the other post-communist EU member countries that privatized pensions – had specifically requested that the EU adjust its deficit guidelines to take into account the financing gap created by pension reform (Casey 2012). When the EU rejected this request, there was additional pressure to backtrack on pension privatization.

It has been speculated that the EU's deficit guidelines are one of the reasons that reversals of pension privatization were concentrated in post-communist Europe rather than Latin America. How significant was the influence of the European Union, and how can we know that EU guidelines were not the main reason that the Hungarian government chose to eliminate its second tier? It is important to note that the European Commission – the executive branch of the EU – opposed Hungary's move to abandon the second tier. A representative for the head economist at the European Commission, Amadeu Altafaj Tardio warned of the dangers of reversing pension privatization:

In Hungary, they seem to reflect the intention to completely abolish the compulsory private pension pillar. Although pension systems are a competence of member states, we have a number of particular concerns. One important issue is long-term sustainability. In this respect, we would be concerned if the wealth accumulated in pension funds were to finance current expenditures, as seems to be the underlying assumption of the draft budget for 2011. Another concern is the way this reversal is carried out. In particular,

---

[26] Neil Buckley, "Hungary's Troubling Pension Reforms," *Financial Times*, November 26, 2010.

it seems that the choice between staying in the second pillar and returning to the first is not as free as it originally appeared, as (1) beneficiaries will be automatically transferred back to the state pillar unless they declare otherwise by the end of January, and (2) those who stay in the second pillar would lose entitlement to a state pension, although employers' contributions will continue to be paid to the budget. Private pension funds also play a useful role in deepening domestic financial markets, which they would no longer be able to fulfill if their viability were undermined.[27]

As the OECD statement reveals, the international community was generally unenthusiastic about these moves by the Hungarian government. Representatives of other international organizations also warned about the dangers of reversal. The head economist at the OECD, Pier Carlo Padoan, expressed similar concerns about the long-term fiscal implications of reversing.[28]

There are several other reasons to think that the EU's deficit guidelines alone are an insufficient explanation for the Hungarian reversal. First, the Hungarian government began the EU accession process in 1994, ten years before it attained membership. Pension privatization was adopted in 1998. If anything, the EU accession process should have exerted a greater influence on the government to keep deficits within the recommended guidelines in order to ensure that Hungary would be allowed to join. Once Hungary became an EU member in 2004, the pressure to conform should have been much less. Removing a country from the EU for a violation of EU policy would be extremely difficult, would likely require a series of major infractions, and has, in fact, never been done.[29] Although Hungary might incur sanctions and other sticks and carrots to encourage compliance, the consequences were less than not being admitted to the EU at all. Second, not all EU countries that privatized pensions also reversed. Croatia, Macedonia, Denmark, and the Netherlands are EU members and have not, to date, cut back on contributions to the second tier of pensions. The Croatian government also happens to have pursued much less extensive pension privatization and have a lower recurring financing gap which is consistent with my theoretical expectations that countries with limited pension privatization are less likely to reverse.

Despite objections to Hungary's economic and political shift under Orbán in 2010, the country retained relatively good relations with the EU under the circumstances. The ascent to power in 2010 of Orbán and the Fidesz Party coincided with Hungary taking on the rotating presidency of the EU for one year. The host country enjoys some agenda-setting powers, although these powers

---

[27] "Hungary, Bulgaria Challenge Rehn on Pensions," *EurActiv*, December 6, 2010.

[28] Thomas Escritt, "Hungarian Parliament OKs Take-over of Second-pillar Pensions," *Investment & Pensions Europe*, December 19, 2010.

[29] At the time of writing, the United Kingdom is the first country to appear to be leaving the EU after the "Brexit" referendum vote in 2016. In the case of the United Kingdom, this decision was, of course, initiated domestically and not an instance of the EU is forcing out a country.

have been more limited since the adoption of the Lisbon Treaty in the early 1990s. Hungary's leadership was hailed by some as a moderate success, with achievements including the conclusion of Croatian accession talks, an agreement on economic governance, and an EU-wide strategy for addressing social problems among the Roma population.[30]

The World Bank played only a limited role in discussions about reversing pension privatization in Hungary, and there is no evidence that Hungarian politicians were overly concerned about the World Bank's position. Hungarian officials did make some attempt to defend their move as being consistent with World Bank recommendations. One Hungarian newspaper ran the headline: "The pension scheme is unsustainable – World Bank analysts urge reform to be reformed."[31] Contrary to what the headline suggests, the specific World Bank recommendations cited in the same article did not include the elimination of the second tier of pensions. Instead, World Bank recommendations included a better system for election contributions in order to lower administrative fees.

Adverse Economic Consequences of the Hungarian Reversal

One reason for governments to begin reversing pension privatization with temporary and partial measures is to gauge the reaction of investors and the public to any such measures. The Hungarian government did not do this. Hungary's reversal did have negative market consequences, although it is difficult to distinguish the effect of nationalizing pension funds from the other dramatic economic measures taken by the Orbán government in 2010. In November 2011, Hungary was downgraded by Moody's, Standard & Poor's, and other investment ranking agencies to so-called "junk status" after a year of what many considered unorthodox economic policies pursued by the Orbán government. The report specifically cited the adoption of a special bank tax and the nationalization of private pension funds in the second tier. Other economic indicators were also troubling. The value of Hungarian bonds and the forint declined, the stock market spread widened, and unemployment remained high.[32]

The private sector expressed concern about investing in Hungary. The secretary general of the Association of Hungarian Mortgage Banks noted the adverse effects of reversal, announcing that "The pension and insurance funds are the investors most likely to buy covered bonds and due to the nationalization this investor base is now smaller than it was."[33] More generally, investors were typically leery. In December 2011, Hungary's five-year spread for government bonds increased dramatically to its highest ever level – at 800 basis

---

[30] "Hungary's European Union Presidency: Back to Partisanship," *Economist*, July 7, 2011.

[31] Szilvia Hamori, "The pension scheme is unsustainable – World Bank analysts urge reform to be reformed," *Nepszabadsag*, June 2, 2006 (translated by BBC Worldwide Monitoring).

[32] "Moody's cuts Hungary to 'junk'," Financial Mirror, November 25, 2011.

[33] "Bankers wary of Hungary covered bonds plan," *EuroWeek*, March 23, 2012.

points – indicating that investors were predicting a high risk of default by the government.[34]

The short-term economic reaction suggests that the Hungarian government might have been wise to consider learning from the experiences of other countries and to phase in reversal measures to see what the market consequences would be. Domestic political factors, however, made the Orbán government less cautious. Again, isolating the effect of reversing pension privatization alone is difficult. At a minimum, however, eliminating contributions to the second tier and moving existing holdings back into the PAYG portion of pensions was an important component of a larger economic strategy that had negative economic ramifications. Orbán's policies had been successful in one important respect: the Hungarian government enjoyed short-term surpluses. The 2014 elections returned the Fidesz Party to power, suggesting that many Hungarian citizens did not disapprove strongly of the substantial shift in policy.

The Polish Reversal of Pension Privatization

In 1999, Poland adopted pension privatization under the left-wing Solidarity Electoral Action government. In 2011, the right-wing Civic Platform government adopted a combination of temporary and short-term measures reducing contributions to the second tier. In the first part of 2014, the Polish government took a further step and appropriated pension assets in individual pension accounts which were being invested in government bonds. The former Finance Minister, Leszek Balcerowicz, was quoted as saying that this was "the worst anti-reform in Poland since the fall of communism."[35]

Although the Polish reversal of pension privatization began less dramatically than in the surrounding countries and has been less extreme than occurred in Hungary, international organizations and the private sector balked when the Polish government reduced contributions to the second tier in 2013 and appropriated private pension holdings invested in government bonds in 2014, transferring millions of citizens' savings from individual accounts back into the national social security system. Poland was considered a leader for responsible fiscal and social policy in the region. Although Poland was not the first to reverse, the government's decision to backtrack on its 1998 reforms was interpreted by some as a particularly bad sign.

The business community and international organizations expressed concern that this trend was spreading across Europe: In one instance a headline from *Forbes* read "How the Hungarian Disease is Spreading across Eastern

---

[34] Gavin Nolan, "An Eastern Front," *Derivatives Week*, December 26, 2011.

[35] Jonathan Kandell, "Can Poland's Private Pension Funds Survive Government's Bond Grab," *Institutional Investor*, May 2014.

Europe."[36] Pension policy was increasingly being linked with whether a government was pursuing responsible fiscal policy. A former advisor to the Polish Chamber of Pension Funds, Dariusz Stańko, stated that "We have the biggest pot of pension money in this part of Europe and are perceived to be leaders in the sector. If we go ahead with this, other countries will follow."[37] In fact, Poland was following the example of other countries, but its reversal appears to have been largely unanticipated by observers.

The reversal of pension privatization in Poland confirms that even under different domestic and economic circumstances than we see in Hungary and Russia, a moderate degree of pension privatization makes the curtailing of the second privatized tier of pensions more likely. Several factors suggest that Poland's version of pension privatization was more likely to survive than in Russia or Hungary. Compared to Russia, the Polish political system is more competitive and has seen more regular alternations in power. Historically, Polish reformers have also shown a concern with public opinion when adopting radical social and economic reforms. Chłoń (2000) has also described the extensive campaign to market Poland's NDC system to citizens – among whom surveys showed support for the new system. We would expect public opinion to play a bigger role than was the case in Russia because both political competition and democracy were stronger. At least initially, public opinion was on the side of pension privatization, suggesting the reform had a good chance of survival. Compared to Hungary, Poland's economic and fiscal situation is better, indicating that the government might have been more able to sustain the shift to a privatized system. Despite these potential advantages over the Russian and Hungarian reformers, the Polish government has also significantly cut back its second tier.

The Polish case provides important insights into when and how domestic stakeholders can stop, or at least slow, the reversal of an important market-oriented reform. Unlike the reversal in Hungary or Russia, the Polish reversal to date has been more gradual and more partial. Poland's second tier may eventually be eliminated entirely, but its path to this outcome will have been very different from neighboring countries. Poland's distinctive path to and from pension privatization is, therefore, politically revealing regardless of future developments.

Reversing and Revising the Polish Pension System in 2011 and 2013

In some ways, the Polish case is a less likely case of reversal. Pension privatization in Poland was adopted after several years of deliberation and consensus

---

[36] Marek Tatała and Fred Roeder, "How the Hungarian Disease is Spreading across Central Europe," *Forbes*, November 12, 2013.

[37] Gail Moss, "Polish Government May Grab Private Pension Money, Predicts Academic," *Investment & Pensions Europe*, April 4, 2013.

among competing political parties, the public, unions, and employers. Armeanu (2010) writes that

Reforms in Hungary, Slovakia, and the early reforms in Romania, which were designed and adopted without consultation with the opposition, were subject to various degrees of reversals. In contrast, in Poland, where all major parties participated in the adoption process, the result was a consensual reform and chances for sustainability are good. (p. 170)

If pension privatization were to survive anywhere, it should have been in Poland. Although pension privatization was a radical social reform, it was not the most politically unpopular or divisive issue in in debates around Polish pension policy. Rather, it has been the reform of the PAYG system that has been the most difficult and controversial and has garnered the most public attention. The Polish government has been able to achieve only a modest increase in the retirement age. In the regular alternations in power between 1996 and 2007, revisions to pension reform have entailed an oscillation between expanding pension privileges under center-left governments and curtailing privileges under center-right governments (Armeanu 2010). Once pension privatization was adopted in Poland, it was not subject to the same alternations and revisions as the PAYG system (Chłoń-Domińczak and Gora 2003).

In 2011, the Civic Platform voted to reduce temporarily contributions to the second tier of Poland's pension system with a plan to increase the contributions several years later, though not to the original level. The legislation passed and decreased contributions from 7.3 to 2.3 percent of wages with plans to gradually increase contributions back to 3.5 percent of wages by 2017 (Fultz 2012; Żukowski 2012).

Contributions to the second tier did increase moderately in 2013, to 2.8 percent of wages, but the plans to continue increasing contributions to the second tier were ultimately abandoned.[38] In 2014, the government appropriated private pension fund holdings that were being invested in government bonds. The Polish government, it seems, had estimated that doing so would cause limited reaction from investors given other global and regional trends in handling mandatory individual retirement accounts.

To date Poland has pursued a more limited reversal of pension privatization than occurred in either Russia or Hungary. Legislation was passed on December 6, 2013 entitled *Amending Certain Acts in Connection with the Determination for Principles for Old-Age Pension Payments from Funds Collected in Open Pension Funds*. The law went into effect on February 1, 2014 and made

---

[38] Gail Moss, "Polish Government May Grab Private Pension Money, Academic Predicts," *Investment & Pensions Europe*, April 4, 2013.

a number of important changes.[39] These included the following measures which can be grouped in two overarching categories:

- Reversal of Second Tier
  - Transferring all holdings invested in treasury securities to the Social Insurance Institution (ZUS); future transfers of retirement contributions to private pension funds (referred to in Poland as open pension funds) would be optional with the default being that a citizen's contributions go to ZUS
- Regulatory changes
  - Prohibition of private pension funds investment in government treasuries in the future
  - Increase in the percentage of holdings that could be in stocks; all restrictions on equity investment will be lifted by 2018
  - Savings would be transferred from private pension funds to the Social Insurance Institutions beginning ten years before retirement
  - Decrease in maximum contribution fee from 3.5 to 1.75 percent

These changes represented a huge shift in the Polish pension system. Notably, the appropriation of investments in government bonds (treasury securities) constituted 51.5 percent of the funds' worth at the time. Half of the private pension funds' total holdings had been transferred back to the Social Insurance Institution by March 2014. This move alone dealt a huge blow to the industry since the money amounted to about $50 billion from thirteen different private pension funds.[40]

The government also announced a four-month period from April 1 to July 31 of 2014 during which Polish citizens currently making mandatory contributions to individual pension accounts could choose to stay in the privatized system or, by default, have their contributions transferred to ZUS.[41] Unlike in Russia, where citizens have two years to decide, or in Hungary, where citizens had only a few weeks, in Poland people were given four months to choose. Also unique to Poland, citizens would have another period, from April 1 to July 31, 2016, during which to choose where their contributions would be directed (the default would still be ZUS) and then subsequently a decision period every four years during the same dates. The Polish reversal left open the possibility of electing to have contributions go to private pension funds during future enrollment periods, in contrast to the Russian and Hungarian governments which designed one-time enrollment periods. Unlike Hungary, the Polish government did not

---

[39] For a detailed description of the changes made by the 2013 legislation, see Narodowy Bank Polski, Financial Stability Report, July 2014, pp. 89–90.

[40] Narodowy Bank Polski, Financial Stability Report, July 2014, pp. 89–90.

[41] For a description of the 2014 pension reform measures in Poland, see: Jonathan Kandell, "Can Poland's Private Pension Funds Survive Government's Bond Grab?" *Institutional Investor*, May 2014.

require citizens to keep making social security contributions but not receive any social security if they chose to stay in the privatized system.

The Polish switchback period was unique in that private pension funds were forbidden from advertising to convince citizens not to opt out of the privatized system. The changes in regulations – according to which investment in government bonds was prohibited – made private pension fund portfolios riskier since a higher proportion of the holdings would be held in stocks. Indeed, the new law required that 75 percent of private pension funds holding be held in stocks; the percentage of stocks requirement would gradually be eliminated by January 1, 2018. The legislation adopted in December 2013 also eliminated a minimum required rate of return. About 16.7 million Polish citizens were in the privatized system and had to choose, by July 31, 2014, whether to stay in the privatized scheme; only 2.6 million citizens (about 16 percent of those eligible) chose to keep their mandatory contributions going toward the privatized system.[42] The number of citizens staying in the privatized system might have been higher if the default had not been switching back, if private pension funds were allowed to advertise, and if the Polish government had not restricted private pension funds ability to invest in lower risk government bonds. Ultimately, public opinion did not appear to be on the side of individual accounts. This was a less radical and sudden departure from pension privatization than occurred in Hungary, but effectively marginalized the second tier which is now a smaller portion of Poland's national retirement system.

Poland staggered its reversal more than Hungary, but when the government did legislate a switch back to the national social security system, it gave citizens less time than in Russia and banned any advertising by private pension funds. In this way, Poland's reversal of pension privatization represents a kind of middle ground between the Russian and Hungarian experiences.

Like Russia and Hungary, the Polish case demonstrates why a moderate degree of reform results in the reversal of pension privatization: politicians have a large fiscal incentive to backtrack and domestic stakeholders do not block these reversals. The Polish case, however, offers unique insight into when and how domestic stakeholders can stop, or at least stall, the reversal of an important market-oriented reform. The potential for domestic stakeholders in the public and private sectors to object to abandoning the second tier of pension privatization helps explain why the government has created a kind of "open enrollment" period every four years during which citizens can switch back. As of 2014, Poland has pursued a more limited reversal of pension privatization than Hungary. Even if Poland ultimately abandons pension privatization altogether, its reversal will be more much more staggered than either the Russian

---

[42] Piotr Bujnicki and Maciej Martewicz, "Polish Pension Fund Opt-In Rush Saves Bourse From Selloff," *Bloomberg*, August 1, 2014; Krystyna Kryzak, "CEE Roundup: Poland, Czech Republic," *Investment & Pensions Europe*, August 20, 2014.

or Hungarian measures and shows a greater concern with potential reactions from the public and investors.

The Polish reversal has been more partial and staggered because of its fiscal situation combined with the role of interests in the public and private spheres. Poland's financial situation was better than other European countries. Poland was the only European country not to go into recession during the financial crisis of 2008.[43] Nonetheless, the Polish government faces the same EU deficit guidelines as other member countries and a significant amount of money was being diverted into mandatory individual retirement accounts as part of pension privatization.

Because pension privatization was adopted more extensively in Poland than in Russia or Hungary, interests in the public and private sectors were more supportive of pension privatization and were more politically influential. The Polish government took special care to observe whether there were negative reactions from either the public or the private sector. The financial sector – including firms operating in the private pension sector – was somewhat more influential. The Polish public, however, did not seriously object to the government's turnabout on pension policy and only a minority chose to stay in the privatized tier.

Poland's reversal of pension privatization, as the third and final case discussed here, brings together a complete picture about how and why three very different countries pursued a similar radical market-oriented reform of social security, but why this reform failed to take hold.

Security through Diversity: The Adoption of Polish Pension Privatization

Poland, like most other post-communist countries in the region, experienced polarized debates about pension reform in the early to mid-1990s. In many ways, the Polish debates over pension reform were similar to those taking place in Hungary and Russia. There was a divide between the pro-pension privatization side and the anti-pension privatization camp and the battle was resolved in favor of the pro-privatization faction (Guardiancich 2004; Müller 1999, 2001). The World Bank played a more active role in Hungary and Poland than in Russia. In Poland in particular, a World Bank economist headed the pension reform task force allowing the Bank more access than usual (Müller 2001).

Proposals to introduce pension privatization first emerged in 1994. As in neighboring countries like Russia and Hungary, debates over policy proposals occurred amongst bureaucrats. The *Strategy for Poland* economic proposal in June 1994 was presented by Prime Minister Kolodko and was the first official document to include a proposal for the introduction of a mandatory funded

---

[43] "Learning from Abroad: Don't Forget Poland," *The Economist*, December 18, 2012.

component, i.e., pension privatization. The proposal also included measures to base pensions on price indexation (instead of wage indexation) which would limit benefits in the PAYG portion. A proposal specific to pension reform was also introduced in 1994 entitled *Security through Diversity* which advocated for a multi-pillar pension system in keeping with the model being advocated by the World Bank at that time.

The *Security through Diversity* report introducing the reform justified these measures in terms of long-term planning and the improvement of social benefits for Polish citizens. The report also highlighted problems with the PAYG system. Reflecting its title, the authors emphasized the importance of combining the three tiers of a pension system recommended by the World Bank (Chłoń et al. 1999).

A bureaucratic debate ensued about pension reform although, unlike in other countries, the debate was focused more on the extent of pension privatization rather than whether pension privatization should be adopted at all (Chłoń et al. 1999). From mid-1994 through the end of 1996, the Minister of Labor and the Minister of Finance were at loggerheads over reform. The Minister of Labor favored a more moderate modification of the first tier and a more limited role for the funded component. The Minister of Finance favored more extensive Chilean-style reforms. In the Fall of 1995, the government sided with proposals for a larger component going toward pension privatization. Bureaucratic disagreements about pension reform were settled in part by replacing the head of the Ministry of Labor who had been opposing the introduction of pension privatization. Chłoń et al. (1999) detail how a new Minister of Labor, Andrzej Baczkowski, was appointed in 1996 and favored proposals for the introduction of a more extensive funded portion of pensions.

Similar to Hungary but unlike the situation in Russia, the Polish government engaged in an extended examination of public opinion and marketing campaign. Surveys conducted in August 1995 and in April and October 1997 indicated that the Polish public had little confidence in the PAYG pension system inherited from the communist era (Chłoń 2000). In 1995, about 25 percent of a nationally representative sample of Polish citizens reported that the system was bad and changes were necessary, with an additional 30 percent reporting that the system was quite bad. By 1997, about 35 percent were reporting that that system was bad and changes were necessary and about 20 percent said that the system was quite bad. A very small percentage of the population in 1995 and 1997 – about 10 percent – thought that the pension system was good and functioned well.

The Polish government was able to sell the reform to the public in large part because of this lack of confidence in the previous PAYG pension system inherited from the communist era.

Disillusionment with the former PAYG system was not unique to the Polish system. Public opinion polls in Hungary suggested there was support for a second tier. In fact, optimism about the new system was high enough that the Hungarian government's primary concern was that *too many* citizens would switch; the system was designed to avoid making switching to the funded portion too advantageous. Palacios and Whitehouse (1998) analyzed the first 50,000 citizens to switch voluntarily to the funded component and indicated both that the government's assessment was correct and that the design of incentives was having the intended effect of encouraging switching. Policy experts explicitly drew on the Hungarian experience to develop "lessons for other transforming economies" (Palacios and Rocha 1998). In short, the Hungarian experience was generally encouraging for Polish policymakers.

An active public relations campaign promoting the new multi-tier pension system began in 1997. At this time the Office of the Government Plenipotentiary for Social Security Reforms, also commonly referred to as the Office for Pension Reform, was charged with promoting the reform as if its passage and implementation were a foregone conclusion (Chłoń 2000).

The experiences of other countries in the region and in Latin America had an important influence on the adoption of pension privatization measures in Poland. Proponents of the reform in Poland organized trips for government officials, members of parliament, and journalists to other reforming countries, including Argentina, Chile, Hungary, and Sweden. The study of other countries' experiences was useful in terms of both informing policymakers about how to design the system and also publicizing the reform (Chłoń 2000). Aleksandrowicz (2007) highlights the Latvian and Swedish models as being especially important, the former as a fellow post-communist country and the latter as a West European model of reform. In many ways, the Polish reforms mimicked the Swedish model. The Latin American models were important for policymakers, but the stigma associated with Latin America made these examples less compelling to the public.[44]

Pension reform legislation was passed in 1997 and 1998 with implementation in 1999. The first set of laws were adopted in June and August of 1997 and included a law on the organization and operation of pension funds which established the second tier (August 28, 1997), a law on employee pension programs (August 22, 1997), and a law on using privatization proceeds to support pension reform (June 25, 1997). The 1997 laws introduced the mandatory funded component – the least controversial part of the reforms – and received only limited public debate (Armeanu 2010; Chłoń et al. 1999). The 1997 legislation passed with nearly unanimous support from the governing Solidarity coalition and the Social Democratic opposition. One particularly telling aspect is that the reforms were adopted just before parliamentary elections in September 1997.

---

[44] Writing during the early post-communist transitions, Przeworski (1991) discusses the stereotype held by some in Central and Eastern European countries that Latin American countries are underdeveloped and unstable.

The timing of the reforms just prior to elections and their unanimous support is indicative that neither the government nor the opposition was concerned about a backlash.

The reform of the PAYG system, adopted with legislation in 1998, was more controversial than the adoption of pension privatization. Two additional laws were adopted in 1998: a law on the social security system (October 13, 1998) and a law on old-age and disability pensions from the Social Security Fund (December 18, 1998). Some experts speculated that the pension privatization option was chosen to divert attention away from parametric changes in the first tier (where notional defined contributions were introduced) and from making more dramatic reductions in benefits in the first tier. The irony is that by introducing pension privatization policymakers may have been making it more necessary to cut pension benefits further in order to help offset the financing gap created by the new scheme.

A left-wing government known for backing market-oriented reforms adopted the measures, but there was also widespread support among different groups. The opposition parties in the *Sejm* also voted in favor of reform, as did both employers and the Solidarity union (Müller 1999; Naczyk and Domonkos 2014). Support for reform in Poland contrasts with Hungary where the adoption of pension privatization was a partisan measure backed and adopted by the left-wing MSzP and opposed by the right-wing Fidesz party. As the opening quote from a World Bank representative suggests, if pension privatization was going to survive anywhere, we would expect it to have survived in Poland.

Poland's pension privatization was passed in two stages with parliamentary elections held in between. The first version of the legislation was adopted by the *Sejm* in the summer of 1997, followed by parliamentary elections in September 1997, and the second version was adopted in the Fall of 1998 under the Solidarity Electoral Action government. The new system went into effect in 1999. In this respect the timing of Poland's pension legislation is revealing. The less controversial component of reforms – introducing a second tier – was passed just before elections. The more controversial and less popular component for reforms – restructuring the first PAYG tier – was passed after elections.

It is remarkable that the second privatized tier which sought to fundamentally alter the social contract was so uncontroversial that it could be adopted just months before a parliamentary election with nearly unanimous support from parties on both sides. This overwhelming political and public support makes it especially surprising that the system did not survive. The unpopularity of reforms to the first tier, which focused on cutting current benefits, speaks to the powerful force of path dependency; structural reform was actually much easier than parametric reform in this case.

The implementation of the funded tier confirmed that the reform was generally popular. The second tier was designed to be mandatory for those born after 1969 and was optional for those born between 1949 and 1969; this meant that up to 11.5 million people could join the new system, including

3.8 million in the younger cohort (who were required to join) and 7.7 million in the older cohort. The new pension system was more popular than had been expected. In 1999, 10.5 million people joined the privatized portion (the second tier) rather than the 6–7 million who were expected to join (Hausner 2001, 2002). This means that 87 percent of people in the older cohort chose to join although they were not required to do so. Polish politicians had judged correctly that there was support for the new system. By 2005, the number of people enrolled in the second tier had risen to 12 million. By 2010, 14.5 million people were participating in Poland's second tier of pensions (Armeanu 2010).

International companies like ING and AEGON dominated the market, with the top four private pension funds controlling 70 percent of the market. The fourteen registered private pension funds were managing \$571 billion (Armeanu 2010). Private pension funds initially received encouraging rates of return. Experts and citizens were dissatisfied with high administrative fees and a lack of transparency, common complaints in countries in which pension privatization has been introduced.

Security through Sustainability: Reversing Pension Privatization in Poland

Because more citizens had enrolled in the second tier than were expected, the financing gap associated with switching from a PAYG to a partially privatized system was higher than expected. Aleksandrowicz (2007) concludes that "The Polish pension system appears to be a victim of its own success. Transition costs 'skyrocketed' as many people decided to contribute to both the first and second pillar" (p. 333). In part, then, the new pension system functioned so well and was so popular that it contributed to its downfall.

The Polish and Hungarian reforms were a definite move toward Latin American-style pension privatization, but policymakers and politicians avoided referring to them as such given the stigma associated with Latin America as a less developed region among Europeans (Orenstein 2000). Notably, the Polish reform was typical of the region in that it was less extensive than in Latin America and was more heavily based on the Swedish model. Whereas countries like Chile had set up a social security system in which all of a citizen's benefits would be based on the contributions and returns in individual accounts, in the Polish case only about 49 percent of future benefits would come from individual accounts (Brooks 2009). This relatively moderate degree of pension privatization determined the financing gap associated with Poland's pension reform and why the reforms did not stick.

Poland's degree of pension privatization put it in the middle range. Based on simulations specifying an individual's length of work and the rate of return on investments among other factors, 49 percent of a Polish citizen's future benefits would come from her individual account (Brooks 2009). That nearly half of one's pension would come from the individual portion suggests a reform that would alter the way citizens think about the social contract and make calculations about their retirement benefits. The degree of pension privatization, combined with the lack of support for the previous PAYG system, suggests that Polish citizens might have truly reoriented the way they thought about their future benefits.

At the same time, Poland's implicit pension debt has risen in line with its aging population. This debt has ranged from 220 to about 255 percent of GDP from 2000 to 2012.[45] Poland's high pension debt was characteristic of the region and strained the government's finances. Poland had a high implicit pension debt and instituted fairly extensive pension privatization. Compared to the other countries in the region, however, Poland had a better financial and economic position in part due to more extensive market-oriented reforms. It was the only EU member country not to go into recession during the 2008 global financial crisis and the country's strong performance even amidst this crisis was, in part, evidence of the success of its transition to the market.

Although Poland generally had enjoyed a better fiscal situation than Hungary, the Polish government had avoided recession in large part by strategically introducing tax cuts in 2009. As a result, the Polish government budget deficit was 7.9 percent, twice that of Hungary (4.2 percent in 2009), and it was nearing the constitutional debt limit of 55 percent (Fultz 2012). Like Hungary and most other European countries, however, Poland has had a deficit throughout the period in which pension privatization has been in effect.[46] Poland's deficits, however, are not as severe as those experienced by Hungary. Even though Poland had a degree of pension privatization comparable to Hungary, the fiscal pressure on the government was much less because of Poland's better fiscal situation.

The pension system, in particular, struggled because of the rising implicit pension debt, a first-tier PAYG system that was only moderately reformed, and the general government's rising deficits during the 2008 financial crisis. There were also complaints about the collection of pension contributions (Chłoń-Domińczak 2004). This can be seen in the deficits incurred specifically by the pension system. The difference between contributions collected and pension benefits paid out rose from 4.82 percent in 1999 (when the reforms were introduced) to a peak of 5.94 percent in 2010. Backtracking did help this fiscal situation, at least in the short term. The reversal measures in 2011, which decreased contributions to the second tier, resulted in a sharp drop in the pension funds deficit to −5 percent in 2011. The financing gap in the pension system dropped

---

[45] Data about Poland's implicit pension debt are taken from Holzmann et al. (2004). Data for later dates have been imputed using the technique in James and Brooks (2001). I use a global dataset including all countries for which data on implicit pension debt are available and regress implicit pension debt on the age over 65.

[46] Data are from the 2013 World Development Indicators.

further, to 4.83 percent in 2011 and to 4.07 percent in 2012. This reduction in the financing gap also meant a reduction in the amount of money that the state had to transfer to the pension system. In 2010, state transfers to the pension system peaked at 1.9 percent of GDP; this amount declined to 1.03 percent in 2011 and to 0.53 and 0.69 percent in 2012 and 2013 (Gronicki and Jankowiak 2013, pp. 11–12).

Nonetheless, the reduction of contributions to the funded tier was only a short-term solution to the fiscal challenges posed by Poland's pension system. The private sectors emphasized that the fiscal benefits would be short-lived and that there were larger implications. In their 2013 report prepared for the Polish business association, Gronicki and Jankowiak (2013) note that the fiscal benefits of reversal are only temporary but that there are also potentially important macroeconomic consequences. They conducted simulations showing that through 2030 GDP would be up to 8.5 percent lower without the benefit of pension privatization.

Fiscal and Political Incentives to Reverse Pension Privatization

The financial crisis heightened politicians' incentive to divert contributions from the second tier back to general pension revenue. The financial crisis and the lack of domestic stakeholders supporting pension privatization explains why Polish pension privatization did not survive despite being adopted with overwhelming support across partisan and social divisions.

The first proposal about how to reform Poland's second tier of pensions emerged in 2009. Then Prime Minister Donald Tusk of the Civic Platform party solicited a proposal from his chief adviser, Michael Boni. The Boni proposal made several suggestions about how to improve the second tier. These included lifting restrictions on investment so that individual accounts could be better tailored to individual needs, a reduction in management fees, different benchmarks for returns (based on performance in the actual stock and bond markets instead of being based on average performance in the previous three years), and a change in the solicitation of clients.[47]

Opponents to the second privatized tier were not satisfied with these adjustments to Poland's pension privatization system. The Minister of Labor and Social Policy, Jolanta Fedak, responded to the Boni proposal by arguing that there should be a two-year suspension of all contributions to the second tier and a reduction of contributions to the second tier from 7.3 to 3 percent. Fedak's proposal was not seriously considered, but revealed bureaucratic disagreements about the future of Poland's pension system.[48] Disagreement about how to proceed on pension reform emerged from within the Tusk government, with contradictory statements being made about which course to pursue. The only

---

[47] Krystyna Kryzak, "Poland: Ongoing Pensions Saga," *Investment & Pensions Europe*, January 2011.

[48] Ibid.

agreement was that something had to be done about the second tier which was, at best, operating suboptimally.

Similar to Russia, the Ministry of Labor and Social Policy introduced a subsequent proposal about the pension system. This echoed the adoption of pension privatization in Poland – and in other post-communist countries like Russia and Hungary – in which the official policy proposals and discussion occurred amongst bureaucratic actors. In 2010, the Ministry of Labor and Social Policy and the Ministry of Finance released a joint proposal about amending the role of private pension funds in the national retirement system. The Ministry of Labor report proposing pension privatization in 1997 was entitled *Security through Diversity*; appropriately. Another report was published in 2011 in which the Ministry of Labor report proposed its reversal.[49] The emphasis in the former was diversifying risk and the emphasis in the latter was on the establishment of a fiscally sustainable system.

In July 2010, Poland's Central Bank offered a muted reaction to the proposals to reverse pension privatization, stating that

If the proposals of the Ministry [of Labor] become effective, they will significantly influence the financial situation of pension fund management companies and may affect the safety and stability of the fully funded part of the pension system. Irrespective of the proposals presented by the Ministry, another matter important for the operation of the pension fund sector is the lack of regulations regarding institutions paying out pensions from funds accumulated in open pension funds, as the first payments of whole life pension annuities will start in 2014. (pp. 87–88)[50]

The stakes for cutting back on contributions were clear: doing so would mean abandoning, either in whole or in part, the privatized pension system.

A report released in 2013 evaluated the effects of the 2011 proposal and further advocated that the government cash in bonds that were being held in the second-tier individual pension accounts. In fitting contrast to the *Security through Diversification* proposal that introduced pension privatization, this report was entitled *Security through Sustainability*. The 2013 report indicated that the purpose of the initial pension privatization reform was to create a system that was financially sustainable. The report specifically indicates that the financial crisis brought into question the ability of a privatized pension system to accomplish those goals. Returns to private pension funds declined and there was an increase in the deficits necessary to cover the financing gap. The report emphasized that a sizable financing gap was expected to continue until 2060.

Initially, the Ministry of Labor explained that Eurostat took into account the effects of pension privatization on the budget by not including its effects

---

49 *Przegląd funkcjonowania system emerytalnego: Bezpieczeństwo dzięki zrównoważeniu*, Ministry of Labor and Social Policy and Ministry of Finance, Warsaw, June 2013. Copy available upon request. Available online at: http://emerytura.gov.pl/wp-content/uploads/2014/03/20130626_przeglad.pdf (accessed December 5, 2013).

50 Narodowy Bank Polski, Financial Stability Report, July 2010.

in the calculation of the general government revenue. This situation changed, however, when the European Union refused to continue making an exception to the deficit guidelines for those countries that had privatized pensions (Casey 2012).

The 2013 *Security through Sustainability* report also suggested that reports from the private sector indicating the positive benefits of pension privatization and the negative benefits of its removal were suspect. The Ministry of Labor specifically criticized the simulations by Gronicki and Jankowiak (2013), which indicated that the authors would not make available the specific design of the simulations making the results questionable. Clearly, each side had a stake in believing that pension privatization had produced macroeconomic and fiscal benefits, or not.

As in Russia and Hungary, the improvement in government finances was only short-term in nature. In the long term, critics of the move argued that the reversal made the country's financial situation more precarious. Leszek Balcerowicz, the former finance minister, stated that "[r]eaching for accumulated pension savings as a way of curing public finances is a medicine that is worse than the illness."[51] The money gained by acquiring pension savings in government bonds (in the mandatory system) provided about $50 billion. Ultimately, even though Poland was relatively better off, the fiscal and political incentive to access the money being diverted to individual accounts proved too great. In this regard, we see a strong similarity between Poland and the other cases of reversals.

Domestic Stakeholders in the Private Sector

As with the adoption of pension privatization in Poland, private pension funds were not involved in the crafting of policy proposals about either its revision or reversal. Despite their lack of involvement in policymaking, the private pension funds most directly profited from a funded pension tier and were most directly hurt by its removal. The objections of private pension funds have been largely ignored by the Polish government.

Initially, opposition from the private sector was softened by the partial and temporary nature of the reversal. Legislation in 2011 only temporarily reduced contributions rather than instituting a government acquisition of funds. Subsequent measures, however, provoked much louder objections. In September 2013, the Polish government announced that it would redeem all of the government bonds that had been sold to private pension funds.[52] Private pension funds objected strenuously to the government's move. The announcement prompted a decline in stocks and bonds and a slew of criticism from the private sector.

---

[51] Norman Cohen and Jan Cienski, "Poland Pension Reform Reversal Highlights Public Disillusion," *Financial Times*, February 5, 2014.

[52] Marcin Sobczyk, "Polish Assets Take as Pension Overhaul Sinks In," *Wall Street Journal*, September 5, 2013.

The Economic Chamber of Insurance Companies – a lobbying group for pension funds – announced that it was "deeply disappointed" and that the bond proposal "raises serious legal concerns."[53] A representative of Aviva, one of the largest of Poland's private pension funds, was quoted as saying that "We are a global investor and we have choices over where to invest and this rocks your confidence."[54]

The Polish Chamber of Pension Funds – another organization representing the interests of Poland's private pension funds – published an official 25-page response to the Ministry of Labor proposal in 2013 in which it took on the government's arguments for redeeming bonds.[55] The report had little effect and the government's bond proposal went ahead as planned.

The Chamber sent a letter to the European Commission, asking it to take an official position on the government's bond plan announced in 2013.[56] Other legal actions were also considered. These challenges would have been similar to the constitutional challenges that Hungarian private pension funds raised when the funded tier was eliminated in 2010.

Private pension funds were banned from advertising in the 2014 period during which citizens could choose whether or not to keep their mandatory retirement contributions in privately managed individual accounts. This prohibition made funds hesitant to speak publicly in general, with some refusing to grant any interviews at all during this time.[57] Unlike the period of the adoption of pension privatization, the government did not initiate a large-scale campaign to inform citizens about the change, likely because the default was to have one's contributions go back to the state social insurance institute.

By mid-August 2014, by which time all transfer requests were received, around two million citizens had elected to keep a portion of their contributions going to an individual account. The reversal also raised concern among pro-market advocates, such as the former finance minister and proponent of radical market-oriented reforms, Leszek Balcerowicz, and the private investment community. One investor likened the Polish seizure of bonds to Argentina's reversal in 2008.[58]

Lobbying by firms in the financial sector and by private pension funds was more successful in Poland than in Hungary. Naczyk and Domonkos (2014)

---

[53] Ibid.

[54] Jan Cienski, "Pension Funds Plan Poland Bonds Fight," *Financial Times*, October 2, 2013.

[55] *Position of the Polish Chamber of Pension Funds regarding the Report of the Ministry of Labor and Social Policy and Ministry of Finance on review of pension system functioning "Security through Sustainability" of 26 June 2013*. Copy available upon request. Available at: http://www.fiap.cl/prontus_fiap/site/artic/20130905/asocfile/20130905170204/en_opinia_raport_23_08_2013_3_.pdf (accessed December 5, 2014).

[56] Jan Cienski, "Pension Funds Plan Poland Bonds Fight," *Financial Times*, October 2, 2013.

[57] Jonathan Kandell, "Can Poland's Private Pension Funds Survive Government's Bond Grab," *Institutional Investor*, May 2014.

[58] Ibid.

argue that Polish lobbying against reversing pension privatization was more successful because the Polish pension market was more heavily invested in equities than in Hungary and therefore had a greater influence on macroeconomic outcomes. In other words, the structural economic impact of the Polish private pension funds was greater. One report concluded that Polish GDP would have been 7 percent smaller in 2013 than it had been in 2012 if it were not for pension privatization (Gronicki and Jankowiak 2013). Others, like the Polish Financial Supervisory Authority, attributed the private pension funds to having bolstered the Warsaw Stock Exchange (Naczyk and Domonkos 2014).

The greater influence of the private pension funds in Poland than in Hungary helps explain the differences in each country's reversal outcomes. Where the Hungarian government instituted a mostly one-time reversal of all mandatory private pension fund holdings, the Polish government began by reducing contributions to the second tier before appropriating mandatory savings held in government bonds. Although time will tell if the Polish government chooses to entirely eliminate its second tier, at the very least the Polish reversal will have been a more staggered process than the Hungarian one.

Experts acknowledged, however, that the reversal did not have negative consequences for Poland's credit ranking. Credit ratings agencies did not express concern about the appropriation of government bonds.[59] The immediate negative consequence was not in Poland's credit rating, but in the bond and equity markets. There was also concern about the potential flight on investors – although the extent to which this is a problem remains to be seen. In September 2013, when it was announced that the government would appropriate pension savings invested in bonds, the Warsaw Stock Exchange plunged. The fall was only temporary, however, with it recovering only a few weeks later.[60]

Lack of Public Support

Levels of public support for reforming the PAYG system and adopting pension privatization were higher in Poland than in other countries (Müller 1999). It was, therefore, not hard to convince Polish citizens that the old PAYG pension system was insufficient and in need of fundamental reform. Nonetheless, the public response to reversals in pension privatization has been relatively limited. There have been no significant protests and only a small proportion of citizens, some 1.8 million of the 16 million eligible to do so, chose to keep their contributions in the privatized portion of the pension system,.[61] Future enrollment periods will show whether or not the privatized system becomes more or less popular over time.

Before reversing pension privatization, there was no way for Polish politicians to know about the public reaction with any certainty. Given a competitive

[59] Ibid.   [60] Ibid.

[61] Piotr Bujnicki and Maciej Martewicz, "Polish Pension Fund Opt-In Rush Saves Bourse from Sell-off," *Bloomberg*, August 1, 2014.

party system and the Polish government's previous concern about selling the public on pension privatization – and the policy's unexpected popularity – Polish politicians were smart to be concerned about the possibility of a public objection to backtracking.

Groups of experts including the Citizens' Committee for Pension Security (Pol. Komitet Obywatelski ds. Bezpieczeństwa Emerytalnego – KOBE) and economists at the Civil Development Forum (FOR Foundation) in Warsaw organized to oppose the reversal (Tatała 2014). KOBE, in particular, held press conferences, frequently talked with the media, and released reports opposing pension privatization. FOR and its members actively used social media like Facebook and Twitter to promote their position. FOR's members included prominent economists like the former minister of finance, Leszek Balcerowicz, who was involved in FOR's efforts to raise public awareness and mobilize public opposition to reversal. FOR backed an online campaign – NieZaglosuje.pl – that was responsible for sending a petition to member of the Polish parliament with the phrase "If you vote for nationalization of our pension savings, I will not vote for you in the forthcoming elections" (Tatala 2014).

Ultimately, however, survey evidence from Poland at the time suggests that the public was largely apathetic about the move. A nationally representative survey commissioned by a bank and conducted in February 2011 revealed that 72 percent of Poles said that the debates about pension reform would not change their retirement saving plans and that only about 20 percent of Polish citizens were saving money.[62] Despite low rates of individuals saving for their own retirement, a survey in February of 2012 revealed that the vast majority of Polish citizens did not trust their social security benefits to provide a good quality of life in retirement. It appears that most citizens expect to work in retirement to support themselves.[63] More recent survey evidence in 2015, however, shows that Polish citizens were overwhelmingly willing to accept lower salaries for higher contributions to the pension system suggesting that they do in fact want and expect support from the state in retirement.[64] Nonetheless, citizens appear ambivalent about state-provided support including pension privatization based on surveys in 2011 and 2012.

The declining performance of Poland's private pension funds in 2010 made it easier to neutralize any potential public opposition to a reversal. In 2010, Poland's central bank reported a decline in private pension funds' profitability, primarily because of a combination of declining revenue and increasing administrative costs (Fultz 2012). These problems were widely cited as reasons to abandon the reform. The government took several steps to dissuade citizens from opting to keep their contributions in the privatized portion of the pension

---

[62] Homo Homini Instytut Badania Opinii, "Polacy o przyszłych emeryturach," February 2011.

[63] Homo Homini Instytut Badania Opinii, "Co będzie miało największy wpływ na komfort życia na emeryturze?" February 11, 2012.

[64] Homo Homini Instytut Badania Opinii, "Aktywni zawodowo Polacy o śmieciówkach," 2015

system. First, and most directly, the government set the default option to be a return of one's retirement contributions back to ZUS. Second, the government also banned advertising by private pension funds during the decision period in 2014. In addition to making it difficult to drum up public support for the privatized system, this measure also suppressed public lobbying efforts. Some private pension funds would not even comment about the reversal measures to the press for fear of violating the prohibition on advertising.

The government's decision to appropriate retirement savings being held in bonds was also accompanied by a prohibition of investing in government bonds and a minimum requirement for the degree of the portfolio invested in equities. Initially, the government required that an enormous 75 percent of the portfolio be held in equities, although this requirement would be eliminated over time. As a result, private pension fund accounts became much riskier. A young bank employee was quoted explaining his decision to switch back to the state saying that, "At this point, the pension fund has become an equity fund, so it's too risky for our retirement savings. And if we have extra savings, we would rather put them in a mutual fund because it charges lower fees."[65]

Media attention in the run-up to the reversal had highlighted the actuarial projections which indicated that replacement rates would decline considerably (Fultz 2012). This also likely eroded public support for retaining a significant component of the privatized system. The Polish government, though, clearly tilted in favor of redirecting citizens' contributions back into the state's social insurance institute, differed in critical ways from the Russian and Hungarian reversals because of a greater concern with the public's reaction. Critically, the 2011 reversal provided for recurring decision periods every four years during which citizens could choose whether to have a portion of their retirement contribution directed to individual accounts which would be privately invested. Furthermore, the requirement that private pension funds invest heavily in equities is designed to be lifted so that choosing the individual account option may be more desirable.

In this way, the Polish reversal also helps reveal why a reversal would not occur. Polish citizens were estimated to receive up to 49 percent of their future retirement benefits from the individual accounts. This percentage was much lower in Hungary and Russia. As a result, the Polish government was more concerned with making the reversal voluntary, less permanent, and providing an option for citizens to remain in the privatized tier if they wished.

Finally, as in Russia and Hungary, international examples had played a very important role in the adoption of pension privatization in Poland and the government was especially careful to consider the potential reaction from investors and citizens. The temporary and staggered nature of the reversal reveals a learning process by politicians which built on domestic experiences

[65] Jonathan Kandell, "Can Poland's Private Pension Funds Survive Government's Bond Grab?," *Institutional Investor*, May 2014.

in combination with the experiences of other countries. The relatively mild response from investors to Hungary's dramatic reversal made backtracking seem like a feasible option in the Polish case.

Polish bureaucrats explicitly referenced the Hungarian example as a reason to be optimistic that the reversal would not have negative consequences. Jakub Borowski, the chief economist at the Polish Agricultural Credit Bank, noted of the Hungarian reversal in 2010 that "[r]eform in Hungary did not trigger massive outflows from foreigners, despite the large macro imbalances and political jitters."[66] Because the Hungarian reversal was much more radical and still failed to provoke the worst-case scenario of investor flight and decline, it was especially credible to argue that Poland could avoid negative consequences too.

Variation in Reversals: The Implications of the Hungarian and Polish Cases

The Hungarian and Polish cases demonstrate the relationship between fiscal pressure, domestic stakeholders, and the degree of reform in shaping the decision to turnabout on a policy that had been adopted with the idea of rewriting the social contract on retirement. Divergent domestic conditions, however, set the two countries on different reversal paths: the Hungarian reversal was a one-time process and complete compared to Poland's staggered, partial reversal.

One-Time or Staggered Reversal. The Hungarian case also reveals why a government would choose to completely abandon pension privatization in one step, rather than choosing a partial reversal, temporary measures, or a staggered process for removing pension privatization. Hungarian politicians were especially in need of short-term revenue and not concerned about public opinion. Particularly in the context of financial crisis, the Hungarian public was less concerned about pensions than about unemployment and general living standards. The Hungarian case, in particular, challenges the argument that reversals in painful market-oriented reforms will be driven by public backlash. Previous work had already confirmed that the public may not be the biggest threat to market-oriented reforms (as in Hellman 1998).

Degree of Reversal. The Polish government has chosen to retain a somewhat larger portion of the privatized tier than Hungary or Russia. The Polish government has also chosen a more staggered and gradual reversal than Hungary and, to some degree, Russia. The differences between Poland and Russia and Hungary help explain why the Polish government staggered its backtracking with a break of three years between the first legislated reversal in 2011 and the subsequent reversal measures in 2014. Specifically, Poland had pursed a more extensive degree of pension privatization and potentially faced a greater backlash from its private sector. Polish citizens had been at least somewhat supportive of pension privatization – or at least not supportive of the old PAYG

---

[66] Neil Dennis, "Polish Pension Reform Affects Portfolios," *Financial Times*, November 24, 2013.

system – meaning that there was a greater potential for public backlash too. Ultimately, neither private nor public opposition proved to be a serious impediment to backtracking on pension privatization even if the potential for backlash explains the more gradual, staggered nature of the reversal.

Domestic Stakeholders. The Hungarian experience also establishes that special interest groups such as private pension funds may not be the biggest threat to market-oriented reforms. Rather, politicians responding to fiscal and electoral timelines simply could not sustain a reform that required a current diversion of revenue, even if reversing reform did not provide a long-term solution. The Hungarian government did somewhat stagger the reversal, but it was almost entirely a one-step move.

The Polish case, however, confirms that partial reversals can be a reaction to domestic stakeholders. Staggered and temporary measures further confirm that a learning process was taking place. Poland differs greatly from Hungary and Russia in a number of different ways. Poland has a more competitive political system and its fiscal standing was much better. The financial sector in Poland has thrived during post-communist times, suggesting that it might have been influential on the government's policy choices. As in Hungary and Russia, however, the Polish government has pursued a moderate degree of pension privatization. This critical similarity explains why – despite all its differences – Poland also chose to largely abandon its second privatized tier of its national retirement system.

Public Opinion. Although no government that reversed pension privatization faced a serious backlash, governments like those of Poland and Russia indicated concern about a potentially negative reaction, unlike the Hungarian government, which did not appear worried about public opinion or a backlash from investors. Why did the Hungarian government not consider a less high-profile way of undermining the 1998 reform? Hacker (2008) details the transformation of social security in the United States to a system based more heavily on private risk and details how this was done not through large pieces of fundamental and high-profile legislation, but through moderate and incremental changes over a period of time. The Fidesz government could have chosen to modify its partially privatized system in a number of ways that would have just as effectively doomed the system without necessitating a sudden turnaround. For instance, the government could have instituted a temporary suspension of contributions that was later converted into permanent measures. Alternatively, the government could have made contributions to the second privatized tier entirely voluntary instead of mandatory. The government could have also phased in the reversal so that an initial partial reduction was later followed by a complete reversal.

Two factors explain why the Fidesz government did not choose a more moderate reversal. First, the Fidesz government really wanted the money, even if it was only short-term revenue, and it had secured a super-majority in the legislature. All of the modifications mentioned above would have delayed getting access to all of the contributions going to individual accounts. A temporary suspension would have allowed the government to gain access to the revenue immediately, but would not have allowed longer-term planning about how to spend these contributions. Second, Argentina, Estonia, Latvia, and Lithuania had all reversed their pension privatization systems – with Argentina being the most radical – without suffering any of the worst-case consequences of doing so. Although these examples likely reassured Poland too, the Polish government did not enjoy Fidesz's super-majority.

The Hungarian and Polish cases confirm that domestic conditions influence how even very similar policy decisions are pursued in nationally distinct ways. These cases therefore offer us a much more nuanced understanding of the political economy of backtracking on an important market-oriented reform. Taken together, and in comparison with the Russian case, these instances of backtracking constitute compelling evidence that more moderate reforms were the most likely to be abandoned when financial crisis struck.

Summary of Case Findings

The cases of Russia, Hungary, and Poland reveal important findings about how the degree of reform influences the likelihood of reversal. Although these countries vary in terms of a number of potentially important causal factors, they are similar in one critical regard: all three pursued a moderate degree of pension privatization. In all three cases, this moderate reform translated into fiscal pressures to reverse that were unchecked by domestic stakeholders.

These three cases of reversal also highlight several other important points. First, pressure from international organizations is an important part of the story, but it is not the whole story. Hungary and Poland are members of the EU whereas Russia is not. Although the EU places fiscal pressure on its members to stay within certain deficit guidelines, this is only part of the reason that reversals are concentrated in Central and East European post-communist countries. Russia did not face similar deficit restrictions from any international body, yet it still experienced a reversal. Additionally, the World Bank's policy prescriptions changed, but this alone gives us only limited insight into why some countries reversed pension privatization while others did not. The World Bank had provided loan assistance to Hungary, Poland, and Russia when they were pursuing the policy of pension privatization. Given Hungary's serious fiscal challenges and IMF loans in 2008, the Hungarian government might have been the most concerned about a reaction from the World Bank and the most emboldened by the shift in World Bank advice which was much less in favor of pension privatization.

Furthermore, these three cases taken together are compelling evidence that partisan politics does not fully explain backtracking. In Hungary and Poland, right-wing governments reversed pension privatization measures that had been previously adopted under left-wing administrations. In both Hungary and Poland, previous alternations in power meant that it was possible that reversals could have occurred at earlier points in time when an opposing side was in power.

Finally, a critical lesson about reversal from the cases of Russia, Hungary, and Poland is that reversals were pursued to different degrees and in different ways. The Hungarian government chose to completely abandon pension privatization in a single piece of legislation. The Polish government chose a multi-stage and partial reversal. Finally, the Russian government has chosen to abandon pension privatization almost entirely as part of its national retirement system (unlike Poland), but did so in two major pieces of legislation (unlike Hungary). Variation in the degree of reversal can be explained, at least in part, by differences in fiscal and economic pressures. The Hungarian government was under much greater fiscal pressure because of its high government debt. Poland and Russia did not face the same fiscal pressures. The Russian government ultimately did pursue a complete reversal, even before the economy began to worsen due to sanctions imposed because of its conflict with Ukraine. Poland enjoyed the best situation and, at least arguably, the least fiscal pressure to access pension contributions in the short term in order to alleviate fiscal constraints.

Whether the reversal was one-step or took multiple pieces of legislation can be explained by the government's concern with a negative reaction from potential domestic stakeholders, including the public and private pension funds. In Hungary, the government showed little concern about a public backlash or any negative response from investors. A large victory by Fidesz in 2010 gave the party a super-majority with which it could pass controversial constitutional changes; in comparison, passing legislation to reverse pension privatization was easier.

Recent developments have confirmed that backtracking is most likely in those countries that pursued moderate pension privatization. Bulgaria initially seemed like an exception to the trend of moderate reformers reversing pension privatization. From 2006 to 2009, the Bulgarian Socialist Party (BSP) had a large majority, securing 70 percent of the seats in the National Assembly, and made no adjustments to Bulgaria's pension privatization. This is somewhat surprising as the BSP has been a traditional communist party opposed to market-oriented reforms. In fact, the Bulgarian government only began debating making reductions in contributions to the second tier in 2011 following the ascent to power of a right-wing government led by the Citizens for the European Development of Bulgaria.[67] The initial proposal to backtrack on pension privatization failed. Rather, in December 2012, under the direction of a right-wing government the National Social Security Institute of Bulgaria – the government agency tasked with managing the country's retirement system – announced

---

[67] "Bulgarian Pension Funds Hold Breath for Nationalization Decision," *Sofia News Agency*, October 10, 2010.

that future reforms included plans to increase contributions to the second tier.[68]

A right-wing government led by the Citizens for the European Development of Bulgaria was re-elected in October 2014 and this time proposals for a reversal of pension privatization succeeded. In December 2014, the Bulgarian government gave citizens the option of opting out of the second privatized tier in a kind of partial and voluntary reversal. Those starting new jobs will have one year to choose whether to participate in the second tier with the default option set to contribute only to the PAYG system.[69] Lawmakers have since proposed alternative measures aimed at lowering the administrative fees associated with individual accounts, but the reversal measures remain in place.[70] The Bulgarian case, then, offers additional evidence of backtracking on a moderate degree of pension privatization.

The Kazakh Exception: Extensive Pension Privatization & Reversal

Kazakhstan is a noteworthy exception to my general expectations about reversals in pension privatization. The Kazakh government entirely privatized pension and has recently chosen to switch instead to a system of notional defined contributions. Kazakhstan counters the post-communist regional trend of pursuing moderate pension privatization and is an exception to my general expectations about reversal. In 1998, the country's government implemented a form of complete pension privatization in which 100 percent of pensioners' benefits would come from individual, privately invested accounts. In introducing such a system, it pursued a greater degree of reform than any other post-communist country. Chile was the only other country in the world to pursue pension privatization as extensively as in Kazakhstan.

Unlike other countries which pursued extensive pension privatization, the Kazakh government has effectively reversed the reform. In January 2013, President Nazarbayev announced that there would be major changes in the country's pension system. The biggest changes would involve the consolidation of ten private pension funds whose management would be transferred back into state hands.[71] In June 2013, a new law "About Pension Provision in the Republic of

---

[68] National Social Security Institute of Bulgaria, "State Social Security in Bulgaria," December 2012 (available at http://www.noi.bg/en/abouten/infomaterials, accessed January 2013).

[69] Krystyna Kryzak, "Bulgaria Set to Follow Hungary, Poland in Raid of Second-pillar Pensions," *Investment & Pensions Europe*, December 22, 2014.

[70] Krystyna Kryzak, "Bulgarian Parliament Adopts Pension Committee Report," *Investment & Pensions Europe*, May 15, 2015.

[71] "The Republic of Kazakhstan: Financial System Stability Assessment," IMF Country Report No. 14/258, Washington, DC: IMF, July 8, 2014; the official government explanation of the new system is available on the website set up for the newly formed Single Accumulative Pension Fund at http://www.enpf.kz (accessed December 2015).

Kazakhstan" was adopted which introduced the *Edinogo nakopitel'nogo pensionnogo fonda*, or Single Accumulative Pension Fund. This new Single Accumulative Pension Fund is a joint stock company owned by the Kazakh state. Its holdings are managed by the National Bank of the Republic of Kazakhstan, meaning that the system is now entirely state-run. The government tracks individual contributions which determine future benefits, but now does so according to a system of notional defined contributions instead of individual accounts. Contributions can be used solely as pension savings and are not legally considered a citizen's property and cannot be inherited.[72] Additional legislation was passed in July 2015 linking future benefits to work history.[73]

The move was accompanied by a public statement from Oraz Zhandosov, one of those responsible for the design of Kazakhstan's pension privatization reform introduced in 1998.[74] Zhandosov gave full public support for the consolidation of funds, noting that a number of mistakes had been made in the design of the initial system. Government officials further noted that the assets in the merged fund would be available for domestic infrastructure projects, similar to recent Russian proposals.[75] Government officials were also sure to emphasize that Kazakhstan would retain its three-pillar system, although there would be changes at each level.[76]

Kazakhstan diverges from my general expectations because the government has operated as a long-standing authoritarian regime under the direction of President Nazarbayev. Notably, the Kazakh government is much less democratic than the Latin American countries which pursued pension privatization. This major difference in regime type between Kazakhstan and the other extensive reformers explains why reversal was relatively easy in this case. Because Kazakhstan is a long-standing authoritarian country, it was unlikely that extensive pension privatization would alter the social contract in a way that made it difficult for President Nazarbayev to reverse course.

The regime of President Nazarbayev, Kazakhstan's leader since the fall of communism, has been characterized as one of soft authoritarianism in which the president relies on different means of persuasion combined with coercion and suppression to maintain power (Schatz 2009). Patronage has long been used to bolster support for the regime particularly in the area of natural resource deals (Cummings 2002). As such, public opinion is important,

---

[72] Valerii Surganov, "Chto prineset pensionnaia reforma? Vvodiatsia 5-protsentnye vyplaty s rabotodatelei i polnoe gosobespechenie sotrudnikov silvykh struktur," *Kapital*, August 6, 2015.

[73] Olzhas Ramazanov, "Kazakhstan gotovitsia k mashtabnoi pensionnoi reforme," *KTK Novosti*, July 9, 2015.

[74] Raushan Nurshayeva and Mariya Gordeyava, "Kazakhstan mobilises pension fund assets to spur growth," *Reuters*, January 23, 2013.

[75] Ibid.

[76] *Kapital*, "V pensionnuiu sistemu Kazakhstana vnesut izmeneniia: Bazovuiu pensiiu budut naznachat' v zavisimosti ot stazha raboty," May 13, 2014.

but does not play the same direct influential role it might in a democratic system. The Kazakh government did not introduce or reverse pension privatization because of pressure from domestic stakeholders. Rather, the long-serving President Nazarbayev rightly estimated that this was a great deal of money which could be used by the state with virtually no public backlash.

Despite the limited potential for public backlash, the government announced the changes as a modernization of the pension system aimed to ensure there would be adequate pensions for all. The government accompanied the changes to the second tier of pensions with changes to the first, unfunded tier by raising the minimum pension.[77] It also helped that returns to the accumulative portion of pensions in 2013 had been poor as the result of a stagnating economy. Public opinion data from other post-communist countries like Russia further suggest that citizens care more about the state-provided unfunded pension and issues like the retirement age. In Kazakhstan, however, the government has even been able to introduce a slight increase in the retirement age – increasing the retirement age to 63 for men and 58 for women (from 60 and 55) – without any major backlash.

In contrast to Russia, it appears that the Kazakh government is less concerned about public opinion – even though both countries are commonly considered to be authoritarian. The Russian leadership chose to phase in changes to the accumulative portion, allowing them to gauge public reaction, and has been very hesitant to raise the retirement age despite long-standing recommendations from experts that doing so was important for the country's long-term financial stability.

Although my focus in the case studies is on identifying and evaluating the causal mechanisms by which reversals occurred and explaining why the nature and degree of reversals varied, examples of countries in which backtracking did not occur are consistent with my expectations. As noted in Chapter 4, the Latin American countries that pursued extensive or full pension privatization have engaged in a number of measures to make the system function better, but politicians in these countries have avoided proposals about eliminating or reducing contributions to the privatized individual tiers. Latin American governments are not more committed to market-oriented reforms in general and have shown a willingness to change economic policies depending on public opinion and the partisanship of those in office. Stokes (1996) notes the extreme case of President Menem in Argentina who campaigned on a platform of social spending only to pursue austerity in his subsequent policies. Indeed, Argentina is a regional exception with regard to pension privatization: unlike its geographic neighbors, the Argentinean government pursued moderate pension privatization and was the first country in the world to dramatically reverse pension privatization.

---

[77] Nikita Korol'kov, "Modernizatsiia pensionnoi sistemy RK: eto blizhaishaia perspektiva i potentsial na budushee," *Kapital*, October 9, 2014.

Those Latin American countries that had extensively privatized pension privatization have not followed suit.

Cases of reversal and nonreversal are consistent with the evidence from cross-national trends that countries with moderate reforms are the most likely to backtrack even when we account for other common explanations. Domestic stakeholders play a central role in keeping a reform in place. If politicians see fiscal benefits in reversing and domestic stakeholders are not invested in the policy, then backtracking is likely to occur.

PART IV

CONCLUSION

8

The Importance of Understanding Pension Policy Reversal

> Economic reforms implemented without an understanding of their political consequences, rather than promoting economic efficiency, can significantly reduce it.
> Daron Acemoglu and James Robinson, 2013[1]

> For if we are wise now, why were we not equally sage before?
> Adam Przeworski, 1991[2]

Pension privatization was remarkable in its attempt to alter a long-standing social contract about who would accept the risk for providing for citizens in their old age. Theories at the time emphasized that changing the social contract based on pension privatization would be difficult because people had come to expect the state to provide certain benefits. When reversals of pension privatization occurred, however, backtracking was not the product of a public backlash. Instead, after pension privatization had been put into place, 10 or 20 years later politicians abandoned these systems when it was fiscally beneficial to do so and in cases in which domestic interest groups did not object. The reversals of pension privatization tell a remarkable story about why market-oriented reforms are adopted and why these efforts may ultimately be abandoned.

I take no stance here about whether pension privatization is the most appropriate reform for any specific country. Indeed, the results are somewhat mixed. Pension privatization appears to work well in some countries and less so in others. Whether or not pension privatization can yield economic and social benefits depends upon domestic conditions and how the system is regulated. We can generally agree, however, that even ideal reforms are suboptimal if they

---

[1] Daron Acemoglu and James A. Robinson. 2013. "Economics versus Politics: Pitfalls of Policy Advice," National Bureau of Economic Research (NBER) Working Paper Series, Working Paper 18921, available at: http://www.nber.org/papers/w18921 (accessed April 17, 2014).
[2] Przeworski (1991, p. 1).

fail to last. This is especially true for social security reform. Making substantial changes to retirement policies every decade is no way to design a national pension system.

The reversals of pension privatization around the world reveal important lessons about when and why reforms will be adopted and when they will survive. I highlight several of these lessons here. Market-oriented reforms are diverse and pension privatization is unique in several regards. Nonetheless, the case of pension privatization offers generalizable lessons for economic policymaking, including the importance of fiscal incentives, the role of domestic stakeholders, and the significance of reform design for long-term policy survival.

Why Governments Reversed a Market-Oriented Reform

The theory presented in this book is not a Goldilocks theory in that conditions must be "just right" for reversal. Rather, the causal story here reveals the complicated and connected influence of fiscal pressures and domestic stakeholders on the formation and sustainability of policy. In some countries, the pressure and ability to reform resulted in moderate reforms that did not fundamentally alter the social contract but were nonetheless fiscally costly for politicians to maintain in light of a financial crisis. The nature of the initial reform adopted matters a great deal: do a little or do a lot but avoid getting unstuck in the middle.

Reversals occurred because of politicians' fiscal incentives to reverse and the lack of domestic opposition that existed in certain countries. The financial crisis of 2008 sparked discussions about where politicians could get short-term revenue. In countries with extensive pension privatization, however, reversal was not a politically feasible option because domestic stakeholders, including citizens and private pension funds, were entrenched in the systems. By contrast, in countries with moderate pension privatization politicians could get valuable short-term revenue by backtracking and faced limited, if any, pushback from domestic stakeholders. Domestic politics filtered these fiscal pressures in ways that resulted in different kinds of reversals across countries. Indeed, a central part of understanding reversals is appreciating how domestic political battles and partisan policy agendas transformed fiscal pressures into reversals.

Although pension privatization is a unique kind of social security reform and a unique kind of privatization, like other market-oriented reforms it creates a system in which the government oversees and regulates closely a system in which private businesses are central actors. As such, the lessons of pension privatization generalize well to other market-oriented reforms. Cross-national statistical analysis suggests that countries with a moderate degree of pension privatization were more likely to backtrack on pension privatization. The quantitative analysis confirms my expectations that those countries that pursued pension privatization to a moderate degree were the most likely to reverse.

I turn to the case studies for a deeper understanding of the political economy of pension privatization reversals and why these reversals varied.

Case studies of the adoption and reversal of pension privatization in Russia, Hungary, and Poland further explicate the causal mechanisms which contributed to reversals and help explain how and why reversals were pursued in different ways and to different degrees. These cases were selected because they are alike in many important regards which explain why they all backtracked on pension privatization, but vary in important aspects which show why they pursued reversals in different ways.

The Russian reversal of pension privatization reveals why moderate reform would lead to backtracking on pension privatization. I have the advantage of having begun to study Russian pension politics before a reversal of pension privatization was even being discussed and am therefore able to provide a detailed picture of why pension privatization was adopted in Russia, the consequences and methods of its implementation, and why ultimately it did not endure. In the case of Russia, pension privatization was adopted and abandoned under the same party of power – United Russia – and under the same leader, Vladimir Putin.

The Russian public was not calling for the government to backtrack on the 2002 pension reforms. Instead, the government saw significant short-term fiscal gains from reversing and did not face any serious opposition to doing so. The financial crisis of 2008 instigated the need for short-term revenue and explains the timing of Russia's reversal. The Russian government pursued pension privatization incrementally, allowing it to gauge whether there would be any significant public backlash. Neither the public sector nor the private pension funds were influential domestic stakeholders with regard to pension privatization. Instead, the government has been able to go back and forth on pension policy with little public reaction and minimal backlash from the private sector.

The Hungarian and Polish cases are similar to the experience of Russia in revealing how moderate reforms make a reversal more likely and are distinct in showing the different paths by which governments reined in pension privatization. In both Hungary and Poland, the 2008 financial crisis sparked discussions about where politicians could gain short-term revenue and resulted in proposals for eliminating or reducing pension privatization. In neither country did citizens appear to be very invested in the privatized portion of pensions nor did private pension funds have the ability or desire to pressure politicians to preserve pension privatization. As a result, both governments reversed their previous course on social security.

The Hungarian government initiated a dramatic and complete reversal in 2010 with little public or legislative discussion. The Hungarian reversal was spurred by a particularly bad domestic fiscal situation and the legislative majority secured by Fidesz in the fall of 2010. Fidesz campaigned on lowering taxes and improving employment. Backtracking on pension privatization gave the government access to short-term revenue that helped politicians keep these promises, at least in the short term. Despite vocal criticism from policy experts, the government passed a swift and complete elimination of the second tier.

The Polish government pursued an incremental and, to date, more partial reversal than occurred in Hungary. In Poland, a less dire fiscal situation and a more competitive political arena prevented politicians from scrapping pension privatization wholesale as the Fidesz government did in Hungary. Survey evidence in Poland was more definitive than in Hungary in showing that citizens were not overly concerned about the reversal of pension privatization. Polish politicians, however, took a more cautious approach by passing legislation to only partially reduce contributions and for a portion of this reduction to be temporary. This leaves open the option for Poland that the second tier could be fully restored at a later date.

Taken together, the global trends and the case studies indicate that fiscal pressures, politicians' time horizons, and the strength of domestic interest groups shape whether or not a reform will survive. In cases in which pension privatization had been adopted to a moderate degree – not in the most or least extensive reformers – the financial crisis that began in 2008 created conditions which made reversal likely: politicians could gain short-term revenue without any significant domestic opposition.

Fiscal Costs and Backtracking on Reform

One important lesson here is that the recurring costs of maintaining a policy will influence politicians' incentives to backtrack. Pension privatization was unique in that the money diverted to individual accounts provided an obvious and quantifiable sum of money to be gained by backtracking. Reversing other reforms – such as renationalizing property – can also provide valuable fiscal benefits. Politicians must always make choices about who to tax and how much and where to allocate spending. When there are sources of revenue that do not require raising taxes or cutting benefits, these should be especially appealing to politicians. Reversing pension privatization freed up short-term revenue without requiring an increase in taxes or decrease in spending which was especially salient because of the financial crisis of 2008.

We should take very seriously whether or not politicians have short-term incentives to maintain policies and the benefits (which may be more than temporary revenue) of backtracking on measures. Even if reversing does not improve a country's long-term fiscal situation, expensive reforms are hard to maintain unless politicians' hands are tied in some way. Politicians generally operate on electoral timeframes so that a move that improves the situation now before the next election and does not produce immediate negative consequences will be a tempting one. This is an inherent challenge in long-term policy planning. What politician really has an incentive to think beyond her own time in office? The solution may not be in trying to eliminate the time inconsistency between long-term goals and politicians' electoral horizons, but instead in thinking about how to make short-term incentives congruent with long-term objectives.

The Role of Domestic Stakeholders

Another important lesson is that even if there are large fiscal incentives to reverse, domestic stakeholders can prevent backtracking. After pension privatization was adopted, there was concern that such a radical shift could not truly remake social security. Brooks (2009) called the concluding chapter of her study "A New Social Contract?" and suggested that the biggest threat to pension privatization would be accusations that the new system was unfair. This was a highly plausible scenario given the potential magnitude of the shift from guaranteed state-provided benefits to systems in which citizens would depend on their own contributions and the returns to those contributions. In Latin America, this concern proved to be true as governments have pursued revisions of the privatized pension systems in part with the justification of making systems fairer. The key, however, was how far the government initially went in terms of making the switch. In fact, in the countries that made the most dramatic shift to pension privatization, the policy is currently surviving and is even undergoing a round of revisions intended to improve its performance. Here, the advocates of pension privatization were correct that a new social contract would be created. Furthermore, a new business–state contract emerged in which private pension funds are playing a central role in national social security.

By contrast, in countries in which pension privatization was only moderately pursued, domestic stakeholders have not emerged to back the reform's survival. In these countries, the public is largely uninformed and apathetic about whether or not pension privatization continues. In Russia, survey evidence showed that traditional socioeconomic indicators and support for Putin do not predict whether or not one supports pension privatization. Furthermore, nearly half of the population was unaware that the reversal was taking place. In Hungary, polls were contradictory, but the Fidesz government's quick elimination of pension privatization suggests that their gamble on public indifference was well-founded. Even in Poland, where the government had worked hard to sell the public on pension privatization and nearly half of social security benefits were to come from the individual accounts, the public has not appeared to be much affected by the change.

Private pension funds are one of the potential domestic stakeholders in pension privatization, but again, in countries with only moderate pension privatization these business interests have played a marginal role in recent pension debates. Rather, the larger financial conglomerates of which most private pension funds are a part have calculated that they make more money from other financial products, making the reversal of pension privatization unfortunate, but not critical, to their survival. As further evidence, investors have not fled countries where pension privatization has been overturned. Even in Argentina, the first country to abandon pension privatization – and to do so completely, there was only a temporary dip in stock market performance.

Contrary to fears that the public will undermine painful, but necessary economic and social reforms, the reversal of pension privatization was instigated by politicians seeking short-term revenue who lacked opposition from domestic stakeholders. This turns on its head the logic of the J-curve in which elected politicians would fail to pursue market-oriented reforms because of popular opposition. Instead, in the case of pension privatization, the public and private sectors could play a much more positive role in helping retain important reforms.

Post-Communist Implications

Reversals in pension privatization have been concentrated in the post-communist countries. Argentina was the first and one of the most dramatic instances of backtracking on pension privatization. The British government has since announced plans to alter its individual accounts system for a more simplified one. Nonetheless, there is an extent to which the reversal of a potentially path-departing change has been a post-communist phenomena.

Reversals of pension privatization are an excellent example of how the post-communist countries of Central and Eastern Europe and Central Asia illustrate the similarities and differences across the region. They are similar, of course, in that many of the post-communist reformers have now eliminated or curtailed their pension privatization systems. They differ, however, in terms of the means and degree to which they backtracked. We see that the post-communist countries are both remarkable in their similarity and in their notable variation.

The important lesson for post-communist politics is twofold. The post-communist lens has undoubtedly shaped both the nature of policy challenges governments face and the types of policies they may adopt. The post-communist countries in this region were industrialized countries with extensive and costly PAYG pension systems that could not be sustained. These governments were also generally – though not universally – inclined to adopt fairly extensive market-oriented reforms like a flat tax and pension privatization. Indeed, pension privatization was adopted and reversed among countries with very different economies and regime types in part because of the communist legacy. The communist legacy meant that governments did not go as far in implementing pension privatization because they faced very costly PAYG systems and could not afford the financing gap that would be generated by more extensive measures.

Within this uniformity, however, is remarkable and meaningful variation which reveals the distinctive nature of domestic politics across the region. Many post-communist countries adopted and reversed a moderate degree of pension privatization, but they did so in very different ways. This variation reflects larger trends. While some countries such as Poland are becoming leaders in the European Union, others, like Hungary, face a wide array of criticism for economic, political, and social policies. Others like Belarus, Russia, and Kazakhstan operate under an authoritarian structure. These differences in political regimes – as well as other important differences including their economic structures – shape their divergent responses to similar challenges. The findings in this book contribute to our understanding of the region by emphasizing that post-communist politics should be seen as a very diverse set of countries facing similar challenges in unique ways.

The case of reversals in pension privatization also contributes to our understanding of authoritarian politics, especially through the Russian case. The extent of pension privatization alongside politicians' short-term fiscal incentives and weak domestic stakeholders in the policy explain why reversals occur. At the next stage, regime type influenced how – and to what extent – pension privatization was reversed. The Russian case demonstrates policymaking in an authoritarian regime. Authoritarian leaders like the Russian leadership care about public opinion and the reaction of private groups. Indeed, this is why we see that reversals occurred in both democratic and authoritarian regimes when pension privatization was not extensive. And indeed survey evidence in Russia reassured the leadership that the public was largely apathetic and uninformed on this issue. We can see, though, a major difference in Russia's authoritarian style of policymaking. In Russia policy battles are often interministerial debates. By the time an official proposal becomes public, it has already been vetted and agreed upon by several major ministries and the presidency. This book shows that authoritarian regimes may pursue the same goals and even policies as democracies but do so in very different ways.

The Importance of Reform Design

The findings about the fiscal costs and role of domestic stakeholders suggest a more overarching – and perhaps obvious – lesson from the reversal of pension privatization. The design of the initial reform matters for how well the policy will work and whether it will stay in place. Scholars and policy experts have always thought the nature of the policy matters, but this lesson bears repeating. A simplistic and implicit (if not explicit) assumption was often made that pension privatization was the same kind of reform everywhere. But not all pension privatization was the same. Some countries went all the way while other pursued only moderate measures. The result was that when a financial crisis hit, the extensive reformers retained the policy while the moderate reformers were not invested enough to do so.

Some advisers to post-communist countries transitioning to market systems in the early 1990s recommended that countries go all the way to ensure that reforms would become entrenched in society and in the political system (e.g., Åslund 1995). Even initially, however, others noted that the most successful reformers were not pursuing the most radical "shock therapy" options but were instead complementing privatization and liberalization measures with more extensive social spending. No country in the region fit the ideal of a rapid reformer nor did any government appear to be strategically selecting early reforms as a means of building political support (European Bank for Reconstruction and Development 1999). Instead of focusing just on rapid or gradual reforms, then, we should consider the nature and consequences of specific policies.

Pension privatization was adopted due to the fiscal pressures posed by PAYG systems, its promotion by transnational policy advocates (especially the World Bank), and because of the purported macroeconomic benefits. The cost of the PAYG system played a central role in whether politicians felt pressure to adopt this radical social security reform and whether they could afford to do so. After pension privatization was adopted, the fiscal costs of maintaining it, along with a consideration of domestic stakeholders, played a central role in whether or not it would be retained. Central to these debates was how initial conditions influenced the degree to which pension privatization was pursued. In countries with a moderate degree of pension privatization, politicians were losing access to significant short-term revenue but domestic stakeholders, including citizens and private pension funds, were not invested in the continuation of the reform.

Current trends suggest that there may be a curvilinear relationship between the degree of reform and the likelihood of reversal. In countries with extensive pension privatization, we have not seen any reversals to date and the most limited reformers have also generally not reversed. Moderate reformers have been the most likely to backtrack. It is possible, however, that the true distinction is between those who extensively reformed and those who did not. To date, several of the countries with the most limited reforms – Sweden, Costa Rica, and Croatia – have not discussed reversing pension privatization. These are only three countries, however, so we cannot make a definitive conclusion about the curvilinear aspect of the relationship between the degree of reform and the risk of reversal. Nonetheless, the results are clear that the interplay between the fiscal incentives to eliminate pension privatization and the absence of domestic stakeholders shapes whether politicians will pursue reversals.

That a moderate degree of pension privatization made reversal most likely reaffirms some of our conventional understanding of market-oriented reform. There is indeed a tension between what politicians would like to do to get access to revenue and what citizens and private actors may want. In countries with extensive pension privatization, the large fiscal benefit of backtracking did not unhinge the reform even among several Latin American countries not known for being uniquely consistent in their pursuit of market-oriented policies. My findings also confirm that there is a time inconsistency problem. Przeworski (1991) describes the potential dilemma faced by politicians who want to pursue necessary market-oriented reforms that might have long-term benefits but which will also impose short-term costs. Citizens may be unlikely to accept the uncertainty and pain of these short-term costs. Regarding pension privatization, politicians want to ease short-term fiscal pressures by gaining access to social security contributions that would otherwise be diverted to individual accounts. Although allowing the individual accounts to grow may address the challenge of providing for retirees in decades to come, politicians may not be willing to accept the short-term costs (reduced spending elsewhere, higher taxes, or higher deficits) that would be required.

In short, if we hope that reforms will survive in the long term, then we should think about how these policies create strong domestic stakeholders in the short term. These domestic stakeholders could come from a variety of places – the bureaucracy, the private sector, the public, or politicians' own interests – but they almost certainly must be in place to avoid politicians capitalizing on the short-term benefits of reversing.

Debates about pension reform – in contrast to some specific policies – are here to stay and we should think more seriously about understanding *ex ante* when reforms are likely to survive or not. Understanding the political consequences of economic reforms is critical. Economic policies like pension privatization have distributional and fiscal consequences which affect their political chances of survival in the long term. Adopting reforms without understanding their political consequences can lead to outcomes that are economically inefficient and socially undesirable, as Acemoglu and Robinson note.

The findings presented here suggest that we should focus on long-term objectives in retirement planning and how citizens, private pension funds, and government bureaucrats will react in the short term to policy changes. Meeting long-term objectives is impossible without short-term implementation. This rather obvious lesson about short-term policy consequences has been overlooked in the pursuit of radical social security transformations. Certainly, policymakers have been concerned with whether pension privatization would work and what its consequences would be. Nonetheless, there appeared to be little serious fear that the reform would be abandoned. The concern instead was that pension privatization would never be adopted; once implemented, many assumed that it would stick. We should shift our thinking instead to think about not just the difficulty of pursuing policies that fundamentally alter social and economic systems, but whether those changes can be made permanent.

Debates about pension privatization are not over and the findings of this book are limited, as is any work, by being written at a particular point in time. Policies will come and go; pension privatization may or may not survive in the long run in other countries. Even as the final draft of this book is being completed, important changes to pension policy are being considered in a number of countries. For the time being, pension privatization is becoming more entrenched in some countries, particularly in the Latin American reformers. As time passes, it appears less likely that these policies will be simply abandoned, although unexpected changes happen all the time.

The central finding of this book gets us closer to understanding which policies are likely to survive and which are only temporary deviations. Although the focus has been on reversals, there is a complementary and optimistic lesson as well: some very well-intentioned and beneficial reforms will survive, will produce short- and long-term benefits, and will help solve challenging and complex problems.

Appendix of Interviews Conducted by Author

I do not report the names of individuals interviewed to maintain their anonymity and confidentiality. Forty-two individuals were interviewed between the period of 2006 and 2013. Anonymized notes from the interviews are available for all of the interviews. I have put a star next to interviews for which anonymized transcripts and/or recordings of the interview are available in Russian upon request. Below I have identified the type of interviewee, the date, and location of the interview. In the event that I conducted more than one interview on a given day, I have numbered the interviewees to indicate that these are distinct interviewees.

Investment company representative, September 14, 2007 (Moscow, Russia)*

Investment company representative, September 17, 2007 (Moscow, Russia)*

Investment company representative #1, September 25, 2007 (Moscow, Russia)*

Investment company representative #2, September 25, 2007 (Moscow, Russia)*

Investment company representative #1, September 26, 2007 (Moscow, Russia)*

Investment company representative #2, September 26, 2007 (Moscow, Russia)*

Investment company representative, October 2, 2007 (Moscow, Russia)*

Investment company representative, October 5, 2007 (Moscow, Russia)

Investment company representative, October 9, 2007 (Moscow, Russia)

Investment company representative, October 30, 2007 (Moscow, Russia)*

Investment company representative #2, October 30, 2007 (Moscow, Russia)*

Investment company representative, November 7, 2008 (Moscow, Russia)*

Private pension fund representative, October 18, 2007* and July 29, 2011 (Moscow, Russia)

Private pension fund representative #1, October 25, 2007, Summer 2011 (Moscow, Russia)*

Private pension fund representative #2, October 25, 2007*, June 30, 2011 (Moscow, Russia)

Private pension fund representative, November 1, 2007 (Moscow, Russia)*

Private pension fund representative, November 29, 2007 (Ekaterinburg, Russia)*

Private pension fund representative, June 23, 2008 (Moscow, Russia)

Private pension fund representative, July 8, 2011 and June 24, 2013 (Moscow, Russia)

Private pension fund representative, July 15, 2011 (Moscow, Russia)

Ministry of Economic Development and Trade, October 2, 2007 (Moscow, Russia)*

Ministry of Economic Development and Trade #2, October 2, 2007 (Moscow, Russia)*

Ministry of Economic Development and Trade, #3, October 2, 2007 (Moscow, Russia)*

Ministry of Economic Development and Trade, October 18, 2007 (Moscow, Russia)*

Ministry of Economic Development and Trade, October 16, 2007*, July 4, 2011, and June 27, 2013 (Moscow, Russia)

Ministry of Health and Social Development representative, July 1, 2008 (Moscow, Russia)

Pension Fund representative, September 6, 2006 (Moscow, Russia)

Pension Fund representative, July 10, 2008 (Moscow, Russia)*

Ministry of Finance representative, July 16, 2008 (Moscow, Russia)

United Russia representative, December 5, 2007 (Moscow, Russia)

Policy expert, September 4, 2006 (Moscow, Russia)*

Policy expert, September 5, 2006 (Moscow, Russia)*

Policy expert, September 7, 2006 (Moscow, Russia)*

Policy expert, September 11, 2006 (Moscow, Russia)*

Policy expert, September 12, 2006 (Moscow, Russia)*

Policy expert, September 21, 2007 (Moscow, Russia)*

Policy expert, December 3, 2007 (Moscow, Russia)*

Policy expert, July 11, 2008 (Moscow, Russia)

Policy expert #2, July 11, 2008 (Moscow, Russia)

Policy expert #3, July 11, 2008 (Moscow, Russia)

Policy Expert (Expert Economic Group), July 11, 2011 (Moscow, Russia)

Policy expert (Center for Strategic Development), July 5, 2011 and June 25, 2013 (Moscow, Russia)

Pension Terminology

Pension Privatization

pension privatization/ second-pillar reforms	Pension privatization is a policy in which mandatory social security contributions are attributed to individual accounts which are privately managed and invested. The terms *pension privatization* and *second-pillar reforms* are used interchangeably throughout the text. The first pillar is the PAYG portion, the second pillar is a mandatory individual account, and the third pillar constitutes voluntary savings. In other work, this type of reform has also been referred to as a type of *multi-pillar* or *multi-tier pension reform*, a *funded pension reform*, and an *individual account pension reform*, but these terms do not refer exclusively to pension privatization and also include other measures.

Other Important Terms

age dependency ratio	refers to the ratio of the working age population to the retired population
defined benefit	retirement benefit guaranteed as a fixed amount
defined contribution	retirement benefit determined by contributions and any returns to those contributions
funded portion of pensions	refers to the portion of the pension system in which current contributions will be used to cover future pension payments

implicit pension debt	the cost of current obligations to retirees under the PAYG system
notional defined contribution	defined contributions based on calculations depending on parameters typically including years of work and contributions
PAYG	pay-as-you-go; refers to pension systems in which current contributions cover current benefits
unfunded portion of pensions	refers to the portion of the pension system in which current contributions cover current benefits

References

Acemoglu, Daron and James A. Robinson. 2013. "Economics Versus Politics: Pitfalls of Policy Advice," *National Bureau of Economic Research* (NBER) Working Paper Series, Working Paper 18921, available at: http://www.nber.org/papers/w18921 (accessed April 17, 2014).

Aleksandrowicz, Paula. 2007. "Pension Reforms in Poland Since Transition – From Path Departure to Path Dependence," *European Journal of Social Security*, 9(4): 323–344.

Andrews, Emily. 2006. *Pension Reform and the Development of Pension Systems: An Evaluation of World Bank Assistance*. Prepared by the Independent Evaluation Group (IEG), Washington, DC: International Bank for Reconstruction and Development and the World Bank.

Appel, Hilary. 2011. *Tax Politics in Eastern Europe: Globalization, Regional Integration, and the Democratic Compromise*. Ann Arbor: University of Michigan Press.

Appel, Hilary and Mitchell Orenstein. 2013. "Ideas Versus Resources: Explaining the Flat Tax and Pension Privatization Revolutions in Eastern Europe and the Former Soviet Union," *Comparative Politics Studies*, 46(2): 123–152.

Armeanu, Oana. 2010. *The Politics of Pension Reform in Central and Eastern Europe: Political Parties, Coalitions, and Policies*. London: Palgrave Macmillan.

Åslund, Anders. 1995. *How Russia Became a Market Economy*. Washington, DC: Brookings Institution.

Augusztinovics, Mária. 1999. "Pension Systems and Reforms in the Transition Economies," In *Economic Survey of Europe*, 3, December. United Nations Economic Commission for Europe, Geneva, Switzerland.

Augusztinovics, Mária and B. Martos. 1996. "Pension Reform: Calculations and Conclusions," *Acta Oeconomica*, 48(1/2): 119–160.

Baker, Andy. 2009. *The Market and the Masses in Latin America*. Cambridge: Cambridge University Press.

Balzer, Harvey. 2003. "Managed Pluralism: Vladimir Putin's Emerging Regime," *Post-Soviet Affairs*, 19(3): 189–227.

Barnes, Andrew. 2003. "Russia's New Business Groups and State Power," *Post-Soviet Affairs*, 19(2): 154–186.

2006. *Owning Russia: The Struggle over Factories, Farms, and Power*. Ithaca, NY: Cornell University Press.

Barnes, Andrew and Juliet Johnson. 2015. "Financial Nationalism and Its International Enablers: The Hungarian Experience," *Review of International Political Economy*, 22(3): 535–569.

Barr, Nicholas and Peter Diamond. 2008. *Reforming Pensions: Principles and Policy Choices*. Oxford: Oxford University Press.

Barr, Nicholas and Michal Rutkowski. 2005. "Pensions." In *Labor Markets and Social Policy In Central and Eastern Europe: The Accession And Beyond*, ed. Nicholas Barr, 135–170. Washington, DC: World Bank Publications.

Baumgartner, Frank R. and Bryan D. Jones. 1993. *Agendas and Instability in American Politics*. Chicago, IL: University of Chicago Press.

Bawn, Kathleen, Marty Cohen, David Karol, Seth Masket, Hans Noel, and John Zaller. 2012. "A Theory of Political Parties: Groups, Policy Demands and Nominations in American Politics," *Perspectives on Politics*, 10(3): 571–597.

Beazer, Quintin. 2012. "Bureaucratic Discretion, Business Investment, and Uncertainty," *Journal of Politics* 74(3): 637–652.

Beck, Thorsten, George Clarke, Alberto Groff, Philip Keefer, and Patrick Walsh. 2001. "New Tools in Comparative Political Economy: The Database of Political Institutions," *The World Bank Economic Review* 15(1) (June 1): 165–176.

Beck, Nathaniel, Kristian Skrede Gleditsch, and Kyle Beardsley. 2006. "Space is More than Geography: Using Spatial Econometrics in the Study of Political Economy," *International Studies Quarterly*, 50(27): 27–44.

Berry, William and Brady Baybeck. 2005. "Using Geographic Information Systems to Study Interstate Competition," *American Political Science Review*, 1(4): 509–519.

Betliy, Oleksandra and Ricardo Giucci. 2011. "Pension Reform in Ukraine. Comments on the Main Features of the Current Draft Law," Policy Paper Series [PP/01/2011]. Kiev, Ukraine: Institute for Economic Research and Policy Consulting.

Bielecki, Jan. 2011. "What Shapes Pension Reform in Emerging Europe?" Presented at the Pension System in Emerging Europe: Reform in the Age of Austerity, European Bank for Reconstruction and Development, London, UK.

Blaydes, Lisa. 2011. *Elections and Distributive Politics in Mubarak's Egypt*. Cambridge: Cambridge University Press.

Box-Steffensmeier, Janet M. and Bradford S. Jones. 2004. *Event History Modeling: A Guide for Social Scientists*. Cambridge: Cambridge University Press.

Bozoki, Andras and John Ishiyama., eds., 2002. *Communist Successor Parties in Central and Eastern Europe*, New York: M.E. Sharpe.

Brooks, Clem and Jeff Manza. 2006. "Why Do Welfare States Persist?," *Journal of Politics* 68(4) (November 1): 816–827.

Brooks, Sarah M. 2009. *Social Protection and the Market in Latin America: The Transformation of Social Security Institutions*. Cambridge: Cambridge University Press.

2007a. "When Does Diffusion Matter? Explaining the Spread of Structural Pension Reforms Across Nations," *Journal of Politics* 69(3): 701–715.

2007b. "Globalization and Pension Reform in Latin America," *Latin American Politics and Society* 49(4): 31–62.

Campbell, Andrea. 2003. *How Policies Make Citizens: Senior Political Activism and the American Welfare State*. Princeton, NJ: Princeton University Press.

Cangiano, Marco, Carlo Cottarelli and Luis Cubeddu. 1998. *Pension Developments and Reforms in Transition Economies*. IMF Working Paper No. 98/151, European I Department and Fiscal Affairs Department.

Cao, Xun. 2010. "Networks as Channels of Policy Diffusion: Explaining Worldwide Changes in Capital Taxation, 1998–2006," *International Studies Quarterly* 54(3): 823–854.

Carpenter, Daniel. 2001. *The Forging of Bureaucratic Autonomy: Reputations, Networks, and Policy Autonomy in Executive Agencies, 1862–1928*. Princeton, NJ: Princeton University Press.

Casey, Bernard H. 2012. "The Implications of the Economic Crisis for Pensions and Pension Policy in Europe," *Global Social Policy*, 12(3): 246–265.

Casey, Bernard and Jörg Michael Dostal. 2008. "Pension Reform in Nigeria: How not to 'Learn from Others'," *Global Social Policy*, 8(2): 238–266.

Chandler, A. 2004. *Shocking Mother Russia: Democratization, Social Rights, and Pension Reform in Russia, 1990–2001* Toronto: University of Toronto Press.

Chawla, Mukesh, Gordon Betcherman, and Arup Banerji. 2007. *From Red to Gray: The "Third Transition" of Aging Populations in Eastern Europe and the Former Soviet Union*. Washington, DC: World Bank.

Chłoń, Agnieszka. 2000. *Pension Reform and Public Information*. Washington, DC: World Bank.

Chłoń, Agnieszka, Marek Góra, and Michal Rutkowski. 1999. "Shaping Pension Reform in Poland: Security through Diversity," *Social Protection Discussion Paper Series No. 9233*, Washington, DC: The World Bank.

Chłoń-Domińczak, Agnieska. 2004. "The Collection of Pension Contributions in Poland," in *Collection of Pension Contributions: Trends, Issues and Problems in Central and Eastern Europe*, Budapest, Hungary: International Labour Office, Sub-regional Office for Central and Eastern Europe.

Chłoń-Domińczak, Agnieszka, and Marek Gora. 2003. "The NDC System in Poland – Assessment after 5 Years," In *World Bank and RFV Conference on NDC Pensions*, Sandham, Sweden: World Bank.

Cook, Linda J. 2007. *Postcommunist Welfare States: Reform Politics in Russia and Eastern Europe*. Ithaca, NY: Cornell University Press.

Crabtree, Charles, David Darmofal, and Holger Kern. 2015. "A Spatial Analysis of the Impact of West German Television on Protest Mobilization During the East German Revolution," *Journal of Peace Research* 52(3): 269–284.

Culpeper, Pepper. 2010. *Quiet Politics and Business Power: Corporate Control in Europe and Japan*. Cambridge: Cambridge University Press.

Cummings, Sally. 2002. *Kazakhstan: The Power and the Elite*. London: I.B. Tauris.

Darmofal, David. 2015. *Spatial Analysis for the Social Sciences*. Cambridge: Cambridge University Press.

Dave, Surendra. 2006. "India's Pension Reform: A Case Study in Complex Institutional Change," Bombay, India: Centre for Monitoring Indian Economy Pvt. Ltd. (CMIE).

DeCanio, Samuel. 2015. *Democracy and the Origins of the American Regulatory State*, New Haven, CT: Yale University Press.

DeCastello Branco, Marta. 1998. *Pension Reform in the Baltics, Russia, and other Countries of the Former Soviet Union.* IMF Working Paper No. 98/11.

Degtyarev, G. (1999) *Pensionnaia Reforma v Rossii: 1991–1999.* Moscow: Institute of Social Economic Problems of the Population, Russian Academy of Sciences.

Denisova, Irina, Orbán, M. and Yudaeva, K. 1999. "Social Policy in Russia: Pension Fund and Social Security," *Russian Economic Trends* 8(1): 12–23.

Dmitriev, Mikhail. 2000. "Should the Pension Reform Program be Changed?" Moscow: Carnegie Moscow Center.

Dmitriev, Mikhail, Pomazkin, D., Stolyarov, A., Sinyavskaya, O., Surkov, S. 2002. *Finansovoe Sostoyanie i Perspektivy Reformirovaniia Pensionnykh Sistemykh v Rossiiskoi Federatsii.* Available at www.pensionreform.ru/24601 (accessed April 20, 2015).

Drahokoupil, Jan, and Stefan Domonkos. 2012. "Averting the Funding-gap Crisis: East European Pension Reforms since 2008," *Global Social Policy* 12(3): 283–299.

Drukker, David. 2009. "Analyzing Spatial Autoregressive Models using Stata," with Ingmar Prucha, Presented at the 2009 Italian Stata Users Group meeting (February 19). StataCorp.

Drukker, David M., Hua Peng, Ingmar R. Prucha, and Rafal Raciborski 2012. "Creating and Managing Spatial Weighting Matrices using the spmat Command," College Station, TX: Stata Corps.

Duvanova, Dinissa. 2013. *Building Business in Post-Communist Russia, Eastern Europe, and Eurasia: Collective Goods, Selective Incentives, and Predatory States.* Cambridge: Cambridge University Press.

Ebbinghaus, Bernhard. 2005. "Can Path Dependence Explain Institutional Change? Two Approaches Applied to Welfare State Reform." Discussion Paper 05/2. Cologne, Germany: Max Planck Institute for the Study of Societies.

Ebbinghaus, Bernhard, Mitchell A. Orenstein, and Noel Whiteside. 2012. "Governing Pension Fund Capitalism in Times of Uncertainty," *Global Social Policy* 12(3): 241–245.

Égert, Balázs. 2012. *The Impact of Changes in Second Pension Pillars on Public Finances in Central and Eastern Europe.* OECD Economics Department Working Paper. OECD Publishing. http://ideas.repec.org/p/oec/ecoaaa/942-en.html (accessed April 17, 2017).

European Bank for Reconstruction and Development. 1999. *Transition Report 1999: Ten Years of Transition.* London: European Bank for Reconstruction and Development.

European Commission. 2012. *An Agenda for Adequate, Safe, and Sustainable Pensions.* Brussels. White Paper.

Ferge, Zsuzsa, and Gabor Juhasz. 2004. "Accession and Social Policy: The Case of Hungary," *Journal of European Social Policy* 14(3) (August 1): 233–251.

Fish, M. Steven. 2005. *Democracy Derailed in Russia.* Cambridge: Cambridge University Press.

Flores-Macías, Gustavo. 2012. *After Neoliberalism? The Left and Economic Reforms in Latin America,* Oxford: Oxford University Press.

Franzese, Robert J. and Jude C. Hays. 2007. "Spatial Econometric Models of Cross-Sectional Interdependence in Political Science Panel and Time-Series-Cross-Section Data," *Political Analysis* 15(2): 140–164.

Freedom House. 2013. *Freedom in the World 2013: Democratic Breakthroughs in the Balance*. New York and Washington, DC: Freedom House.

Frye, Timothy. 2010. *Building States and Markets after Communism: The Perils of Polarized Democracy*. Cambridge: Cambridge University Press.

Fultz, Elaine. 2012. "The Retrenchment of Second-Tier Pensions in Hungary and Poland: A Precautionary Tale," *International Social Security Review* 65(3): 1–25.

Gál, Róbert. 2012. *Annual National Report 2011: Pensions, Healthcare, and Long-term Care (Hungary)*. Analytical Support on the Socio-Economic Impact of Social Protection Reforms (ASISP) for the European Commission DG Employment, Social Affairs, and Inclusion.

Gál, Róbert, András Simonovits, and Géza Tarcali. 2001. "Generational Accounting and Hungarian Pension Reform," Social Protection Discussion Paper Series No. 0127, Washington, DC: The World Bank.

Ganev, Venelin. 2007. *Preying on the State: The Transformation of Bulgaria after 1989*. Ithaca, NY: Cornell University Press.

Geddes, Barbara. 2003. *Paradigms and Sand Castles: Theory Building and Research Design in Comparative Politics*, Ann Arbor, MI: University of Michigan Press.

Gehlbach, Scott. 2008. *Representation through Taxation*. Cambridge: Cambridge University Press.

Gehlbach, Scott, and Edmund J. Malesky. 2010. "The Contribution of Veto Players to Economic Reform," *Journal of Politics* 72(4): 957–975.

George, Alexander L. and Timothy J. McKeown. 1985. "Case Studies and Theory of Organizational Decision Making," in *Advances in Information Processing in Organizations*, Vol. 2, pp. 21–58. Greenwich, CT: JAI Press.

Gessel, Rainer, Katharina Müller, and Dirck Süß. 1998. "Social Security Reform and Privatisation in Poland: Parallel Projects or Integrated Agenda?" First published as a BOFIT Discussion Paper No. 8/98 at European University Viadrina Frankfurt (Oder).

Goode, Paul J. 2004. "The Push for Regional Enlargement in Putin's Russia," *Post-Soviet Affairs*, 20(3): 219–257.

Gourevitch, Peter. 1986. *Politics in Hard Times: Comparative Responses to International Economic Crises*, Ithaca, NY: Cornell University Press.

Gronicki, Mirosław and Janusz Jankowiak. 2013. *Otwarte Fundusze Emerytalne i Gospodarka Polski w Latach, 1999–2013*. Warsaw: Lewiatan.

Grzymała-Busse, Anna. 2002. *Redeeming the Communist Past: The Regeneration of the Communist Successor Parties in East Central Europe*. Cambridge: Cambridge University Press.

Guardiancich, Igor. 2004. "Welfare State Retrenchment in Central and Eastern Europe: the Case of Pension Reforms in Poland and Slovenia," *Managing Global Transitions* 2(1): 41–64.

Guardiancich, Igor. 2013. "Pension Privaitzation in CEE: World Bank's Failure and European Inconsistencies." Presented at the ETUC and ETUI, Challenges and Future Perspectives of Pension Funds in Europe.

Hacker, Jacob. 2008. *The Great Risk Shift: The New Economic Insecurity and the Decline of the American Dream*. Oxford: Oxford University Press.

Hacker, Jacob and Paul Pierson. 2014. "After the 'Master Theory': Downs, Schattschneider, and the Rebirth of Policy-Focused Analysis," *Perspectives on Politics* 12(3): 643–662.

Haggard, Stephan and Robert Kaufman. 2008. *Development, Democracy, and Welfare States: Latin America, East Asia, and Eastern Europe.* Princeton, NJ: Princeton University Press.

Haining, Robert P. 2003. *Spatial Data Analysis: Theory and Practice.* Cambridge: Cambridge University Press.

Hanson, Philip and Elizabeth Teague. 2005. "Big Business and the State in Russia," *Europe–Asia Studies* 57(5): 657–680.

Häuserman, Silja. 2010. *The Politics of Welfare State Reform in Continental Europe: Modernization in Hard Times.* Cambridge: Cambridge University Press.

Hausner, Jerzy. 2001. "Security Through Diversity: Conditions for Successful Reform of the Pension System in Poland." In *Reforming the State,* eds. János Kornai, Stephan Haggard, and Robert R. Kaufman, 210–234. Cambridge: Cambridge University Press.

　2002. "Poland: Security through Diversity," in *Social Security Pension Reform in Europe,* eds. Martin Feldstein and Horst Siebert. Chicago, IL: University of Chicago Press for National Bureau of Economic Research.

Hellman, Joel S. 1998. "Winners Take All: The Politics of Partial Reform in Postcommunist Transitions," *World Politics* 50(2): 203–34.

Hemerjick. Anton. 2012. *Changing Welfare States.* Oxford: Oxford University Press.

Herman, Zita. 2013. "Hungary – Social Partners Involvement in the Reforms of the Pension Systems." Dublin, Ireland: European Foundation for the Improvement of Living and Working Conditions (Eurofound).

Herrera, Yoshiko M., and Devesh Kapur. 2007. "Improving Data Quality: Actors, Incentives, and Capabilities," *Political Analysis* 15(4) (October 1): 365–386.

Hirschman, Albert. 1970. *Exit, Voice, and Loyalty: Response to Decline in Firms, Organizations, and States.* Cambridge, MA: Harvard University Press.

Holzman, Robert, and Richard P Hinz. 2005. *Old-Age Income Support in the 21st Century: An International Perspective on Pension Systems and Reform.* Washington, DC: World Bank.

Holzmann, Robert, and Palmer, Edward, eds. 2006. *Pension Reform.* Washington, DC: World Bank.

Holzmann, Robert, Robert Palacios, and Asta Zviniene. 2004. *Implicit Pension Debt: Issues, Measurement, and Scope in International Perspective.* Social Protection Discussion Paper Series. World Bank.

Honaker, James, Gary King, and Matthew Blackwell. 2011. "Amelia II: A Program for Missing Data," *Journal of Statistical Software* 45(7): 1–47 Available at: http://www.jstatsoft.org/v45/i07/ (accessed April 20, 2017)

Hujo, Katja, and Mariana Rulli. 2014. "The Political Economy of Pension Re-Reform in Chile and Argentina." Research Paper 2014–1. United Nations Research Institute for Social Development (UNRISD).

Hyde, Matthew. 2001. "Putin's Federal Reforms and their Implications for Presidential Power in Russia," *Europe–Asia Studies,* 53(5): 719–743.

Immergut, Ellen M., and Karen M. Andersen. 2007. "Editor's Introduction: The Dynamics of Pension Politics." In *The Handbook of West European Pension Politics,* ed. Ellen M. Immergut, Karen M. Anderson, and Isabelle Schulze. Oxford: Oxford University Press.

James, Estelle, and Sarah Brooks. 2001. "Political Economy of Structural Pension Reform." In *New Ideas About Old Age Security: Toward Sustainable Pension*

Systems in the 21st Century, ed. Robert Holzmann, 133–170. Washington, DC: World Bank.

Javeline, Debra. 2003. *Protest and the Politics of Blame: The Russian Response to Unpaid Wages*, Ann Arbor, MI: University of Michigan Press.

Jenkins, Jeffrey A. and Eric M. Patashnik, eds. 2012. *Living Legislation: Durability, Change, and the Politics of American Lawmaking*. Chicago, IL: University of Chicago Press.

Jensen, Donald N. (2001) "How Russia is Ruled." In *Business and the State in Contemporary Russia*, ed. Peter Rutland, 33–64 Boulder, CO: Westview Press.

Kane, Chekih, and Robert Palacios. 1996. "The Implicit Pension Debt," *Finance and Development* 33(2): 36.

Karasyov, D., and Y. Lublin. 2001. "Trends in Pension Reform in the Russian Federation: A Brief Overview," *International Social Security Review* 54(2–3).

Kasek, Leszek, Thomas Laursen, and Emilia Skrok. 2008. "Sustainability of Pension Systems in the New EU Member States and Croatia: Coping with Aging Challenges and Fiscal Pressures," *World Bank Working Paper No. 129*, Washington, DC: World Bank.

Kay, Stephen J. 2000. "Privatizing Pensions: Prospects for the Latin American Reforms," *Journal of Interamerican Studies and World Affairs* 42(1, April): 133–143.

2009. "Political Risk and Pension Privatization," *International Social Security Review*, 63(3): 1–21.

Kerner, Andrew. Conditionally accepted. "The Ownership Society: Financial Returns and Popular Support for Markets in Post-Pension Reform Latin America," *British Journal of Political Science*.

King, Gary, Robert Keohane, and Sidney Verba. 1994. *Designing Social Inquiry: Scientific Inference in Qualitative Research*. Princeton, NJ: Princeton University Press.

Kingdon, John. 2003. *Agendas, Alternatives, and Public Policies*, second edition. Harlow, UK: Longman.

Kitschelt, Herbert et al. 1999. *Post-Communist Party Systems: Competition, Representation, and Inter-Party Cooperation*. Cambridge: Cambridge University Press.

Konitzer, Andrew and Stephen K. Wegren. 2006. "Federalism and Political Recentralization in the Russian Federation: United Russia as the Party of Power," *Publius*, 36(4 Autumn): 503–522.

Kornai, János. 1991. "The Hungarian Reform Process: Visions, Hopes, and Reality," in *Crisis and Reform in Eastern Europe*, Ferenc Fehér and Andrew Arato, eds., 27–98. New Brunswick and London: Transaction Publishers.

Kornai, János. 1992. *The Socialist System*. Oxford: Oxford University Press.

Kritzer, Barbara E. 2008. "Chile's Next Generation Pension Reform," *Social Security Bulletin* 68(2): 69–84.

Kritzer, Barbara E., Stephen J. Kay, and Tapha Sinha. 2011. "Next Generation of Individual Account Pension Reforms in Latin America," *Social Security Bulletin* 71(1): 35–76.

Kubicek, Paul. 1996. "Variations on a Corporatist Theme: Interest Associations in Post-Soviet Ukraine and Russia," *Europe–Asia Studies*, 48(2): 27–46.

Levitsky, Steven and Lucan Way. 2010. *Competitive Authoritarianism: Hybrid Regimes After the Cold War*. Cambridge: Cambridge University Press.

Light, Matthew. 2012. "What Does It Mean to Control Migration? Soviet Mobility Practices in Comparative Perspective," *Law & Social Inquiry*, 37(2): 395–429.

Lijphart, Arend. 1971. "Comparative Politics and the Comparative Method," *American Political Science Review* 65(3, Sep.): 682–693.

Lindblom, Charles. 1982. "The Market as Prison," *Journal of Politics*, 44: 324–336
    1977. *Politics and Markets: The World's Political Economic Systems*. New York: Basic Books.

Linos, Katerina. 2013. *The Democratic Foundations of Policy Diffusion: How Health, Family, and Employment Laws Spread Across Countries*. Oxford: Oxford University Press.

Madrid, Raúl L. 2003. *Retiring the State*. Stanford, CA: Stanford University Press.

Maleva, Tatiana and Oksana Sinyavskaya 2005. *Pensionnaya Reforma v Rossii: Istoriya, Rezultati, Perspektivi*. Moscow: Pomatur.

Maltzman, Forrest and Charles Shipan. 2008. "Change, Continuity, and the Evolution of the Law," *American Journal of Political Science* 52(2 April): 252–267.

Markus, Stanislav. 2007. "Capitalists of All Russia, Unite! Business Mobilization Under Debilitated Dirigisme," *Polity* 39(3, July): 277–304.

Marques, Israel. 2016. *Political Institutions and Preferences for Social Policy in the Post-Communist World*. Dissertation. Columbia University.

Mesa-Lago, Carmelo. 2008. *Reassembling Social Security: A Survey of Pensions and Healthcare Reforms in Latin America*. Oxford: Oxford University Press.

Meseguer, Covadonga. 2004. "What Role for Learning? The Diffusion Privatisation in OECD and Latin American Countries," *Journal of Public Policy* 24(3): 299–325.
    2005. "Policy Learning, Policy Diffusion, and the Making of a New Order," *The ANNALS of the American Academy of Political and Social Science*, 598: 67.

Meseguer, Covadonga and Abel Escribà-Folch. 2011. "Learning, Political Regimes and the Liberalization of Trade," *European Journal of Political Research* 50: 775–810.

Meseguer, Covadonga and Fabrizio Gilardi. 2009. "What is New in the Study of Policy Diffusion?," *Review of International Political Economy* 16(3): 527–543.

Mettler, Suzanne and Joe Soss. 2004. "The Consequences of Public Policy for Democratic Citizenship: Bridging Policy Studies and Mass Politics," *Perspectives on Politics* 2(1): 55–73.

Minns, Richard. 2001. *The Cold War in Welfare: Stock Markets Versus Pensions*. London: Verso.

Moe, Terry. 1990. "The Politics of Structural Choice: Toward a Theory of Public Bureaucracy," in Olivier E. Williamson, ed., *Organization Theory: From Chester Barnard to the Present and Beyond*. Oxford: Oxford University Press.
    2005. "Power and Political Institutions," *Perspectives on Politics*, 3(2 June): 215–233.

Mudrakov, V. I. et al. 2002. *Negosudarstvennoe pensionnoe obespechenie naseleniya Rossiskoi Federatsii*. ed. V. I. Mudrakov Moscow: Prosveshenie.

Müller, Katharina. 1999. *The Political Economy of Pension Reform in Central-Eastern Europe*. Cheltenham, UK: Edward Elgar.
    2001. "The Political Economy of Pension Reform in Eastern Europe," *International Social Security Review* 54(2–3): 57–79.
    2003. *Privatising Old-Age Security*. Cheltenham: Edward Elgar Publishing.
    2008. "The Politics and Outcomes of Three-pillar Pension Reforms in Central and Eastern Europe" In *Pension Reform in Europe*, eds. Camila Arza and Martin Kohli, 87–106. London: Routledge.

Murphy, Kevin M., Andrei Shleifer, and Robert W. Vishny. 1992. "The Transition to a Market Economy: Pitfalls of Partial Reform," *The Quarterly Journal of Economics* 107(3): 889–906.

Myles, John and Paul Pierson, eds. 2001. "The Comparative Political Economy of Pension Reform." In *The New Politics of the Welfare State*, 305–333. Oxford: Oxford University Press.

Naczyk, Marek and Stefan Domonkos. 2014. "The Global Financial Crisis and Changing Coalitional Dynamics in East European Pension Politics." Presented at the Annual Meeting of the American Political Science Association, Washington, DC, August 28–31.

Naczyk, Marek and Bruno Palier. 2014. "Feed the Beast: Finance Capitalism and the Spread of Pension Privatization in Europe." Paper prepared for the 26th Annual Conference of the Society for the Advancement of Socio-Economics, Chicago, July 10–12.

Nadler, Richard. 2000. "Portfolio Politics: Nudging the Investor Class Forward," *National Review*, 52(23): 38–40.

Nelson, Joan. 2001. "The Politics of Pension and Healthcare Reform in Hungary and Poland." In *Reforming the State*, eds. János Kornai, Stephan Haggard, and Robert R. Kaufman, 235–266. Cambridge: Cambridge University Press.

Nooruddin, Irfan. 2011. *Coalition Politics and Economic Development: Credibility and the Strength of Weak Governments*. Cambridge: Cambridge University Press.

North, Douglass. 1990. *Institutions, Institutional Change, and Economic Performance*. Cambridge: Cambridge University Press.

Olson, Mancur. 1965. *The Logic of Collective Action: Public Goods and the Theory of Groups*. Cambridge, MA: Harvard University Press.

Orenstein, Mitchell A. 2000. "How Politics and Institutions Affect Pension Reform in Three Postcommunist Countries," World Bank Policy Research Working Paper 2310 (March).

2008. *Privatizing Pensions: The Transnational Campaign for Social Security Reform*. Princeton, NJ: Princeton University Press.

2011. "Pension Privatization in Crisis: Death or Rebirth of a Global Policy Trend?," *International Social Security Review* 64(3): 65–80.

2013. "Pension Privatization: Evolution of a Paradigm," *Governance* 26(2): 259–281.

Orlov-Karba, Pavel. 2005. *Vse o Pensionoi Reforme v Rossii*. Moscow: Gardariki.

Orzsag, Peter, and Stiglitz, Joseph. 2001. "Rethinking Pension Reform: 10 Myths about Social Security Systems." In *New Ideas About Old Age Security: Toward Sustainable Pension Systems in the 21st Century*, ed. Robert Holzmann, 17–56. Washington, DC: World Bank.

Palacios, Robert, and Montserrat Pallarès-Miralles. 2000. *International Patterns of Pension Provision*. Social Protection Discussion Paper Series. Washington, DC: World Bank.

Palacios, Robert and Roberto Rocha. 1998. "The Hungarian Pension System in Transition," *Social Protection Discussion Paper Series, No. 9805*. Washington, DC: The World Bank.

Palacios, Robert and Edward Whitehouse. 1998. "The Role of Choice in the Transition to a Funded Pension System," *Social Protection Discussion Paper Series, No. 9812*. Washington, DC: The World Bank.

Patashnik, Eric. 2008. *Reforms at Risk: What Happens After Major Policy Changes are Enacted.* Princeton, NJ: Princeton University Press.

Pierson, Paul. 1994. *Dismantling the Welfare State? Reagan, Thatcher, and the Politics of Retrenchment.* Cambridge: Cambridge University Press.

1998. "Irresistible Forces, Immovable Objects: Post-industrial Welfare States Confront Permanent Austerity," *Journal of European Public Policy* 5(4): 539–560.

2000. "Increasing Returns, Path Dependence, and the Study of Politics," *The American Political Science Review* 94(2): 251–267.

Piñera, Jose. 2000. "A Chilean Model for Russia," *Foreign Affairs* 79(5): 62–73.

Polanyi, Karl. 1944. *The Great Transformation: The Political and Economic Origins of Our Time.* Boston, MA: Beacon Press.

Przeworski, Adam. 1991. *Democracy and the Market: Political and Economic Reforms in Eastern Europe and Latin America.* Cambridge: Cambridge University Press.

2008. "Introduction," in *Selected Works of Michael Wallerstein: The Political Economy of Inequality, Unions, and Social Democracy.*

Przeworki, Adam, Michael E. Alvarez, José Antonio Cheibub, and Fernando Limongi. 2000. *Democracy and Development: Political Institutions and Well-Being in the World, 1950–1990.* Cambridge: Cambridge University Press.

Queisser, Monika. 1998. *The Second Generation Pension Reforms in Latin America.* Paris: Development Centre Studies, OECD Proceedings.

Remington, Thomas. 2001. *The Russian Parliament: Institutional Evolution in a Transitional Regimes, 1989–1999.* New Haven, CT: Yale University Press.

2003. "Majorities without Mandates: The Russian Federation Council since 2000," *Europe–Asia Studies,* 55(5): 667–691.

2011. *The Politics of Inequality in Russia.* Cambridge: Cambridge University Press.

2014a. *Presidential Decrees in Russia: A Comparative Perspective.* Cambridge: Cambridge University Press.

2014b. "Reforming Welfare Regimes in Russia and China: The Case of Pensions," Presented at the annual conference of the Midwest Political Science Association, Chicago, IL, April 3.

Roberts, Andrew. 2010. *The Quality of Democracy in Eastern Europe: Public Preferences and Policy Reforms.* Cambridge; Cambridge University Press.

Robertson, Graeme. 2011. *The Politics of Protest in Hybrid Regimes: Managing Dissent in Post-Communist Russia.* Cambridge: Cambridge University Press.

Robertson, Graeme and Emmanuel Teitelbaum. 2011. "Globalization, Regime Type and Labor Protest in Developing Countries," *American Journal of Political Science* 55(3): 665–677.

Rocha, Roberto and Dimitri Vittas. 2002. "The Hungarian Pension Reform: A Preliminary Assessment of the First Years of Implementation," in *Social Security Pension Reform in Europe,* Martin Feldstein and Horst Siebert, eds. Chicago, IL: University of Chicago Press for National Bureau of Economic Research.

Rodrik, Dani. 1991. "Policy Uncertainty and Private Investment in Developing Countries," *Journal of Development Economics* 36(2): 229–242.

Roland, Gérard. 2000. *Transition Economics: Politics, Markets, and Firms.* Cambridge, MA: MIT Press.

Rose, Richard. 1990. "Inheritance Before Choice in Public Policy." *Journal of Theoretical Politics* 2(3): 263–291.

Russian Union of Industrialists and Entrepreneurs (RSPP). 2001. "Alternative Proposal of the RSPP for a Pension Reform Concept," May 31 (copy available upon request).

Rupnik, Jacques. 2012. "How Things Went Wrong," *Journal of Democracy*, 23(3): 132–137.

Rutland, P. 2000. "Putin's Path to Power," *Post-Soviet Affairs* 16(4): 313–354.

Sahay, Ratna and Rishi Goyal. 2006. "Volatility and Growth in Latin America: An Episodic Approach," IMF Working Paper WP/06/287, International Monetary Fund.

Schatz, Edward. 2009. "The Soft Authoritarian Tool Kit: Agenda-Setting Power in Kazakhstan and Kyrgyzstan," *Comparative Politics* 41(2 January): 203–222.

Schattschneider, E.E. 1935. *Politics, Pressure, and the Tariff: A Study of Free Private Enterprise in Pressure Politics, as Shown in the 1929–1930 Revision of the Tariff*, Upper Saddle River, NJ: Prentice-Hall.

Schwarz, Anita M. 2011. "New Realities of Pension Policy in Central Europe," *Human Development Group, Europe and Central Asia Region*. Washington, DC: The World Bank.

Schwarz, Anita M., Omar S. Arias, Asta Zviniene, Heinz P. Rudolph, Sebastien Eckardt, Johannes Koettl, Herwig Immervoll, and Miglena Abels. 2014. *The Inverting Pyramid: Pension Systems Facing Demographic Challenges in Europe and Central Asia*. Washington, DC: The World Bank.

Schweiger, Christian. 2014. "Poland, Variable Geometry and the Enlarged European Union," *Europe–Asia Studies* 663): 394–420.

Sharafutidinova, Gulnaz. 2010. "Federal Governance in Russia: How Putin Changed the Contract with His Agents and the Problems It Created for Medvedev," *Publius: Journal of Federalism* 40(4): 672–696.

Shipan, Charles and Craig Volden. 2008. "The Mechanisms of Policy Diffusion," *American Journal of Political Science* 52(4 October): 840–857.

Simmons, Beth and Zachary Elkins. 2004. "The Globalization of Liberalization: Policy Diffusion in the International Political Economy," *American Political Science Review* 98(1 February): 171–189.

Simmons, Beth, Frank Dobbin, and Geoffrey Garrett, eds. 2008. *The Global Diffusion of Markets and Democracy*. Cambridge: Cambridge University Press.

Simonovits, András. 2000. "Partial Privatization of a Pension System: Lessons from Hungary," *Journal of International Development* 12: 519–529.

2002. "Hungarian Pension System: The Permanent Reform," Institute of Economics, Hungarian Academy of Sciences.

2006. "Optimal Design of Pension Rule with Flexible Retirement: The Two-Type Case," *Journal of Economics* 89(3): 197–222.

2009. "Hungarian Pension System and its Reform," Discussion Papers MT-DP – 2009/8, Institute of Economics, Budapest, Hungary: Hungarian Academy of Sciences.

2011. *The Mandatory Private Pension Pillar in Hungary: An Obituary*. Budapest, Hungary: Institute of Economics, Hungarian Academy of Sciences.

2012. "Pension Strategy for Hungary, 2014," *V4 Revue*, November 2.

Singh, Anoop and Martin Cerisola. 2006. "Sustaining Latin America's Resurgence: Some Historical Perspectives," IMF Working Paper WP 06/252. International Monetary Fund.

Skowronek, Stephen. 1995. "Order and Change," *Polity* 28(1 Autumn): 91–96.

Solov'ev. A.K. 2015. *Pensionnaia Reforma: Illiuzii i Real'nost'*, 2nd edition, Moscow: Prospekt.

Standard & Poor's. 2010. *Global Aging 2010: An Irreversible Truth*. New York, NY: Standard & Poor's.

Stanko, Dariusz. 2003. "Polish Pension Funds, Does the System Work? Cost, Efficiency and Performance Measurement Issues," Graduate School of Economics, Osaka University, and the Warsaw School of Economics, Chair of Social Insurance.

Stone, Deborah. 2012. *Policy Paradox: The Art of Political Decision Making*. New York: W.W. Norton & Company.

Stokes, Susan. 1996. "Public Opinion and Market Reform: The Limits of Economic Voting," *Comparative Political Studies* 29(5): 499–519.

Stroup, Sarah. 2012. *Borders among Activists: International NGOs in the United States, Britain, and France*. Ithaca, NY: Cornell University Press.

Tapia, Waldo. 2008. "Comparing Aggregate Investment Returns in Privately Managed Pension Funds," 21. *OECD Working Paper on Insurance and Private Pensions*. Paris: OECD.

Tatała, Marek. 2014. "'Pension System Reform and Reform Reversal: The Polish Lesson," 4Liberty.eu Review, 1(October): 198–210.

Taylor, Brian. 2011. *State-Building in Putin's Russia: Policing and Coercion After Communism*. Cambridge: Cambridge University Press.

Tompson, William. 2002. "Putin's Challenge: The Politics of Structural Reform in Russia," *Europe–Asia Studies* 54(6): 933–957.

USAID. 1999. *Pension Reform in Hungary: Useful Experiences for Ukraine*. Kyiv, Ukraine: PADCO/USAID, Social Sector Restructuring Program.

Van den Noord, Paul, and Richard Herd. 1993. *Pension Liabilities in the Seven Major Economies*. Paris: Organisation for Economic Cooperation and Development.

Vasoo, S. and James Lee. 2001. "Singapore: Social Development Housing and the Central Provident Fund," *International Journal of Social Welfare* 10: 276–283.

Velculescu, Delia. 2011. "Pension Reforms in Emerging Europe: the Uncertain Road Ahead." *Presented at the International Monetary Fund*, New York, NY, April 1, 2011.

Vittas, Dimitri. 2000. *Pension Reform and Capital Market Development*. Washington, DC: World Bank Publications.

Vittas, Dimitri, Heinz Rudolph, and John Pollner. 2010. "Designing the Payout Phase of Funded Pension Pillars in Central and Eastern European Countries," Policy Research Working Paper 5276, Europe and Central Asia Region, Private and Financial Sector Development Department & Central Europe and the Baltics Country Department, April, Washington, DC: The World Bank.

Walker, Jack. 1991. *Mobilizing Interest Groups in America: Patrons, Professions, and Social Movements*. Ann Arbor, MI: University of Michigan Press.

Way, Lucan. 2008. "The Real Causes of the Color Revolutions," *Journal of Democracy* 19(3): 55–69.

Weyland, Kurt. 2006. *Bounded Rationality and Policy Diffusion: Social Sector Reform in Latin America*. Princeton, NJ: Princeton University Press.

Whitehouse, Edward. 2011. "Reversals of Systemic Pension Reforms in Central and Eastern Europe: Implications," OECD Social Policy Division.

Williamson, John B., Stephanie A. Howling, and Michelle L. Maroto. 2006. "The Political Economy of Pension Reform in Russia: Why Partial Privatization?," *Journal of Aging Studies* 20(2): 165–175.

Wilson Sokhey, Sarah. 2010. *The Politics of Post-Communist Pension Reform: The Influence of Business Lobbying on Policy Outcomes*. Dissertation, The Ohio State University.

2015. "Market-Oriented Reforms as a Tool of State-Building: Russian Pension Reform in 2001," *Europe–Asia Studies*, Vol. 67 (5): 695–717.

Word Development Indicators. 2014. Washington, DC: World Bank.

World Bank. 1994. *Averting the Old Age Crisis: Policies to Protect the Old and Promote Growth*. Oxford: Oxford University Press.

Yakovlev, Andrei. 2006. "The Evolution of Business–State Interaction in Russia: From State Capture to Business Capture?," *Europe–Asia Studies*, 58(7): 1033–1056.

Yakushev, Evgenii and O. Kolobaev. 2002. "Negosudarstvenie pensionie fondi v Rossii – pervie 10 let," *Finansovie Uslugi*, 9–10.

Żukowski, Maciej. 2012. *Annual National Report 2011: Pensions, Healthcare, and Long-term Care (Poland)*. Analytical Support on the Socio-Economic Impact of Social Protection Reforms for the European Commission DG on Employment, Social Affairs, & Inclusion.

Index